STEPHENSON- Nazi organisation   324.

D1426594

THE NAZI ORGANISATION OF WOMEN

The Nazi Organisation of Women

JILL STEPHENSON

CROOM HELM LONDON

BARNES & NOBLE BOOKS
TOTOWA, NEW JERSEY

©1981 Jill Stephenson
Croom Helm Ltd, 2-10 St John's Road, London SW11

British Library Cataloguing in Publication Data

Stephenson, Jill
  The Nazi organisation of women.
  1. Nationalsozialistische Deutsche Arbeiter-
  Partei
  2. Women — Germany — Societies and clubs —
  History — 20th century
  3. Women in politics — Germany — History —
  20th century
  I. Title
  329.9'43   DD256.5

  ISBN 0-85664-673-3

First published in the USA 1981 by
BARNES & NOBLE BOOKS
81 ADAMS DRIVE
TOTOWA, NEW JERSEY, 07512

ISBN 0-389-20113-8

Printed and bound in Great Britain by
Redwood Burn Limited
Trowbridge & Esher

For Steve

ACKNOWLEDGEMENTS

It is a pleasure to acknowledge the advice and assistance I have received from individuals and institutions while preparing this book. The main sources were made available by the Bundesarchiv, Koblenz, the Berlin Document Center and the Institut für Zeitgeschichte in Munich; for access to their facilities I am most grateful. I would also like to thank the Hoover Institution, California, for sending me essential microfilm. My warmest thanks are due to the staff of the Wiener Library, London, for their unfailing hospitality as well as their invaluable help. Edinburgh University Library readily met many demands, particularly through its photographic and inter-library loan departments. For financial assistance to enable me to carry out research abroad and to utilise the documentary sources most efficiently, I am indebted to the Travel and Research Fund of Edinburgh University and also to the British Academy, which generously made me a grant. I received invaluable information and help from Dr Gisela Miller, Hamburg, and Dr Marta Baerlecken-Hechtle, Düsseldorf, and I am also grateful to Mrs Louise Willmot, Oxford, Conan Fischer, Heriot-Watt University, Dr Peter Stachura, Stirling University and Mrs Cecilia Smith, Edinburgh University, for their advice. Professor Dietrich Orlow and Professor W.S. Allen were kind enough to answer queries which I addressed to them. Once again I have trespassed on Professor V.G. Kiernan's time; he generously read part of the text in draft. And, also, I owe a special debt to Mrs Sheila Somerville, for her patience as well as her efficient typing of the text. My husband, too, has shown patience, tolerating the domestic regime which this book's completion has demanded. Its shortcomings are, of course, no one's responsibility but my own.

CONTENTS

INTRODUCTION

This is not a history of the Nazi Party; others, on whom I have greatly depended, provide this.[1] Nor is it intended to be of the 'women's history' genre. Rather, it is a brief account of the origins, development and functions of the women's groups associated with the NSDAP from near its beginning until its end, which, it is to be hoped, will do more than 'only serve the negative purpose of demonstrating the dominance of men in Nazism',[2] even if that conclusion is inescapable. For one thing, vague or misleading remarks have been made about the early years of Nazi women's activity by some writers, including myself,[3] which Chapters 1 and 2 should clarify. And consideration of Nazi women's organisations is timely because of the publication, late in 1978, of a book by the former leader of the official women's organisations in the Third Reich, Gertrud Scholtz-Klink. *Die Frau im Dritten Reich*[4] gives a clear picture neither of 'women in the Third Reich' nor of the organisations over which Frau Scholtz-Klink presided. By reproducing a large number of contemporary publications and some (often abbreviated) documents interspersed with at times bitter comments, she has certainly not produced 'the pioneering work of the highest order' that her publisher has claimed;[5] on the contrary, she has shown that while she has, over the years, forgotten a few things, she has learned nothing. She would have done well to read the genuinely pioneering study of her system by Clifford Kirkpatrick, first published in 1938,[6] whose insights and appraisals are, not always but often enough, still valid today. But as a contemporary, pre-war study, Kirkpatrick's is necessarily incomplete.

While this book aims to provide a more complete picture of the Nazi women's organisations from their start, in the early 1920s, until their end in 1945, its purpose is above all to contribute to the study of National Socialism as a movement which attracted and held the enthusiasm of a small minority of Germans who, given the chance from 1933, attempted to impose their will on the majority. The paradoxical character of the NSDAP, as a revolutionary force pledged to restore Germany to a mythical past from which it could develop towards an ideal present and future, attracted to it from 1919 those who wanted to return to the point where, they felt, Germany had taken a wrong turning. Unification in 1871 had been part of the 'correct' development, as far as it had gone, but the ensuing rapid industrialisation had brought urbanisation and the politicisation of the working class by Marxist Social Democrats. It had also, by its insatiable demand for cheap and docile labour, brought large numbers of women into exhausting, dirty and even dangerous work which threatened the healthy development of the 'race' by damaging and debilitating Germany's mothers. The massive increase in women's employment outside the home in the thirty or so years before the First World War[7] had also, by this analysis, threatened family life in other ways, by diverting housewives and mothers from their essential duties in the home for much of their life. Women were too busy or too tired to learn how to run a home in an orderly way, to protect their own health as childbearers, and to care adequately for their children. Improved methods of birth control from the later nineteenth century had led women to try to mitigate their problems by restricting the size of their family[8] – yet again, in the Nazi view, endangering the future of the 'race'. The quality of German life, too, was under threat, with women, 'the guardians of German culture', distracted by work, political agitation and the growth of a consumer society from their alleged age-old function of cherishing the nation's distinctive songs, dances, costumes and crafts.

The Nazi revolution would restore women to the idyllic destiny from which they had been diverted before the First World War and which was, said the Nazis, deliberately derided by the Marxists, internationalists, liberals and feminists who seemed, in the post-war period, to have emerged as the victors from Germany's pre-war political and social conflicts. And if women had been deflected from their destiny – which was only the fulfilment of the instinctive aspirations of the female nature, it was said – even before the war, the experience of the war and the trauma of the revolutionary upheavals in a number of Germany's cities in 1918-19 convinced increasing numbers of men and women that the circumstances of post-war Germany would only intensify the distortion. The kind of changes that could be achieved to counteract modern evils through the new parliamentary system would do no more than tinker with the symptoms, for example, the 'filth' that was given free rein in literature and drama by the lifting of censorship.[9] Nothing less radical than a revolution – a *national* revolution, not a Marxist one – could bring Germany back to the path of 'correct' development. This was what the Nazi Party was fighting for in the *Kampfzeit* (time of struggle, up to 1933). Axiomatically, women could not participate actively in the struggle, since allowing them to do so would be simply to follow the false example set by the Nazis' adversaries. One of the spectres that remained with Nazi activists for years was the horror of women's participation in the attempted revolution of 1918-19, and Rosa Luxemburg — although she was a victim rather than a perpetrator of violence — became a symbol of the evils threatening German society. Years later, she and others were remembered with fear and loathing as an example of what National Socialism was pledged to prevent.[10]

These sentiments contributed to the development of what may cautiously be called the Nazi view of women's role in the nation and in the Party. As Hans Frank was to say, there were 'as many "National Socialisms" as there were leaders',[11] and the variations on the theme of women's place were legion. But it is generally safe to say that in the Nazi view women were to be 'wives, mothers and homemakers'; they were to play no part in public life, in the legislature, the executive, the judiciary or the armed forces. Hitler himself frequently expressed opposition to women's participation in politics, claiming that it sullied and demeaned the female nature, as he saw it.[12] It was partly Hitler's personal attachment to the image of women as 'mothers of the nation' which delayed and then vitiated the introduction of labour conscription for women during the Second World War,[13] although in his *Götterdämmerung* mentality early in 1945 he was prepared to see women enlisted as soldiers and sent to the front.[14] While leading Nazis differed about the extent to which women should be employed outside the home and to which they could usefully contribute to the Party's campaigns, they generally accepted that from earliest childhood girls should be brought up to accept motherhood as their 'natural calling', and that all other roles they might assume or functions they might exercise should be consistent with childbearing and child-rearing. Again, this preoccupation derived largely from increasing anxiety in Nazi and non-Nazi circles alike in the 1920s about Germany's falling birth-rate.[15]

While growing numbers of men were drawn to National Socialism in the 1920s because of these ideas among others, there were women, too, who found the Nazis' traditionalist approach to women's role attractive. For them, it was enough to sympathise with and support the Party's 'fighting menfolk', and although small numbers of women joined the new local branches of the NSDAP which sprang up all over the country from the mid-1920s, most pro-Nazi women regarded it as inconsistent with their own and the Party's view of women's role to join a political party. But there were, almost paradoxically, a number of women with distinctly feminist views who gravitated to National Socialism because of its anti-Marxism, its ultra-nationalist and racist aspect, or for local or family reasons. It is clear that they either ignored the

Party's pronouncements about women's role or else refused to take them seriously. In the critical years between 1930 and 1933 the Party gave them plenty of encouragement in their self-delusion at a time when its leadership was hoping to make a favourable impact on the female voter in its bid for power the legal way. Gregor Strasser, the Party's organisational chief at this time until his unexpected resignation in December 1932, particularly seemed to welcome and encourage women's participation in election campaigns. And so women supporters of National Socialism in the 1920s, up to 1933, might or might not wholeheartedly support the Party's general view of women's place in society, and might or might not be members of the NSDAP.

Women's group activity developed something of a split personality because it embraced these different kinds of women. It also started and grew spontaneously and in a variety of forms because the inherent male chauvinism of the movement led to exclusive concentration on the men's struggle against the Weimar 'system'. Often enough, a woman whose husband or brother was a Party member would join in giving *ad hoc* support to the men in the area, providing food, making and mending uniforms, or, as in Hanover in 1922, for example, making a flag bearing the Party's symbol.[16] These activities set the tone for what would throughout the rest of the Nazi era be known as 'womanly work', the kind of mundane, practical assistance which women, as homemakers, could readily provide, and which men really could not be asked to contemplate. This division of labour reflected the Party's general view of women's functions and underlined its insistence on the segregation of the sexes at work and at play. Women's talents and capacities were different from men's, and, like men's, they should be utilised to the full and not squandered in vain attempts by women to take over men's work or emulate men's achievements. Because of initial neglect of women's contribution to the Party's work, which led to its growth independently of male control, this segregationist policy led perhaps not to 'secondary racism',[17] but certainly to organisational apartheid. The male chauvinist mentality of the NSDAP's men ensured that women who were attracted to the Party were condemned to 'separate development', which allowed them to work out their role in the Party's service to a great degree as they chose.

The evolution of Nazi women's groups of different kinds caused problems for the Party once it belatedly acknowledged their existence and assistance, in the later 1920s. To solve these, Gregor Strasser ordered the dissolution of all existing women's groups in 1931 and created, in their stead, the *NS-Frauenschaft* (NSF – Nazi Women's

Group), the first official Nazi women's organisation under central Party control. Strasser's role here and in the subsequent development of the NSF casts interesting light on his character and methods. Unlike many leading Nazis he clearly felt that the women's organisation could contribute usefully to the Party's work; this was no doubt why he was at pains to create a uniform, harmonious organisation out of the diverse warring factions which had evolved in the 1920s. Others, too, valued the 'women's work'. The SA depended on women's soup kitchens to feed its members when they were on duty, especially if they were unemployed, and for a time the SA welcomed the rudimentary first-aid service provided by Nazi women for 'heroes' hurt in brawls.[18] As the Depression hit Germany's larger towns particularly hard from 1930 onwards, welfare work by women who collected money, cast-off clothing and household utensils, who gave material and moral support to the families of political detainees, and who provided food and warm clothing for destitute Germans, whether they were Party supporters or not, was regarded as vital in both practical and propaganda terms.[19]

As the Party's apparatus and ambitions grew, so it came to create new, permanent institutions to replace the voluntary, *ad hoc* work done by women enthusiasts. The SA in Berlin, for example, developed its own specialist medical corps and increasingly — and ungratefully — rejected the assistance which women's groups continued to provide.[20] The founding of the Nazi welfare organisation (*NS-Volkswohlfahrt* — NSV) in Berlin in winter 1931-2 similarly led to a downgrading of the spontaneous assistance for long provided by women's groups. And in July 1932 the order that the Hitler Youth should have a monopoly of organising Nazi girls threatened to deprive the NSF of its traditional function of bringing the young into the movement, under the guidance of their elders. After tooth-and-nail resistance from the women,[21] this order was enforced in 1933, but only by replacing the existing leadership in the NSF in the first of a series of changes which culminated in the appointment of Gertrud Scholtz-Klink as NSF leader in February 1934.[22] By the time she took office, the women's organisation had been shorn of most of the functions it had exercised in the *Kampfzeit*, and in spite of official propaganda to boost its image it never recovered from these losses. The demarcation disputes in which the NSF became involved, with the NSV and the Hitler Youth especially, during the 1930s and into the war, were a reflection of the extent to which NSF leaders refused to be reconciled to these losses, and to which they recognised the damage they had inflicted on the NSF's authority and prestige.

For the rest of the Third Reich, the NSF was to concentrate on winning over the uncommitted 'valuable' female population to National Socialism, in Germany itself and in the new possessions Germany acquired in the later 1930s and early 1940s. Here, it suffered not only as a result of the restricted role which the Party Leadership now allowed it, but also from the strange limbo in which the NSDAP, of which it was a part, found itself from 1933. The substantial support which the Party had won in elections in 1932-3 was still the support of a minority of the electorate, and many of these voters, influenced by the catastrophic economic circumstances prevailing in Germany in the early 1930s, could hardly properly be classed as 'Nazis'. For many, the NSDAP was the party of last resort in desperate times. Failure to recognise this was one factor which seduced the NSDAP into a grandiose but doomed attempt to win the co-operation and approval of the mass of 'Aryan' Germans for every measure of Hitler's Government in peace and war, by persuasion and with a minimum of coercion. There was also the optical illusion created by the rush of opportunists to join the Party and its affiliated organisations, including the NSF, after Hitler's appointment as Chancellor on 30 January 1933. But most of all, the Party found itself confined to this utopian purpose by Hitler's betrayal of it. By taking over the machinery of the State intact, Hitler and a few chosen henchmen were able to govern through traditional German institutions.

This was the final negation of Gregor Strasser's grand design of building the Nazi Party as a microcosm of society which would be able to assume control of society in all its facets once the political struggle was won and power was achieved at the centre. But this aim, like so much of Strasser's work, was scrapped after his resignation, not eight weeks before Hitler became Chancellor. In the moment of political victory, the disarray in the NSDAP, to which the dismantling of Strasser's system materially contributed, enabled Hitler to disregard its long-held aspirations, to bypass it and to throw in his lot, temporarily at least, with the old elites in the civil service and the army. From this point onwards, the NSDAP and its affiliated groups were left to try to impose the regime's will on the population *without* antagonising it. With the 'racially undesirable' and 'politically unreliable', coercion and brutality could be used and were used; with the inherently 'valuable' population, and especially with women, the mothers of the nation, it was barely an option. Propaganda and 'tireless' persuasion were the approved methods to which the Party and above all the NSF were restricted.

The strategy for applying this frustratingly ineffective technique began with *Gleichschaltung* (co-ordination). All political, social, charitable and other groups which were objectionable to the NSDAP were dissolved and the remainder purged and brought under Nazi leadership, in new monolithic combines. The destruction of the trade unions and the gathering of their former members in Robert Ley's German Labour Front created the largest of these. On a smaller scale, all members of the various former teachers' associations, for example, were under strong pressure to join the Nazi Teachers' League, and they succumbed in large numbers at this time of high graduate unemployment.[23] After some confusion resulting from the repeated changes of NSF leadership in 1933-4, Gertrud Scholtz-Klink set about trying to bring all 'valuable' German women into a new combine, the *Deutsches Frauenwerk* (DFW – German Women's Enterprise), under the leadership of the NSF.[24] In theory, the complex task of influencing the mass of German women was to be achieved by making them accessible to NSF propaganda and control through their membership of the DFW. It has to be doubted if this ambition was in any sense realistic: housebound housewives could not be put under the same kind of pressure to join an official organisation as could be used to make workers of all kinds conform, especially in time of widespread unemployment. But even apart from this the NSF's pretensions to organise all German women were hamstrung from the start by the class basis of the NSDAP's appeal and by the way in which the *Gleichschaltung* of the women's organisations reinforced this.

The NSDAP had always drawn the bulk of its support from the various elements in the middle class. Even in the Depression the organised working class 'remained unimpressed by Nazi slogans', although some proletarian women became Nazi supporters.[25] With the destruction of communist and socialist organisations as the first priority of *Gleichschaltung*, working-class women, like the men, lost their main focus of group activity. Some working-class women, like women of other classes, belonged to Church groups, and most did not belong to organisations of any kind; this applied especially to women in rural areas. The NSF would find the dead weight of apathy on the part of the traditionally unorganised virtually impossible to mobilise, and the continuing influence of the Churches extremely hard to undermine. And it immediately forfeited the interest of working-class women who had engaged in some kind of group activity by the way in which it constructed the DFW exclusively on the remains of middle-class women's groups which would quickly become expendable but which provided a ready-made basis — with members, funds, premises, magazines — for a new all-embracing combine. From the start, the middle-class character of the DFW, in terms of its immediate membership, inherited from the old groups, in terms of its leadership, attitudes and activities, denied it the support of more than a handful of working-class women, and contradicted its stated aim of bringing all German women under its aegis. The limited appeal of the DFW ensured that its ambition to become the mass organisation of German women would never be realised.

But if the Party and its women's groups were middle-class in orientation and appeal, this did not mean that all, or even most, middle-class women were attracted to them. There were enthusiasts, and there were also women who joined because they regarded membership as a useful insurance policy, particularly if they had a professional career to conserve. Often enough they merely paid their subscription and were classed, on investigation, as 'inactive' members; it was a continuing source of frustration to NSF and Party officials that women from the 'educated classes' generally held aloof from the women's organisation. And middle-class women were certainly not in the forefront of those responding to Party and NSF appeals for volunteers to help the German war-effort from 1939.[26] Only a minority of women — in contrast with men — tends to favour single-sex group activity, and a single-sex monopoly organisation with a heavy emphasis on propaganda and indoctrination at once made itself unattractive to large numbers of women, whatever their class. Some women joined no doubt because they wanted to be members of a music group or sports club or sewing circle, and had to choose between the Nazi-sponsored one, under DFW control, or nothing. But, even so, German women were, contrary to the popular view,[27] peculiarly resistant to National Socialism, and probably, because of their relative inaccessibility, much more resistant than men. And there was another reason: German women, like women elsewhere, remained more attached than men to religion. The spiritual authority of the Churches, particularly the Catholic Church in rural areas, retained the allegiance of large numbers of women in the face of competition from the NSF. It was hardly a contest: the Nazis could not hope to win against one of the traditional forces in society which many had believed they were coming to power to safeguard against 'atheistic Marxism'.[28] Unable to use coercion to win recruits to the DFW, the NSF found, uncomfortably, that it was largely preaching to a converted minority, still cut off from the antagonistic or, more likely, uninterested 90 per cent and more of the female population of Germany.

Annexations before and during the war provided the Party and its affiliates with pastures new, with millions more ethnic Germans to Nazify. If this lifted morale, the effect was only temporary as the same problems emerged in the new territories as had dogged the NSDAP's efforts in the 'old Reich'. After a wave of initial enthusiasm by a susceptible minority, there remained the mass of the apathetic who, without necessarily being anti-Nazi, wished simply to remain private, unorganised citizens. And attempts to mobilise the organised for extra efforts in wartime revealed a disquieting amount of negativism among even them. It became increasingly clear that many of those who had joined the women's organisation had done so less out of burning enthusiasm for the Nazi cause than because they felt that self-interest would be served by belonging to the official women's organisation; most women of this disposition wanted not so much to be ordinary members as to hold an office of some kind.[29] Favour and status, then, were the preoccupations of many who actually joined the DFW; it may be that the overwhelmingly middle-class character of the organisation determined this, with women who felt they had a position in society to maintain reluctant to be mere ordinary members — working members — of the DFW. The war highlighted the plight of the NSF and DFW by clearly showing up who were activists and who were passengers, and there was no doubt that the former were in the minority. They were left with the unpopular task of trying to maintain morale at home in the face of growing discomfort and the manifest injustice of the way in which the subject of labour conscription was treated by Hitler above all. The NSF's middle-class leaders were highly critical of how the system bore most heavily on working-class women, with large numbers of middle-class women managing to remain immune.[30] The enthusiasts who were left to carry the burden of popular discontent obviously regarded themselves as the representatives of all German women, but government and Party policies had long since worked to deny them the chance to play this role in any way effectively.

It was perhaps fitting that the women's organisation should revert, towards its end, to something akin to what its predecessors had been in the 1920s, small local groups working in difficult circumstances to mitigate distress, this time among fellow citizens who were victims of air-raids or the more or less willing subjects of evacuation policies. With shortages and the rupture of the communications' network towards the end of the war, the NSF's activities must have borne an uncanny resemblance to those of the *Kampfzeit*,[31] with little or no central control of individual local policies. And it was clearly in emergency circumstances, in small groups of dedicated activists, that the Nazi women's work flourished. The extent of central authority effectively wielded by Gertrud Scholtz-Klink from her office in Berlin had always depended on the degree to which a Gauleiter had or had not intervened, but the chains of command in the women's organisation had been established at an early stage and had at least nominally held until well into the war. Their purpose had been to try to ensure that the work of the women's organisation throughout the country was conducted in a uniform way, to serve at the local level the demands of the regime as enunciated by the NSDAP and detailed by the staff of bureaucrats gathered in Gertrud Scholtz-Klink's central office. This contrasted sharply with Strasser's creation of the NSF in 1931 as essentially the women's branch of the Party, serving its needs at the local level. Strasser had himself set in motion the centripetal forces,[32] which would ultimately and stultifyingly culminate in a top-heavy administrative centre whose edicts were intended to determine the nature of local women's group activity everywhere. But this conclusion was the logical one only to men, like his successors, with minds less flexible than his own. Unimaginative men with totalitarian aspirations produced a bureaucratic jungle in the women's organisation, as elsewhere; but here they were helped by their choice, as women's leader, of an equally unimaginative woman. No doubt the obsession with order and uniformity – which competing jurisdictions and a barrage of paperwork successfully vitiated – was yet another deterrent to potential recruits to the women's organisation at the local level. Those who joined up and stayed the course had as their reward a brief taste of initiative and freedom from the centrally-imposed straitjacket in the last months of the war, before the total eclipse.

Notes

1. Dietrich Orlow, *The History of the Nazi Party 1919-1933*, Newton Abbott, 1971 (hereafter Orlow I); Dietrich Orlow, *The History of the Nazi Party 1933-1945*, Newton Abbott, 1973 (*hereafter Orlow II*); Albrecht Tyrell (ed.), *Führer Befiehl . . .* , Düsseldorf, 1969; Peter Hüttenberger, *Die Gauleiter*, Stuttgart, 1969; Peter Diehl-Thiele, *Partei und Staat im Dritten Reich*, Munich, 1971.

2. M.S. Jones, review of Peter Stachura (ed.), *The Shaping of the Nazi State*, London, 1978, in *New German Studies*, vol. 6, no. 2, said this about Jill Stephenson, 'The Nazi Organisation of Women, 1933-39' (hereafter Stephenson 1978).

3. Claudia Koonz, 'Nazi Women before 1933: Rebels against Emancipation', *Social Science Quarterly*, March 1976, pp. 558, 561-2; Claudia Koonz, 'Mothers in the Fatherland: Women in Nazi Germany' in Renate Bridenthal and Claudia Koonz, (eds.), *Becoming Visible*, Boston, 1977, pp. 453-5, 457; Dörte Winkler, *Frauenarbeit im 'Dritten Reich'*, Hamburg, 1977, p. 38; Jill McIntyre, 'Women and the Professions in Germany, 1930-40', in Anthony Nicholls and Erich Matthias (eds.), *German Democracy and the Triumph of Hitler*, London, 1971, p. 196; A. Jill R. Stephenson, 'Women in German Society, 1930-40', PhD thesis, Edinburgh University, 1974, Chapter 6, 'The Nazi Organisation of Women', pp. 331-47.

4. Gertrud Scholtz-Klink, *Die Frau im Dritten Reich*, Tübingen, 1978.

5. Grabert-Verlag, note on the dust-jacket.

6. Clifford Kirkpatrick, *Woman in Nazi Germany*, London, 1939 is the British edition; the American edition was published in 1938.

7. *Statistisches Jahrbuch für das Deutsche Reich*, 1927, p. 25.

8. D.V. Glass, 'Family Planning Programmes in Western Europe', *Population Studies*, 1966, p. 225; J. Peel, 'The Manufacturing and Retailing of Contraceptives in England', *Population Studies*, 1963-4, pp. 117, 122.

9. Jill Stephenson, *Women in Nazi Society*, London, 1975, p. 10.

10. NSDAP Hauptarchiv (hereafter HA), reel 13, fol. 254, Gau History Halle-Merseburg, p. 1; Berlin Document Center (hereafter BDC), Akten des Obersten Parteigerichts (hereafter AOPG), 2684/34, letter from Walter Buch to Dr Krummacher, 20 September 1933; see below, p. 145.

11. Quoted in Joachim C. Fest, *The Face of the Third Reich*, London, 1970, p. 164; Winkler, op. cit., p. 28, also makes this point.

12. Stephenson, op. cit., p. 12n23.

13. See below, pp. 180-1.

14. See below, p. 206.

15. Stephenson, op. cit., pp. 38-40; F. Grosse, review of Ernst Kahn, *Der Internationale Geburtenstreik*, Frankfurt, 1930, in *Die Arbeit*, 1931, p. 308.

16. Institut für Zeitgeschichte Archive (hereafter IfZ), MA 736, Bruno Wenzel, *Zur Frühgeschichte det NSDAP in Niedersachsen*, n.d.

17. David Schoenbaum, *Hitler's Social Revolution*, London, 1967, p. 187.

18. Conan Fischer, Heriot-Watt University, has been kind enough to give me information about this.

19. Mrs Cecilia Smith, Edinburgh University, is writing a thesis on the Nazi welfare organisation, the NSV. She was kind enough to give me information about this.

20. See below, p. 47.

21. See below, pp. 86-91.

22. See below, pp. 98-112.

23. 'Mädchenbildungs- und Lehrerinnenfragen in der Pädagogischen Presse', *Die Frau*, June 1934, pp. 570-1; Stephenson, op. cit., pp. 151, 159-60.

24. See below, pp. 132-43.

25. H.A. Winkler, 'German Society, Hitler and the Illusion of Restoration 1930-33', *Journal of Contemporary History* (October 1976), p. 2.

26. See below, pp. 142, 149-50, 181, 185.

27. Joachim C. Fest, *Hitler*, London, 1977, p. 369, writes of 'growing hordes of sharply politicized women' supporting the NSDAP in 1928; c.f. below, pp. 25-7, 30, 40, 44 for figures. David Pryce-Jones, 'Mothers for the Reich'. *Times Literary Supplement*, 2 July 1976, propagates several of the myths.

28. See H.A. Winkler, op. cit., for a discussion of the support the NSDAP won from those who wanted a return to the pre-1914 system.

29. HA/13/253, 'Rundschreiben Nr. 157/42', 1 July 1942, gives a good illus-

tration of organised women's desire for titles and badges.

30. See below, p, 185.
31. See below, pp. 203-5.
32. See below, pp. 65-6, 68-71.

1 EVOLUTION AND CREATION

Nazi Women's Work Begins

The inauguration of the Nazi Party's own archive in January 1934 to gather material from which the NSDAP's history in the *Kampfzeit* could be constructed[1] brought requests during May 1935 that the Gau (region) offices of the *NS-Frauenschaft* provide information about the Party's women's activities before 1933. By the end of 1936 a number of 'Gau Histories' of the NSF had been duly submitted to the Party Archive; these were pieces of varying length and detail, since women's group activity in the NSDAP had developed in an even more irregular way than the growth of the Party itself across Germany in the 1920s.[2] It was probably inevitable that the official history of the NSF which was based on these submissions and which appeared for popular consumption in 1937 should be highly generalised and anodyne.[3] The authors had felt obliged to edit out even minor indiscretions about the NSF's past which appeared in the Gau Histories, to maintain the Party's public image of harmony and uniformity, while no reference whatever was permitted to the chronic rivalries which had bedevilled the Party's embryonic women's organisation from its inception. There was nothing unique about the 'internal bickering [which] characterised the Women's Auxiliary in Thalburg';[4] but it was hardly the stirring, harmonious stuff of which the Party's official history would be made. The authorised version was cosmetic, and therefore misleading.

The reality was not as damaging as the extent of the cover-up might suggest. But the essentially haphazard way in which Nazi women's groups had evolved was not what the Party Leadership wished to recall once it was in power. The often spontaneous growth of diverse tiny groups, at varying times in different places, did not accord with the preferred myth of the inexorable conversion of Germans to the all-conquering creed of National Socialism through the messianic appeal of Adolf Hitler. Certainly, some of the NSF's Gau historians show greater talent as propagandists than as chroniclers, investing their 'history' at every turn with glowing accounts of the willingness of countless German women to make sacrifices for the 'Idea' of National Socialism. But the individuality of local development, and the elevating of local personalities to a high place in the historical hierarchy – regardless,

sometimes, of whether they had since fallen from grace — was unacceptable to central Party bureaucrats who insisted on an image of
unity, co-operation, obedience and, with Hitler and a few others ex-
cepted, anonymity. The official ideal was not the enthusiastic indivi-
dualist but the selfless and unsung heroine.[5]

The bland official histories of the women's organisation serve the
purpose of showing how the Nazi leadership wished this aspect of the
Party's development to be viewed, making a useful contrast with the
highly subjective Gau Histories on the one hand and what can be pieced
together from contemporary sources on the other. The official com-
ment that 'the number of women who gravitated towards National
Socialism rose steadily in the years 1921 to 1926 . . . The women in
small local bands gathered together under the leadership of women
National Socialists in work groups',[6] is incontestable, but also incomplete. It gives no hint of the rather large women's groups in the Gaus
Saxony, Munich and Berlin by the late 1920s, where internal conflicts were vitiating the value of the women's contribution to the
Party's struggle. Nor does it suggest that in, for example, what became
Gau Kurhessen even as late as 1930 'one really cannot talk of there
being a Women's Organisation'.[7] And the official account equally gives
no place in the allegedly monolithic development of National Socialism
to the general *völkisch* (racist-nationalist) ferment after the First World
War which spawned a variety of extremist groups among which, at first,
the Nazi Party was only one of many.

The earliest emergence of women's activity in support of the NSDAP
has to be viewed against the confused and confusing background of the
Party's history up to its refounding in February 1925. The original
German Workers' Party was essentially Bavarian in membership and
appeal, but particularly after it came under Hitler's domination in
summer 1921 it increasingly attracted support from groups and individuals with similar objectives in other parts of Germany. It was probably, paradoxically, a sign of Hitler's early success as a propagandist
that the NSDAP, along with a number of other *völkisch* groups, was
banned in most states of the Reich during 1922 and 1923, even before
the November 1923 *Putsch* attempt, and in Bavaria itself after it. The
ensuing proliferation of alternative extremist groups of a 'right-wing'
nature, partly as cover-organisations for continuing NSDAP activity and
partly as genuinely new *völkisch* groups, created a muddle of fragmentation which only began to be rationalised after Hitler's release from
Landsberg jail in December 1924, the accompanying lifting of the state
prohibitions on the NSDAP, and Hitler's reassertion of his unchallenged

leadership in his *Bürgerbräukeller* speech at the end of February 1925.[8]

During this complicated phase of the Party's development there were two broad strands of women's group activity. In the first place there were the few women who were paid-up Party members and the larger number of female supporters who were wives, daughters or other adherents of male Party members. On the other hand, there were women in *völkisch* groups which were not directly associated with the Nazi Party but which shared its aims and prejudices. The common motivation for pro-Nazi and general *völkisch* women's group activity in the early 1920s derived from the trauma of the lost war and the Versailles Treaty, followed by ruinous inflation, resentment at the 'betrayal' at home which was associated with the attempted socialist revolution at the end of the war, and revulsion at the growth of 'Bolshevism', which might mean anything from mild Social Democracy to full-blooded Communism, in Germany and abroad. Patriotism of an unattractively chauvinistic nature, professed Christianity of a thoroughly uncharitable variety, virulent anti-semitism and abhorrence of moral 'permissiveness', which was associated with 'Bolshevism', were the main sentiments which drew these women together and towards National Socialism, which was pledged to destroy the cancer at the root of Germany's ills — the 'liberal-democratic-Marxist' conspiracy. In the 1920s group allegiance among women of this disposition was fluid, but by the end of the decade, and particularly once the Nazis' bandwagon began to roll at speed after their September 1930 election success, an increasing number of *völkisch* women were turning to National Socialism as the most vital and potentially successful anti-left extremist group.[9]

Judged purely by Party membership figures, there were very few women Nazis indeed in the 1920s. On the eve of the September 1930 election breakthrough 7,625 female members accounted for barely six per cent of the entire membership; almost half of these lived in seven Gaus in the Berlin-Brandenburg, Saxon and Bavarian areas, while there were fewer than 500 NSDAP women altogether in the five western Rhineland Gaus.[10] But these figures do not accurately reflect the extent of female support for the Nazi Party. The official account's reasonably plausible explanation is that women sympathisers saw their function in affording material comfort and moral support to their fighting menfolk rather than in joining the Party since 'the active political struggle, the most pressing task of the NSDAP before the *Machtübernahme* (Nazi takeover of power), [was] the men's affair'.[11] For many, too, it was enough for a family to pay a man's Party subscription without having to find the money for a woman, too, to join.[12] But the Party which

anathematised conventional political activity by women from its beginning to its end nevertheless welcomed women who wished to join.
The earliest membership list, for January 1920, includes some 18
women out of a total of 190,[13] although in the same year audiences
addressed by Hitler were as much as 20 to 30 per cent female.[14] But as
NSDAP local branches (*Ortsgruppen*) were founded outside Bavaria,
too, women joined as full members, with three or four figuring in the
1921 membership list of the new Hanover branch,[15] while a Frau
Passow featured among the twelve original members of the new
Göttingen branch in 1922.[16]

As local branches developed, the women Party members joined with
women sympathisers in auxiliary groups to render assistance to the
Party's men in the area, generally in terms of providing sustenance and
mending clothes. Often begun on an *ad hoc* basis by the wives of Party
members,[17] these activities soon became organised so that canteens for
Storm Troopers (SA men), particularly, and sewing rooms for making
and repairing uniforms and other clothing operated on a regular basis
in many local branches. As they worked, the women discussed points of
Party policy and those who were sufficiently familiar with the basic
tenets went out to canvass and distribute literature at election time.
The Party's women also went around the houses in their area collecting
clothes and money for needy Party members, particularly for SA men
and for the families of the unemployed, not least 'when the husband
had lost his job for political reasons'.[18] And when SA men were involved — as they increasingly were — in ugly brawls with political
opponents, the local Nazi women's group would treat the cuts and
bruises sustained. This function far more than the others earned pro-
Nazi women public abuse and vilification, but, at least in retrospect,
many of them claimed that persecution only strengthened their pride
and their purpose.[19]

Like the Party itself, the women's groups adopted the leadership
principle, often because there was an energetic woman in a local branch
who took the initiative and organised activities. Frau Passow in
Göttingen was one such, and in Naumburg, in Gau Halle-Merseburg,
the lead was taken by Agnes von Bülow and her daughter. In Leipzig
Lotte Rühlemann led an active *Frauengruppe* (women's group) which
managed, in addition to its local commitments, to gather a small contribution early in 1927 to send to a grateful Goebbels in Berlin to assist
'last week's wounded'. Sometimes the leadership was given by a
Gauleiter's wife. Frau Hinkler, whose husband was an early Gauleiter
in Halle-Merseburg, played a leading part in starting women's group

activity there; and in Plauen/Vogtland not only was the Saxon Gauleiter Martin Mutschmann's wife one of the earliest members of the *Frauengruppe der NSDAP*, founded in January 1923, but the family interest was enhanced by the adherence of Mutschmann's mother as well.[20]

During the confused period of Hitler's imprisonment some individual women's groups emerged which pledged loyalty to him even while the Party was outlawed. As far north as Lübeck a 'National Socialist German Women's Movement' was founded in 1924 which had its own organisation and constitution, but acknowledged Hitler's unchallenged leadership and, even in the difficult prevailing circumstances, formally required its members to join the NSDAP.[21] In Nuremberg, the *Völkischer Frauenbund* (racist-nationalist women's association), created in July 1924 from the remnants of the local women's group of the German Workers' Party, retained its name until the major reorganisation of 1931, but in practice functioned as the local Party's women's group. At the start it pledged allegiance to Hitler, Ludendorff and, in addition, the repulsive local anti-semite Julius Streicher, who frequently addressed the group during 1924 and 1925. Then, the association counted a membership of 146, and from this position of strength sent representatives in 1925 to attend the founding of a similar group in Bamberg. The Nuremberg group seems to have worked amicably under the authority of the NSDAP's local branch leadership in the nucleus of the later Gau Franken.[22]

While women's auxiliary groups emerged in parts of Germany where NSDAP local branches were being founded and worked in support of these branches, and, as a rule, under the authority of their male political leadership, there was at the same time the parallel development of independent *völkisch* women's groups, some of which aspired to growth on a national scale. As early as 1914, Guida Diehl – later to figure fleetingly in the NSF – had founded the Newland Movement (*Neulandbund*) as a patriotic, ultra-conservative 'renewal movement' aiming at a religious revival and the moral regeneration of Germany.[23] Charlotte von Hadeln had broadly similar aims when she founded the *Bund Königin Luise* (BKL – Queen Luise League), a patriotic, non-party organisation, in 1923. Like Guida Diehl, she aimed to promote the virtues of Christian motherhood and morality, and to campaign against 'filth', socialism and the restrictions imposed by the Versailles Treaty.[24] Some members of both these groups eventually turned to National Socialism as a dynamic and growing party which reflected their own prejudices and aspirations, as did women who had been associated with the *Schutz- und Trutzbund* (Protective and Offensive Association)[25] in the early 1920s, including Lotte Rühlemann of Leipzig.[26]

Of the motley collection of extremist groups of 'patriotic' women which sprang up in the early 1920s, one would have particular significance for the NSDAP, primarily because of the determination of its leader to achieve a close association with Hitler's Party. The *Deutscher Frauenorden* (DFO — German Women's Order) was founded in Berlin in 1923 by Elsbeth Zander, and soon began to establish local branches in other areas; among the earliest were the group founded by Elsbeth Zander's close associate, Hanna Schnabel, in Chemnitz, Saxony, in 1923,[27] and the Mecklenburg group which was in being in 1924.[28] Because Elsbeth Zander was suddenly removed from a leading position in the Nazi women's organisation after a decade of political involvement, in 1933, and because Party offices strenuously resisted the repeated attempts made thereafter to contact her or enquire about her current activities,[29] it is not easy to construct a picture of her early career beyond the description 'journalist'.[30] But three things seem clear: first, she was extremely ambitious; she was also a natural leader who had the personal and oratorical power to rouse women and command their loyalty, and while she subscribed to the general aims of the other *völkisch* women's groups she seems to have been more genuinely radical than, for example, Guida Diehl and Charlotte von Hadeln, both of whom were unequivocally conservative. For all these reasons, Elsbeth Zander became attracted to the dynamic *völkisch* movement of National Socialism, and for the same reasons she was considered a valuable ally by the Nazis for several years, until her usefulness was expended.

While it began life unaffiliated to any political party, the DFO's preferences were well demonstrated when it sent delegates to the abortive Weimar 'unity conference' in summer 1924 and pledged its support to three heroes, Graefe, Hitler and Ludendorff, whose initials provided its somewhat unoriginal motto — *Glaube, Hoffnung, Liebe* (Faith, Hope, Love).[31] The official account of 1937, which accorded the DFO a unique place in the early development of a Nazi women's organisation, preferred to ignore the DFO's shared loyalty, asserting that 'during the Führer's imprisonment, the DFO placed itself deliberately and unconditionally behind Adolf Hitler'.[32] Indeed, Elsbeth Zander worked hard to increase the DFO's contacts with the Nazi Party, travelling to speaking engagements in different parts of Germany. As early as 1924 she addressed the *Völkischer Frauenbund* in Nuremberg,[33] and thereafter felt able to count Julius Streicher as an ally; in May 1926 she invited him to address a large women's meeting in Berlin, and also asked that he send her 'instructive material' about 'assaults on German girls' in Nuremberg, to help her to enlighten the girls in the DFO's youth groups about the perils they might face at the hands of Jews.[34]

But Elsbeth Zander's ambitions were not restricted to achieving occasional contacts with NSDAP notables. Already in May 1925 she had written to Hitler himself asking for the maximum publicity to be given for the DFO's forthcoming national rally, since 'it would assuredly be of great importance if a good number of women from National Socialist circles took part'.[35] Her efforts began to pay off in 1926, with the formal accrediting of the DFO as the Party's women's auxiliary group at the Weimar Party Congress in July 1926, and her own recognition by the Party as legitimate and unchallenged leader of the DFO.[36] Where this arrangement left the other essentially local women's groups working for the NSDAP was not clarified; this was not a question which would have impinged on Hitler's mind, although it was probably at the forefront of Elsbeth Zander's. For the DFO, an immediate benefit was that the Party's newspaper, the *Völkischer Beobachter*, began to carry news items about it and to urge SA men and Party members to support its activities. And Goebbels, the Berlin Gauleiter and therefore the Party's political leader in the area where the DFO was most active, showed readiness to speak at major DFO meetings, for example the commemoration service on 9 November 1926, for the 'martyrs' of 1923, and at a similar meeting a year later he was fulsome in his praise for the DFO's work for the Party.[37] Goebbels's attitude here is of interest, since in a few years it was to alter markedly, and the early cordial relationship between the DFO, with its headquarters in Berlin, and the Greater Berlin Gau of the NSDAP was to turn very sour indeed.

In the mid-to-late 1920s, however, the DFO seemed a considerable asset, a ready-made women's organisation with a leader who had thrown herself and her group wholeheartedly into the Party's work. That the great loyalty which she inspired in some of her followers would be offset by growing animosity on the part of others, and that she would turn out to be incapable of efficiently managing an enlarged organisation while the DFO grew in size, at the same time jealously guarding her own authority and status, was perhaps not foreseeable; it was certainly not foreseen. And so when, in December 1927, Elsbeth Zander asked Hitler to place the DFO under the direct jurisdiction (*reichsunmittelbar*) of the NSDAP, 'to facilitate closer co-operation',[38] he agreed. From January 1928 the DFO was affiliated to the Nazi Party.[39] New formal regulations for the DFO, which were agreed with the Party Leadership, described its aims as being: the removal of women from the disorders of party politics; training women in all aspects of nursing and welfare work; giving material aid to large families, political detainees and Germans abroad, especially those in the 'occupied areas' taken from Germany at Versailles; and training girls to become 'racially conscious' German women and responsible members of the *Volksgemeinschaft* (national community). The conditions for admission to the DFO were a minimum age of eighteen and some proof that the applicant was of German 'Aryan' stock. Confirming the new relationship between the DFO and the NSDAP, admission to the DFO was restricted to female Party members, while Elsbeth Zander's status was enhanced by her designation, with Party approval, as *Reichs-führerin* (National Leader) of the DFO.[40]

Elsbeth Zander's apparent willingness to submit her own organisation to the authority of the NSDAP must have seemed a stroke of good fortune to the male-orientated Party which had paid negligible attention to attracting female support but which now, from the mid-1920s, committed to achieving power by constitutional means, would have to try to appeal to female as well as male voters. Without any noticeable effort by the Party leaders – beyond making the occasional appearance at DFO functions – the Nazi Party had acquired a women's organisation which already had branches in various parts of the country and over which Elsbeth Zander seemed to exercise unquestioned authority. The DFO's new regulations adequately reflected the views held by the Party Leadership about the role women should play in the community, and the Party would benefit from the automatic acquisition of new members now that joining it was obligatory for existing as well as aspiring DFO members. Elsbeth Zander apparently had some difficulty in persuading her followers of the benefits of the new arrangement, since a number were reluctant to pay – albeit a reduced subscription – to join the Nazi Party. But she insisted that this requirement by the Party Leadership be met, on pain of expulsion from the DFO,[41] and this threat seems to have worked. While figures for the early women's groups associated with the NSDAP have to be treated with more than ordinary caution, it seems reasonable to suggest that the new relationship between the Nazi Party and the DFO gave the latter renewed impetus and therefore, because of the Party membership requirement, also benefited the former: in August 1930 a police report mentioned that the DFO had about 160 local branches with about 4,000 members altogether.[42] On this basis, the DFO seems to have accounted for a good half of the female membership of the NSDAP which stood at 7,625 in September 1930.[43] Elsbeth Zander, with her enhanced status as the women's leader recognised by the Nazi Party, was clearly a valuable ally to be treated with respect.

Her own view of the 'common cause' to which both the DFO and the NSDAP were pledged seemed to accord with Hitler's; it was, she said, 'not the construction of a new party, but the education of new people', a process in which she believed a women's organisation had a large part to play. Bringing up the young in the faith, combating Jewish influence in art, literature and university studies, as well as performing social welfare tasks of a variety of kinds, including the provision of nurseries and holiday homes for children from urban areas, were all duties which, she said, German women should take upon themselves. But the 'holiest' task of the DFO was to lie in what Gertrud Bäumer, the middle-class feminist, would later characterise as the provision of an ambulance service for injured Party members in the brawls and shooting incidents which amounted to 'nothing other than civil war'.[44] Not surprisingly, Elsbeth Zander placed a higher value on the provision of sick bays and rest homes for SA men and the training of nurses of the order of the 'Red Swastika' — as opposed, presumably, to the Red Cross — in basic first aid,[45] and there is no doubt that in 1927 and 1928, at least, this service was welcomed by the SA and the Party generally. Not until the SA in Berlin had developed its own specialist medical corps did the disadvantages of an inadequately-trained and fiercely autonomous band of women helpers from the DFO begin to seem intolerable, in 1931.[46]

While the DFO was winning Hitler's recognition and growing in strength, new women's groups associated with local Party branches also emerged, as the NSDAP's organisational network expanded across Germany in the later 1920s, particularly once the reorganisation of 1928-9 achieved both greater centralisation of authority and stimulated the development of 'new affiliates and front organisations'.[47] These women's groups worked in essentially the same way as the DFO, with first-aid for injured SA men, the provision of clothing and food for the Party's indigent, and constant attempts to raise funds for these activities which generally came under the heading 'charitable work'. Again like the DFO, these individual local women's groups founded 'youth groups' or 'girls' groups', to recruit girls to the movement at an impressionable age and to train them from the start in the kind of activities in which they would take part when they graduated to the senior organisation. Many of the activities undertaken clearly prefigured the work that would be organised on a much larger scale in the Third Reich both in the NSF and also in the Nazi welfare organisation, the NSV.

For example, what was already termed 'winter aid' work was deemed particularly necessary among needy Party comrades, especially those with large families, as Christmas approached and as, by 1930, unemployment figures climbed steeply. Sending city-dwelling children on holidays in the countryside was another project which continued beyond 1933, while helping mothers and thriftily making and mending clothes and shoes would also be a continuing preoccupation. All of these activities figured prominently in the Gau Histories for the 1920s.[48]

While the NSDAP's organisation was relatively thin on the ground, in the mid-1920s, there was plenty of room for the founding of new women's groups, whether of the DFO, with its central office in Berlin, or on a purely parochial level, like the groups founded in Kassel in July 1925, Frankfurt in April 1927 or Hamburg in May 1927.[49] But a great expansion in the Party's coverage of the country in the later 1920s, coupled with the official recognition of the DFO as the Party's women's auxiliary, led increasingly to competition between rival jurisdictions. Elsbeth Zander clearly believed that Hitler's recognition of the DFO gave her *carte blanche* to assume the leadership of all women's groups associated with the Party, but this had not been stated, nor, it may be guessed, was it intended. Some groups already in existence did not object strongly to takeover by a more important organisation with a national network which presumably would mean enhanced status for them, too. As early as 1926 the von Bülows of Naumburg had agreed to this course, and in Göttingen Frau Passow's group eventually acceded to the DFO leadership's repeated requests to join the DFO *en bloc*. The Gau History records that this association proved a happy one, with Elsbeth Zander a welcome visitor to Göttingen. In Gau Saxony, the Mutschmanns' group in Plauen, too, agreed to join the DFO, and from 1928 there was a substantial increase in the number of DFO groups in the Gau, particularly in the larger towns.[50]

But not all the women's groups which had emerged spontaneously to assist local branches of the NSDAP were prepared to submit to takeover by the DFO after they had done the initial spadework. In Gau Upper Franconia, for example, seven separate groups existed not as part of a women's organisation but as auxiliary groups affording assistance to their respective NSDAP local branch.[51] The *Völkischer Frauenbund* in Nuremberg retained its singular character and local autonomy, too.[52] And in Gau Saxony, in the face of major DFO expansion, Lotte Rühlemann steadfastly maintained the independence of her *Frauengruppe Leipzig* and refused to have anything amicable to do with the

DFO, while nurturing implacable personal animosity towards Elsbeth Zander.[53] While a member of the *Schutz- und Trutzbund* in the early 1920s, Lotte Rühlemann had established a women's group in Leipzig. Discerning, no doubt, the greater potential for success of a more dynamic movement, she threw in her lot with the Nazis and in November 1926 placed her group under the direct authority of the NSDAP's Leipzig local branch.[54] Starting life in a small way with 'sewing evenings' at which the clothing of Party members and local unemployed people was repaired, the *Frauengruppe Leipzig* went on to organise social events on an increasingly ambitious scale, particularly at Christmas.[55] Lotte Rühlemann's success in resisting encroachment by the Saxon DFO organisation, while working closely with the local NSDAP branch, was signalled by her appointment in 1931 as the first Gau NSF leader in Saxony,[56] a post in which she was still to be found ten years later.[57]

The piecemeal and haphazard development of the 1920s led by the end of the decade to there being different groups of women pledged to assist the growing and increasingly successful Nazi Party. Groups which had been established in the early and middle 1920s had grown in size, with the Greater Munich Gau's DFO boasting 220 members by 1930,[58] while in Saxony there were a number of groups with rather less than 100 members each.[59] But these were relatively saturated areas; elsewhere, there was plenty of scope for the founding of new women's groups, whether of the DFO or of a purely parochial nature. The Göttingen DFO, for example, helped to create groups in neighbouring Northeim and Münden.[60] The process continued up to and beyond the *Machtübernahme*, especially in areas like the Rhineland where National Socialism was slower in being established,[61] and indeed continued into the 1940s, as new areas were annexed or conquered and Party organisations developed where there was a 'racially desirable' population. Throughout the lifetime of the Nazi Party there were women's groups at different stages of development. Before 1931 and the founding of the *NS-Frauenschaft*, the main problem was that there were also different kinds of group. The DFO, with its Berlin headquarters distant from the Party's capital in Munich, was by far the largest single women's group associated with the Party, with its independent leadership and mushrooming branches in the later 1920s. The various *ad hoc* groups attached to local Party branches had, by contrast, no overall organisation. And there was, in addition, a significant number of women Party members who did not belong to any women's group at all.[62]

This element of variety need not in itself have proved a disadvantage, although the characteristic monopoly-mania of the Nazi leadership suggests that it would not have been long tolerated in any case. But while Nazi women's groups were sparsely distributed there was little contact between them, and therefore little friction. Once, however, there was growth on a significant scale, there was friction, most noticeably in Saxony, Berlin and Munich. This was either caused or exacerbated by Elsbeth Zander's ambition to absorb all Nazi women's groups into the DFO, coupled with both her own inherent shortcomings and the relative autonomy which she had managed to retain for the DFO at the time of Hitler's acceptance of its affiliation to the Party. Placing her organisation in a *'reichsunmittelbar'* relationship to the NSDAP meant to Elsbeth Zander that the DFO could enjoy the benefits of close association with the Nazi Party while accepting only the ultimate authority of the Party's Munich Leadership over it. Neither Gauleiters nor lesser Party officials had any control over the DFO – as they had over the parochial women's groups – which became increasingly intolerable as DFO groups claimed to be working for the Party while refusing to accept the authority of its political leaders. Together, these elements provided the context for the major reform of the women's organisations in 1931.

Until then, the different groups of women continued their work, apparently oblivious to the paradoxes of their position. Much of their work for their 'fighting menfolk' indeed accorded with the Nazi view of women's role in society. Providing free meals for unemployed Party members and – however trivial it was in large political terms – buttering 'vast quantities of slices of bread . . . before SA expeditions', and mending clothes were obviously 'womanly work'. Visiting the families of 'political detainees' – usually in prison for acts of violence – and providing elementary first-aid for the SA's injured, too, broadly fitted the description. But other aspects of Nazi women's activities in the *Kampfzeit* were less plausibly 'womanly': for example, their intensive canvassing work in elections[63] as the Weimar Republic's political crisis deepened conflicted with Hitler's insistence on keeping women completely out of politics. Further, the activism and, particularly in DFO groups, the independent-mindedness of these enthusiasts seem incongruous among women who were fighting for an inherently anti-feminist cause. Many of them, it is clear, did not take seriously Party pronouncements about restricting women's sphere of activity, and the degree of latitude which they were allowed in their own groups no doubt convinced them that these would not apply to the faithful when the time came to put Nazi ideas into practice.

Because she remained fully in charge of her own organisation, Elsbeth Zander was more a prey to this illusion than some; she could listen to Goebbels's words to the Berlin DFO — 'the struggle is the men's affair, being a mother is woman's' — and still persist in talking about 'women standing side by side with men in the struggle'.[64] She, and others, failed to realise that Nazi women had achieved considerable independence only by default. The aggressively *männerbündisch* (male chauvinist) character of the NSDAP from its inception had led to the complete neglect of women's activities within the Party, so that women who were nevertheless attracted by National Socialism were left to work out their own role and to play it largely as they chose. This applied as much to a parochial group under a vigorous leader — like Lotte Rühlemann in Leipzig — as to the more autonomous DFO. By the time the Party's men acknowledged that women could make a distinctive contribution to the struggle, the pattern of the 'women's work' had been set, whether individual local Nazi leaders welcomed the form it took or not. The women themselves have been written off as naive, but that is at best an oversimplification. Far from being under false illusions, many of them welcomed the male leaders' much-publicised views about women's role as 'wife and mother' and little else; they looked forward to the day when 'women's rightists' of any colour would be silenced, including those in their own ranks. Women with feminist sympathies who had been drawn to National Socialism for other reasons — anti-semitism, anti-socialism, fierce nationalism, *völkisch* mysticism, for example — either did not believe that they would be affected by a campaign against socialist and liberal 'women's rightists', or else imagined that they could somehow persuade the Party leaders to change their mind. When, in 1933, it emerged that the men had meant what they said, a number of disillusioned women supporters voiced their protests;[65] they, along with women in the Party whose assertiveness had been an asset when it had helped to win women's votes, found that once Hitler had achieved political power they were expendable.

There were other paradoxes, too. In a Party where 'Nordic' rites were supposed to replace Christian ones, it seems incongruous that there were particularly energetic efforts by the women's groups to provide Christmas festivities. But while this was obviously an appropriate propaganda tactic in areas — in the south and the Rhineland, for example — which were resistant to Nazi penetration because of strong clerical influence, it is also clear that many Nazi women activists had a genuine personal religious conviction. Many women had gravitated towards *völkisch* movements precisely because of a revulsion at everything associated with socialism – including 'atheistic Marxism'. To many of them, upholding 'Christian morality' in the face of the menace of 'Bolshevist licence' – with easy divorce and legal abortion available in the Soviet Union[66] – implied also defending Christianity itself. In 1931, the first 'Principles of the *NS-Frauenschaft*' propagated the idea of 'a German women's spirit which is rooted in GOD, nature, family, nation and homeland', in that order.[67] Even after 1933, many officials and even two leaders of the NSF classed themselves as either Catholic or Evangelical,[68] as distinct from the Party's preferred usage, *gottgläubig* (theist).

Probably the strongest factor in drawing women to National Socialism was its militantly anti-left stance, and this ensured that the Party's women, like the men, were predominantly middle-class, particularly lower middle-class, from families of declining status and slender means. But there was also a modest element of working-class support for the Party, which grew as the Depression bit. The Social Democratic Party (SPD) and the Communist Party (KPD) could each claim to speak for the working class, but large numbers, particularly among unorganised workers, supported neither of them; at most, half of all wage-earners voted for the SPD and the KPD together.[69] Women workers were less likely to be organised than men, and working-class women as a whole were less likely to vote for the SPD or the KPD than men – if at all.[70] Nazi women's political activity was from the start largely concerned with supporting the men in street fights with Communists and proselytising in large cities, challenging the KPD and the SPD for a share of their constituency. Believing that deeds would be more effective than words, they hoped to win over the families of the unemployed by 'winter aid' activity, providing hot meals and clothing, especially for the children, and organising trips to the countryside for underprivileged city-dwelling youngsters. It was claimed that converts were made in this way, and that wives would convince their husbands that National Socialists cared more for the working class than the Marxist parties. One of Elsbeth Zander's major strengths was said to be her talent for winning over working-class women,[71] and certainly the DFO's early strongholds – in Berlin, Munich and the industrial cities of Saxony – were areas with a substantial working-class population.

Even so, in the early years particularly, it was the middle-class element which was dominant, with some relatively well-educated women among the early local leaders. On balance, it seems that the women supporters of the NSDAP tended to be slightly older than the men;[72] how far the experience of the miseries of the home front during the war, and the 'stab-in-the-back' myth, traumatised adult women and predisposed them to seek a radical rather than a traditional conservative solution to their grievances is not clear, but it seems plausible that those who lost sons, husbands and fiancés and also suffered severe privation would be inclined to look beyond the conventional forms that had already proved fallible. The very extravagance of some Nazi promises would seem attractive to embittered middle-aged, middle-class German women in the 1920s. These women, who were anti-socialist to the core, were among the most enthusiastic helpers of the SA, ministering to their needs in their squalid brawls; and yet, the SA was not only the radical element in the Party, but was, increasingly from 1926, strongly proletarian in membership.[73] Perhaps, then, some Nazi women deliberately cast themselves in the traditional role of leisured middle-class ladies dispensing bounty to the deserving among the lower orders – and to them the men fighting 'Bolshevism' in the streets and working for Adolf Hitler's victory certainly seemed deserving. The very designation of their welfare activities as 'charitable work' suggests that there may well have been an element of this in the strange alliance of conformist middle-class women with groups of roughnecks.

This, then, may have been the motivation for some of the women who were drawn to National Socialism even before it became a powerful national political force. For the rest, the reasons were – as Gau Histories and personal testimonies suggest – a complex mixture of family involvement, strong anti-left political prejudice, or a genuine commitment to National Socialism or to a particular personality within the movement, for example, Hitler himself, Julius Streicher, or, with members of the DFO, Elsbeth Zander. For some, the simple desire to engage in some kind of group activity was sufficient motive. Nazi ideology, such as it was, was clearly insignificant in attracting women to the cause; altogether, the practical, not to say mundane, nature of most of the women's activity suggests that enthusiasm for active involvement in a patriotic, anti-socialist cause in support of their fighting menfolk was a far more powerful motive than attraction to an at times crude and contradictory political faith.

Strasser and the Crisis in the DFO

The formal recognition of the DFO as the Party's women's auxiliary, coinciding with general organisational changes within the NSDAP,[74] led in spring 1929 to Gregor Strasser, as Reich Organisation Leader, being made nominally responsible for DFO affairs at the national level, for the administrative convenience of the Party. Before long he was expressing regret at his involvement in an area which was full of problems, but over which he had little control.[75] The Party Leadership (*Reichsleitung*) had recognised the DFO as the women's group with the right and duty to minister to the sick and needy in local branches, and to the SA particularly, but it had arrogated to itself no right of intervention in the internal affairs of the DFO in return. Perhaps this was the price consciously paid for the influx of DFO women into the Party; more likely, it was the result of a lack of interest by the male leaders of the Nazi Party who were pleased enough to accept the DFO's aid without troubling to concern themselves with its affairs. To this extent, the Nazi Party brought upon itself the problems raised by its women's groups in the late 1920s. Strasser unwittingly found himself the target of a barrage of irate correspondence from those both attacking and defending the conduct of the DFO, and of Elsbeth Zander particularly, and manifested visible discomfort at being unable, through his lack of direct authority over the DFO, to deal effectively with the hornets' nest of problems that was uncovered.

Strasser's skill in coping with these problems in spite of his limited room for manoeuvre, and in dealing with the various personalities who bombarded him with proposals, advice and complaints about the women's organisation, sheds interesting light on his own character.[76] He was extraordinarily agile and tactful with those whom he did not wish to offend when he was unable to meet their requests, but when a correspondent failed to comprehend how diplomatic he was being and overstepped the bounds of complaint which he would tolerate, he could be icily polite in his displeasure. His capacity for work and for its orderly conduct are evident in the volume of correspondence of an apparently trivial but potentially explosive nature with which he was prepared to contend, and the patently relaxed manner in which he did it. He never wavered from his insistence on the need, which he discerned but which others were too obtuse to appreciate, to retain Elsbeth Zander's goodwill — which meant upholding her status — because she personally commanded the loyalty of a substantial number of women in the DFO who might have been lost to the Nazi cause had she been antagonised. Strasser's sensitivity to this is the essential background to the mounting conflict between DFO groups and other Nazi women — in the 'women's groups' (*Frauengruppen* or *Frauenarbeitsgemeinschaften* — FAGs) — in the years 1929-31. It is to the credit of Strasser alone that his attempted solution, the major reorganisation of autumn 1931, resolved the most damaging and disruptive problems in the women's organisation, even if it did not remove them all.

The difficulties which Strasser had to face arose in spite of a ruling by the January 1929 *Führertagung* (leaders' conference), which Elsbeth Zander attended,[77] that there should be only one women's group in each local branch of the Party, whether it was a DFO group or an FAG.[78] Contrary to expectations, this line of demarcation failed to eliminate friction between the DFO and the other women's groups working for the Nazi Party. This was partly because of Elsbeth Zander's stubborn ambition to monopolise Nazi women's auxiliary activity, but was also because a growing number of Gauleiters and local branch leaders were finding the self-confidence of the DFO a positive nuisance, as its members insisted on working for the Party but not under the control of its local political leadership. A trial of strength developed between Elsbeth Zander and the DFO on the one hand and members of the parochial women's groups on the other which seemed in 1931 to be running against the DFO, as a number of Gauleiters and lesser Party officials supported its rivals. Only Strasser's determined upholding of Elsbeth Zander's position, coupled with his dissolution of the DFO when the NSF was created in autumn 1931, saved her from the *coup de grâce*, to the chagrin of her enemies.

Although there was indeed friction in some areas between the different kinds of group, many of the problems which emerged from about 1929 originated within DFO branches themselves. In more than one case, a group of DFO members had become disillusioned either with the local leadership or, more seriously, with Elsbeth Zander's conduct of the organisation as a whole. Discontent manifested itself earliest in the DFO's heartland in Berlin, where a group of women – including one of Elsbeth Zander's earliest associates, Hedwig Kruk[79] – seceded from the DFO early in 1929 because they were dissatisfied with Elsbeth Zander's treatment of them. They did not disband or leave the Party, but rather established themselves as a separate *Frauengruppe* and continued to provide assistance for the Berlin Party and the SA.[80] This was the nucleus of the Berlin *Frauen-Arbeitsgemeinschaft* which was recognised by Goebbels as the official women's auxiliary of the Party and given an office in his headquarters in Hedemann Street.[81] This was a clear breach of the 1929 *Führertagung* ruling; and it also provided Elsbeth Zander's most bitter enemies with a power-base from which to wage a determined vendetta against her and her organisation.

Again, in Munich, the DFO was welcomed and given publicity in the

Völkischer Beobachter in 1929 and 1930, and its work for the Party was praised by Gauleiter Adolf Wagner.[82] But, as in Berlin, so in Munich a disaffected group of DFO members, highly critical of Elsbeth Zander, left the DFO in May 1930 *en masse* and founded the Munich FAG under Frau Kury. Their chief grievance was that the Munich DFO sent most of its subscription income to DFO headquarters in Berlin, and therefore lacked the means to help SA men in Munich. The new 50-strong FAG proposed to step into the breach by providing warm food and clothing for members of the SA and the Hitler Youth in Gau Greater Munich.[83] Its success in winter 1930-31 was signalled by the attendance at its Gau conference in March 1931 of a number of leading Gau Party officers, and particularly by the glowing terms in which Gauleiter Wagner praised the work of the FAG, expressing the hope that many more FAG local branches would soon be founded in his Gau.[84] Frau Kury was listed as the representative of the Party's specialist group for women in the organisation plan of the Gau Munich office which was circulated to district and local branch offices in July 1931.[85]

This was a poor reward for the 220 members of the Munich DFO and their leader, Rosa Stierhof-Schultes, who had worked energetically to rally women to take collections and mend clothes for unemployed Party members.[86] She had already complained in autumn 1930 that 'elements' were trying to damage the Munich DFO.[87] Now, in April 1931, she wrote to Strasser about Gauleiter Wagner's 'double-dealing', about his ingratitude to the DFO after all its hard work, and about the 'scandalous' rivalry which had developed between the DFO and the FAG in Munich. The DFO's position had been undermined to an intolerable extent, she said, so that only the Party leadership could restore it.[88] Still she continued to work for the Party, desperately trying to raise funds for the stream of needy comrades pouring into Munich as the Depression worsened.[89] But Adolf Wagner had made his choice between the DFO and the FAG in his Gau, as he was entitled to do, and to reinforce it he banned the DFO from making collections for the Gau's funds for the destitute in summer 1931, bringing renewed complaints from Rosa Stierhof-Schultes.[90]

Wagner's methods may have been crude, but his choice was understandable. Like a number of Gau and local branch leaders, he found that he preferred the assistance of an FAG, which was under his direct authority, to a DFO group, which was autonomous in the regions and recognised only the authority of Elsbeth Zander at DFO headquarters. In fact, only where a DFO group was prepared to work closely with the local Party leadership, deferring to Party authority if a political leader required it, was a Gau or local branch Party leader likely to favour the presence of a DFO group in his area at all. The DFO was, by the late 1920s, at a distinct disadvantage, in spite of its national organisational network and Hitler's recognition of its special position. For while the fragmentation and the essentially parochial character of the various groups which opposed Elsbeth Zander and the DFO meant that a concerted campaign against her would be difficult, it also meant that her enemies had no identifiable organisation or central leadership which could be challenged once and for all. Each jurisdictional battle had to be fought out at the local level, often with the Party's political leadership on the side of the DFO's rival.

This was not to say that the anti-DFO groups operated in isolation; on the contrary, they corresponded with each other and kept in touch with developments outside their own area, to an increasing extent in 1930 and 1931. Lotte Rühlemann in Leipzig was, for example, a friend of one of the early activists in the breakaway *Frauengruppe* in Berlin, Klothilde Schütz. In November 1930 Lotte Rühlemann was pleased to report that the Frankfurt DFO leader had resigned from the DFO along with her local secretary and treasurer because they had repeatedly tried to contact Elsbeth Zander by letter and telephone, with a total lack of success. Lotte Rühlemann had also met two disillusioned DFO members from Wiesbaden who had been trying fruitlessly to arrange to talk with Elsbeth Zander – 'the same old story', she commented. She herself had recently helped to start an FAG in nearby Plauen, the earliest base of Nazi women's activity in Saxony; 'I don't know if the DFO there has by now fallen asleep', she said.[91] She was to report a couple of months later that a DFO group did still exist, alongside the new FAG, in Plauen – contrary to the *Führertagung* decision – and that this was creating confusion. Lotte Rühlemann's own energetic style as leader of the Leipzig *Frauengruppe* was by now being cramped by the appointment of Hanna Schnabel of Chemnitz as the DFO's Gau leader in Saxony.[92] All this information sent to Klothilde Schütz, herself an inveterate letter writer, would be passed on to other opponents of Elsbeth Zander. His patience sorely tried by her intrigues, Strasser would in September 1931 lose it altogether and berate Klothilde Schütz in the strongest terms for writing to women in many parts of Germany to incite them to opposition to Elsbeth Zander.[93]

Not least because of the *Führertagung* ruling, other DFO leaders besides Rosa Stierhof-Schultes were left high and dry. In June 1931, Elsbeth Zander herself complained to Strasser about the forced dissolution of DFO groups in Pomerania, the Ruhr area and Hanover by local Party leaders who had then promptly ordered the women concerned 'to turn themselves into women's groups of the NSDAP, that is into FAGs'. Quite apart from the unrest that this was causing, it was, she said, 'contrary to every agreement'.[94] But the Party's political leaders across the country seem to have interpreted decisions and agreements rather differently from Elsbeth Zander and her followers. The Halle Party leader had felt within his rights in ordering the dissolution of the local DFO group and the adherence of its members to the Halle *Frauengruppe*, and complained repeatedly to the *Reichsleitung* that the group refused to obey him, claiming that only an order from Munich could force it to comply.[95] This is a clear example of the DFO's interpretation of the extent of Party control over it signified by the acceptance of its '*reichsunmittelbar*' relationship. In disputed cases, Elsbeth Zander's advice to her supporters was to approach Gregor Strasser himself, so that an obstructive Gauleiter or local branch leader could be forced to respect the integrity of the DFO, and Frau von Glasow, DFO leader in East Prussia, for one, took this line of attack.[96]

If the DFO seemed increasingly on the defensive in 1931, and its leaders constantly complaining about their treatment at the hands of local Party officials, it was largely because of action taken arbitrarily against it by Party leaders who were frustrated by their total lack of control over it in the areas where they were supposed to have unchallenged jurisdiction over the Party's work. This was, after all, what the leadership principle was all about. The local branch leader had, of course, only very limited authority, but if he was supported by his Gauleiter in action against the DFO – or if the action was taken by the Gauleiter himself, as it sometimes was – then the DFO was bound to be the loser. Part of Strasser's dilemma was that while he recognised the value of the DFO, even if only reckoned in Party membership figures, he certainly did not want to challenge Gauleiters' territorial authority over a relatively trivial issue. For the Gauleiter, at a time when Party affiliates were being strongly encouraged, an FAG was ideal because not only did it avoid the problems raised by the DFO's semi-independent status, but, because the FAGs had no national organisation, they were also free from the problem – which affected control over the Party's other affiliates – of dual allegiance, to the Gauleiter on the one hand and to the affiliate's national leadership in Munich on the other.[97] The advantage of an FAG was that it could be allowed as little or as much autonomy as suited a political leader, according to his own circumstances.

While the guerrilla warfare between the DFO and the FAGs affected Party branches in many parts of Germany, from the Ruhr to East Prussia, from Pomerania to Munich, some areas where women's activity was well established were completely untouched by it. Göttingen, with its relatively long history of Nazi women's activity, did not suffer at all from the 'unrest in the *Frauenorden* . . . out in the Reich'.[98] And Baden's Gauleiter, Robert Wagner, could not have been more pleased with his DFO organisation which was under the 'splendid' leadership of Frau Klink. As he told Strasser, not only were there no rival women's groups in Baden, but 'disputes and quarrels, yes, and even gossip, have been as good as excluded', while 'the Baden DFO has already performed very gratifying work, particularly in the field of welfare'. Care of the sick and injured and of the children of destitute Party members, as well as the opening of canteens for the unemployed and the provision of clothes for the needy had been left — with complete success — in the hands of 'our excellent women's organisation'.[99] This unsolicited testimonial can have done Baden's DFO leader no harm at all; the peaceful regime of her organisation would be a strong recommendation in securing for her, eventually in February 1934, the leadership of the NSF, as Gertrud Scholtz-Klink.[100] Her example showed that a DFO organisation which would collaborate closely with its local Party could be appreciated. In Baden, far from the DFO's capital in Berlin, Gertrud Klink enjoyed both independence and authority, provided that she recognised the ultimate jurisdiction of the NSDAP Gau Baden. This pattern provided the model for her tenure of office as National Women's Leader in the Third Reich.

While Baden on a large scale and Göttingen on a smaller one were models of tranquillity, no doubt the 'women's work' proceeded in other Party branches, too, in as orderly a fashion as the official history later claimed. But by 1931 there was enough conflict in important areas like Berlin, Munich and Saxony, as well as in numerous smaller branches, for the problems of the women's groups to seem intractable within their existing structure. The attempt to draw lines of demarcation by the *Führertagung* decision had failed to bring harmony because so many Party leaders jumped at the chance of dissolving their local DFO group, regardless of how long it had been in existence and how much it had helped the Party in earlier difficult days. And if the Party's men were not dissatisfied with their local DFO, often enough the Party's women were. Much of the problem derived from the balance of the opposing forces: Elsbeth Zander probably had as many enemies as friends. Had she been under attack from a few factious individuals

only, they could probably have been isolated and neutralised; but
Party bosses of varying degrees of importance could not be completely
disregarded. Had Elsbeth Zander had fewer enthusiastic adherents, then
she and her organisation could have been abandoned by the Party; but
at a time when women Party members numbered only 7,625, the influx
of 600-700 members a month into the DFO, and therefore also into the
Party, which was reported in spring 1931,[101] was very welcome, especially at a time when the Party Leadership was concerned about its
poor image among voting women and about its political opponents'
apparently superior success in attracting women's support in elections.[102]

While Strasser was well aware of Elsbeth Zander's value as a leader
of women, he was also under no illusion about her shortcomings as a
leader of an organisation. Although outwardly defending her against
her enemies, and condemning the most active of these as being moti-
vated by 'personal hatred',[103] he was fully alive to her incompetence in
financial affairs[104] and wholeheartedly agreed with Kurt Klare, a friend
who told him of the widespread criticism of the DFO's *Opferdienst*,
that this magazine was ridiculous and embarrassing.[105] By autumn 1930
Strasser's mind was already turning towards a plan which would mean
the complete reorganisation of the women's groups, since it was clear
that the problems and antagonisms were too deeply-rooted to be
patched up or ironed out. Lotte Rühlemann had heard that the DFO
and the FAGs were to be amalgamated under new regulations as from
New Year 1931,[106] but the serious accident sustained by Gregor
Strasser at this very time put him out of action for some months and
his plans for the women's organisations into cold storage.[107]

In the first half of 1931 a succession of damaging revelations involving the DFO vindicated Strasser's view that a radical reform of the
women's groups was necessary. Had he not been prevented by critical
illness from introducing his new scheme early in 1931, the acrimony
that erupted during the summer might have been averted. On the other
hand, it was never going to be easy to persuade DFO and FAG members
to sink their considerable differences and co-operate amicably in a new
organisation embracing them all. Even more, it may have required the
crises that developed in 1931 to persuade Elsbeth Zander to agree to
the dissolution of the DFO at all. At this time, she seems to have been in
poor health, suffering from congestive heart failure,[108] which may partly
explain why she seemed to be negligently inactive at times.[109] But
whatever the reasons for her increasingly obvious inadequacy and the
growing dissatisfaction with the DFO in many parts of Germany, it

was clear that the women's groups were becoming a liability at a time when the Party was anxious to concentrate its resources on winning widespread popular support rather than dissipating its energies on internal quarrels.

While Strasser was convalescing, Elsbeth Zander at last had to grapple with the mounting chaos at DFO headquarters. In February 1931 she entrusted the rationalisation of the DFO's finances, particularly, to a Pastor Lossin.[110] News of this cheered Strasser who had, he said, been trying to persuade Elsbeth Zander to set her affairs in order 'for years, without effect'.[111] Although financial incompetence in the DFO was not restricted to Berlin,[112] what Lossin uncovered there more than confirmed his worst suspicions that negligence had reached a criminal level, while corruption on a large and blatant scale raised the embarrassing prospect of the need to take legal action against the culprits. Lossin improved the image of the *Opferdienst* and managed to win back subscribers who had drifted away in disgust. But the DFO was lamentably deep in debt. Local tradesmen refused to supply goods to its headquarters since they no longer expected to be paid, while rent, salaries and insurance contributions were all seriously in arrears. Elsbeth Zander, as the individual legally responsible, faced bankruptcy proceedings.[113] The ensuing publicity would inevitably have damaged the NSDAP at the very time when the Party was striving to capitalise on its success in September 1930 and drive towards the overthrow of the Weimar 'system'.

Lossin's efforts at restoring some order to the DFO's office were prodigious and remarkably successful,[114] in spite of Elsbeth Zander's continuing interference.[115] But Strasser was now convinced that while the DFO's regime could be rationalised, its reputation in Berlin could not be salvaged. He seems, in fact, to have regarded Lossin's success as a mixed blessing, since it threatened to reprieve an organisation which by summer 1931 Strasser regarded as defunct. And Lossin's deteriorating relations with Elsbeth Zander only complicated an already difficult issue.[116] Strasser's main concern with the DFO — and it was only a fraction of his responsibilities — was to achieve its dissolution in the reform which he had conceived before his accident and over which he was now negotiating with Elsbeth Zander.[117] Still not fit enough to travel,[118] Strasser sent his lieutenant, Paul Schulz, to Berlin to handle the delicate task of persuading her to agree to his plans, warning that it was essential to treat her with the utmost care, to ensure her agreement.[119]

As if to confirm Strasser's diagnosis, new problems involving the

DFO in Berlin surfaced at this time, in April to June 1931. The ramifications of what at first sight looked like one more round in the skirmishing between the Berlin FAG, led by Frau Grüder, and the DFO were far-reaching. The tremors of the Stennes crisis, which erupted out of the mounting discontent of the SA in the capital,[120] inevitably affected the DFO because of its long and close association with the Berlin SA.[121] Klothilde Schütz wrote to Goebbels in April 1931 to accuse Elsbeth Zander of complicity with Stennes,[122] and others, too, claimed that the DFO's Berlin headquarters was a stronghold of Stennes sympathisers.[123] Elsbeth Zander herself complained to Strasser that many of the DFO's financial problems were attributable to demands made by Stennes on DFO funds, demands which, she said, 'alone and powerless' she had been unable to resist.[124] But whether she was victim or accomplice, it was incontrovertible that the DFO had supported the SA and worked closely with Stennes, and thus seemed to have been aiding the enemies of the Berlin Party leadership, something which was not lost on Goebbels. These events, and the revelations about the DFO's domestic chaos, coincided with a major campaign against the DFO by the Berlin FAG because, as Frau Grüder complained to Goebbels, in one area of Berlin an FAG had been dissolved and replaced by a DFO group.[125]

This was only an excuse to open hostilities on a grand scale. Frau Grüder had assembled a dossier of complaints about the national leadership of the DFO, from various sources, and she dispatched it to Schulz in Munich during April.[125] As the Gauleiter who had recognised the FAG and given it houseroom, Goebbels undoubtedly sympathised with its view of the DFO, particularly once the Stennes crisis broke. He was in the intolerable position of being – even as Gauleiter – unable to intervene in the affairs of the DFO in Berlin, however damaging they might be to the Party there at this critical time. And so while he may have been genuinely grateful when presented with an opportunity to urge Strasser to act against the DFO, there is also the possiblity of his collusion in the production of the damning complaint which was lodged with him against the DFO in early June 1931 by Dr Conti, leader of the SA's professional medical service in Berlin.[127] To all appearances, Goebbels was petitioned from many sides, by the Berlin FAG, by the tireless Klothilde Schütz, and, more seriously, by Conti, to restrain the DFO's excesses. But since he was powerless to take decisive action, it is tempting to speculate that he advised Conti to commit his charges to paper in the form of an official report to himself as Gauleiter, so that he could send it on to Strasser with an urgent plea for the speedy dissolution of the DFO, as he promptly did.[128]

Conti's report explained that his own medical service had superseded the DFO's rudimentary first-aid provision for the Berlin SA, but that the DFO had refused not only to accept this but also to work under the supervision of SA doctors. Now the DFO proposed to open a home for sick and injured SA men, but Conti opposed this because of the total inadequacy of a similar venture already undertaken by the Berlin DFO. Conti waxed scathingly eloquent about the so-called 'nurses' of the DFO, with their lack of training and 'brown, nurse-type fantasy uniforms'; he deplored the 'rowdy and vulgar' manner in which they comported themselves and complained that the unprepossessing picture presented by these 'uniformed pseudo-nurses' had the damaging effect of deterring state-registered nurses from joining the SA's medical service. Conti himself would have restricted DFO activities and put their premises off limits to the SA, had he not been prevented from doing so by his erstwhile superior, Stennes. This reference to a connection between the DFO and the disgraced rebel was cautious but no doubt intended to provoke the drawing of damning inferences. Conti ended his lengthy complaint by squarely attributing the responsibility for all his problems with the DFO to Elsbeth Zander, whom he described as a 'psychopath'. If the Berlin Gau leadership would not alter the situation, he said — and he knew that it could not — then he would institute proceedings against Elsbeth Zander in the Party's court to try to prevent her from further jeopardising the Party's reputation and the SA's activities in the capital.[129]

Whether by arrangement or out of genuine shock at Conti's disclosures, Goebbels wrote at once to Strasser urging him, in the light of the report's revelations, to dissolve the DFO and 'according to proposals you have already made, [create] a new organisation of women Party members'. Any delay would be 'extraordinarily dangerous, particularly for the Berlin organisation', and as a measure of his own concern he was, he said, writing at once to his subordinates[130] to advise them not to allow the DFO to make collections for the Berlin Party, nor to engage in auxiliary work with the SA without the express permission of Dr Conti.[131] Outraged by this restriction, Frau Sagawe, the DFO leader in Berlin protested to Strasser that the DFO in Berlin had been 'completely shelved' and that the FAG alone was permitted to work for the Party there; she seems to have had no inkling of the reasons for this. She appealed to Hitler, through Strasser, to remember how the DFO 'has done its duty for seven long years', while the FAG had not been involved in the hard, early struggles of the movement.[132] But this was, as she must have known, a misrepresentation, since the hard core of the FAG consisted of disaffected secessionists from the DFO; in Berlin, in Munich and elsewhere FAGs had only been created, so the Leipzig *Frauengruppe* believed as an article of faith, because of dissatisfaction with already established DFO groups.[133]

Whether Conti's threat to use *Uschla* (intra-Party courts system)[134] proceedings against Elsbeth Zander — with the accompanying public scandal that could be involved — acted as a stimulant, administered by Goebbels to Strasser, or whether a successful conclusion to Schulz's negotiations with Elsbeth Zander created the appropriate moment for action, in early July 1931 Strasser issued an order with skeleton plans for a new *Nationalsozialistische Frauenschaft* to replace all existing women's groups associated with the Party on 1 October 1931. From the point of view of the Berlin FAG only one provision mattered: Elsbeth Zander was to become 'National Adviser to the *Reichsleitung* on Women's Affairs'.[135] This, it seemed, was a clear sign that far from Elsbeth Zander's being removed from any position of influence in Berlin, she was now to be made leader of all Nazi women, with the authority over non-DFO groups to which she had long aspired. In fact, Strasser was treading a vary narrow path, trying to suggest to DFO members that their leader was indeed being promoted, to secure both their and her compliance with the reform, while actually ensuring that the NSF would be firmly under Party control at all levels, terminating the DFO's anomalous and damaging autonomy. These finer points were missed by a large number of Elsbeth Zander's opponents; none felt more aggrieved than the members of the Berlin FAG.

There is no indication of whether either Goebbels or Conti was involved in the final phase of the FAG's attack on Elsbeth Zander. Nor is the position of Paul Schulz clear; he had received the FAG's file of complaints against the DFO leadership in April,[136] and had presumably passed it on to his superior. Now in August 1931 the Berlin FAG sent Strasser an updated version of the dossier, with further letters and depositions on oath, as well as a digest of the earlier complaints and a covering letter from Frau Grüder, with a statement calling Elsbeth Zander unfit to lead the NSF signed by 44 irate men and women.[137] For good measure, two members of the FAG wrote a further long letter to Strasser at the same time to tell him that it was 'frankly grotesque' that they should now be subordinate to the person who had 'ruined the DFO in Berlin through bad management' and who had gravely upset many Party members of both sexes not only because of her lack of competence but also because of her inherent 'moral unfitness'.[138] These themes reappeared again and again in the dossier, with statements testifying to Elsbeth Zander's untruthfulness, laziness, incompetence, and her tolerance of disorderly and filthy premises. To the Berlin FAG, said Frau Grüder, the prevailing regime in the DFO's leadership was 'in practical as well as moral terms an insult to National Socialist sentiment', while Elsbeth Zander was totally unacceptable as leader of the NSF because she would pose a 'constant menace to the integrity and purity of our Movement'.

Some of the charges were of a professional nature, with echoes of Conti's report in the complaints about DFO 'sisters' with no proper training, dressed in brown nurses' uniforms and masquerading as qualified nurses. Elsbeth Zander's reported excuse for the deceit was 'I have to show Herr Hitler something'. In addition, the arbitrary treatment of office staff, the thoughtless squandering of money, the deplorable standards of the *Opferdienst*, and more besides, were all attested to by various sources, including Leipzig, Lotte Rühlemann's base, to show that this was not merely the biased impression of the Berlin FAG alone. But the Berlin FAG twisted the knife with accusations about the 'slovenliness' which was 'Fräulein Zander's chief characteristic', and the 'relationship' which she had had with the DFO's chauffeur, Tonack, which was clearly too scandalous to be described. SA and SS men complained of shabby treatment by the DFO, especially if they had opposed Stennes. But the SA itself emerged in a dubious light, with stories of its members appearing at meetings dressed up in women's clothes.[139]

On 26 August 1931, these accusations and the covering letters were sent to Gregor Strasser, with the threat of using the *Uschla* system against Elsbeth Zander to prevent her from assuming the leadership of the NSF.[140] But the case came to nothing, and Elsbeth Zander took up her new duties in Munich on 1 October 1931, as scheduled. It seems likely that Strasser either threatened, or actually resorted to, *Uschla* proceedings against the Berlin FAG's ringleaders on the grounds of their flagrant indiscipline. This, at any rate, was the tactic he adopted with Klothilde Schütz, informing her on 11 September 1931 that he had commenced *Uschla* proceedings against her because she persisted in sending round letters to acquaintances all over the country to incite them to resist 'a measure of the *Führer*'s', Elsbeth Zander's new appointment.[141] He had already told her very clearly that his reorganisation plans had been devised 'as a matter of duty in the interests of the Movement', that he would carry them through in the same spirit, and that he could not countenance 'criticism and opposition . . . if they result purely from personal antipathies.[142] For Strasser, Elsbeth Zander's agreement to the new order was the *sine qua non* of its effectiveness, and he had designed the NSF so as to achieve this while also, by winding up the DFO and removing her from Berlin to Munich, rendering her relatively harmless. He was not going to have his painstaking work jeopardised by a pressure group of self-styled loyalists who seemed not to comprehend the discipline which the hierarchical tightly-organised Nazi Party demanded. There can be little doubt that he responded to the Berlin FAG's threat of *Uschla* proceedings promptly and ruthlessly; none of the leading lights in the Berlin FAG achieved office in the Berlin NSF.

The Founding of the *NS-Frauenschaft*

The timing of Strasser's announcement on 6 July 1931, that a new *NS-Frauenschaft* was to supersede the existing Nazi women's groups, may well have been conditioned by events in Berlin – the chaos uncovered by Lossin in the DFO's office, Goebbels's request for speedy action, and the implacable campaign against Elsbeth Zander by the Berlin FAG. But the idea, which had been brewing for some time, was his, and the careful structuring of the NSF to eliminate the worst problems of the existing situation bears his hallmark. Above all, the way in which he broke the news in public is distinguished by its tact:

> The hitherto existing women's organisations, which have only ever been able to embrace a section of National Socialist women, cannot, with the best will in the world, perform [the necessary] tasks . . . [143]

But before his revelation could be made, Strasser had had to persuade Elsbeth Zander that, for the sake of the movement, the DFO – her creation, her personal political vehicle – must be dissolved and its members brought together with both those who had held aloof from Nazi women's group activity and those who had been positively hostile to the DFO. Still convalescent, Strasser delegated this task to Paul Schulz, who reported on 30 April that he had broken the news to Elsbeth Zander, and that she was 'shocked'. Having stressed firmly that the decision was irreversible, Schulz softened the blow by telling Elsbeth Zander of her proposed new title, *Reichsreferentin für Frauenfragen bei der Reichsleitung* (National Adviser on Women's Affairs to the Reich Leadership).[144] This must have been as attractive a prospect for Elsbeth Zander as it was a rude shock to her enemies.

The July announcement gave only the broad outlines of the new order, which suggests that Strasser rushed it out in response to circumstances before he was ready to unveil the detail. This he expected to reveal in September 1931, but it was not published until 1 November, a month after the scheduled inauguration of the NSF throughout the country on 1 October 1931. The result was a degree of confusion in many Gaus and local branches, with heated speculation by the women affected. Strasser had exposed himself to a renewed barrage of complaints, queries and proposals from friends and enemies of the DFO alike. But he seems to have braced himself for this, consistently adopting a polite but brief reply to most correspondents, whatever their hobby-horse, pointing out that there would soon be further details about the new organisation of the women's groups which would clarify the position, and hoping that the writer would have patience until these appeared.[145]

In the meantime, an outline of the proposed reform was provided. Nazi women were in future to be first and foremost Party members, carrying out the 'women's work' of the Party under the direct authority of the local branch leader. All women Party members would 'automatically comprise the NSF within a local branch . . . without its own independent organisation and without the right to levy subscriptions'. The local branch leader was empowered – but not obliged – to appoint to his executive an adviser on women's affairs who would be responsible for supervising the NSF's work. There would, in addition, be a staff of advisers on women's affairs in Munich, led by Elsbeth Zander, which would work out general policy guidelines for the NSF's work and transmit these to the Gau leaderships and, through them, to the local branches. The existing groups were to continue their work until 1 October, and then dissolve themselves – DFO groups and FAGs alike – their members automatically becoming members of the NSF in their local branch of the NSDAP.[146] The failure to achieve compliance with the ruling that there should be only one group, of whichever kind, in any local branch, resulted in the consuming of all the groups into a system which would have a complete monopoly of women's activities within the Party.

The entire tone of the order demonstrates the extent of Strasser's anxiety to appease Elsbeth Zander, in order to ensure her co-operation. The full title of the NSF, explicitly intended to give 'recognition to the years of fruitful work by the *Frauenorden* and its manifest generosity over the rearrangement', was to be *Nationalsozialistische Frauenschaft (Deutscher Frauenorden)*. Strasser was less than truthful in claiming that the new order was the result of consultation between himself and Elsbeth Zander, but he probably saved her face to some degree. Also, by firmly asserting that the DFO's leadership was in full agreement with every aspect of the new scheme − including the dissolution of the DFO[147] − he did convince some DFO supporters that this was a victory for the DFO over its rivals, and that Elsbeth Zander's new position meant promotion.[148] This was intended to ensure that DFO groups accepted their dissolution and submergence in the NSF with a good grace, even with a will − as the DFO in Hamburg did[149] − and that Elsbeth Zander was convinced that her new position warranted the closing down of the DFO's headquarters in Berlin and her transfer to Party Headquarters. Strasser was particularly anxious that nothing should prevent this,[150] since only Elsbeth Zander's physical removal from Berlin could ensure a solution of the problems there.

The disadvantage was that Elsbeth Zander's enemies, too, believed that she was being promoted to a position of authority over the NSF. While this brought a final climax to the conflict in Berlin, it was also a source of anxiety to women elsewhere. But in reporting this to Strasser, Lotte Rühlemann showed that she − as a personal friend, apparently − was more alive to his subtlety than most. While writing to regret that she would not be able to work with Elsbeth Zander after all that had happened in the past, she hinted that if Elsbeth Zander's new post was to be purely 'organisational' then she would be able to co-operate. If, however, the title *'Reichsführerin'* carried any real authority over the NSF, she would have to decline the invitation made to her by the Saxon Gau Party leadership to assume responsibility for reorganising the women's groups in the entire Gau, and she had no doubt that her subordinates, too, would find it impossible to work under Elsbeth Zander. Although she couched her objections in the mildest of terms her inflexibility on this issue[151] was something of a gamble, given Strasser's sharp reaction to others' complaints about Elsbeth Zander.

In reply, Strasser did not call Lotte Rühlemann's bluff, if such it was; instead, he discreetly but unequivocally intimated that Elsbeth Zander's apparent promotion carried with it no authority over the NSF, and that all her actions would require his approval. The executive control of the NSF would lie with the Gau and local branch leaders, while Elsbeth Zander's position would be purely advisory; there was no question of her being 'some kind of Reich leader of all women'. As he told another anxious enquirer, Elsbeth Zander would have no power to issue orders to individual NSF groups, but it was Hitler's express wish that she should bear the title 'Adviser to the Reich Leadership'.[152] Hitler was, no doubt, manifesting his customary sentimental attachment to an 'old campaigner' who had stood by him in more difficult days. But Strasser's singleminded aim was to put Elsbeth Zander where he could, at last, control her activities and prevent further damage. Convinced that Lotte Rühlemann would understand his position, he told her that he would regard it as 'appropriate and valuable' if she accepted appointment as 'official expert' on women's affairs in Gau Saxony.[153] This finally signalled her triumph over her rival, the DFO's Hanna Schnabel, who became one of her district leaders, and the two seem to have managed to resolve their long-standing differences.[154]

The friends as well as the enemies of the DFO were confused about the projected reform; but Gauleiter Robert Wagner's problem was quite singular. He was so pleased with the Baden DFO that he asked that it be exempted from the new regulations, in case any change should 'endanger' the highly satisfactory arrangement in his Gau. His reading of Strasser's July order convinced him that the NSF would not be able to work as effectively as the Baden DFO currently did,[155] and in spite of a soothing reply from Strasser[156] he simply refused to implement the new system in October 1931. It was left to his mystified deputy to ask Strasser for clarification, since the executive orders issued eventually on 1 November seemed to conflict with what was happening — or, rather, not happening — in Baden.[157] The reply curtly ruled out any possibility of Baden's being an exception to new order,[158] which was now, belatedly, implemented, with the result that Gertrud Klink simply continued as the Gauleiter's chosen women's leader in Baden, operating the system which he found so pleasing.[159]

Robert Wagner was exercised, however, by a point which also worried others. Bringing together in one organisation all women Party members, whether they were active workers or not, seemed to him to be bound to dilute the strength of what, in his Gau, was a dedicated, tight-knit working group.[160] The DFO's leader in Gau Ostmark agreed, remarking drily that by no means all women Party members had chosen to join in group activity, and those who had not had seemed content to carry a Party card and bestir themselves little;[161] Lotte Rühlemann agreed with this diagnosis.[162] But the July ruling also had a positively disadvantageous side, as Strasser's mailbag soon revealed. In both the DFO and the FAGs, much of the voluntary work in soup-kitchens and first-aid teams had been performed by women who were not Party members but were nevertheless 'convinced adherents, and so mostly the wives and sisters of paid-up male members'. Were these valuable workers – many of them in financial straits, unable to afford a Party subscription – to be excluded from the new organisation? The local branch leader in Geislingen, Gau Württemberg-Hohenzollern, reported that under the new regulations his NSF group would number at best 20, whereas there were currently over 100 women working for the Party, whose valuable efforts were not to be jeopardised.[163] The Dortmund FAG leader made a similar anxious observation.[164]

Perhaps Strasser's delay beyond September 1931 in issuing the detailed regulations for the NSF was the deliberate result of a desire for feedback about his general proposals. Certainly, the November regulations contained the proviso that 'wives and daughters of those Party members who are in no kind of financial position to pay their own subscription can . . . be brought into the NSF'.[165] But some women took the opportunity to make the kind of partisan proposals which Strasser was specifically concerned to avoid. The Ostmark Gau DFO leader complained that 'the *Reichsleitung* is throwing out the baby with the bathwater' in dissolving the DFO, and urged acceptance of a plan which would, in effect, turn the DFO wholesale into the NSF, dissolve the FAGs, and bring all Nazi women and girls under the existing DFO leadership.[166] The Breslau DFO leader resented the provision that the direction of the 'women's work' would in future be in the hands of the male political leadership.[167] While these women completely failed to appreciate Strasser's determination to bring the women's activities firmly under the Party's control and to treat the former groups reasonably equitably, to cause the least offence possible, there were other DFO leaders who did not understand at all what the new regulations meant. The leader in Misslareuth, near Plauen, wrote to ask Elsbeth Zander – the only leader she recognised – how they would affect the particular circumstances of her local branch.[168]

The reorganisation of the women's groups came at a time when the Party itself was expanding rapidly, so that in a number of places, for example, Gau Hessen-Nassau-North, the Party leadership took the opportunity of the fresh start to found a women's organisation for the first time.[169] Similarly, in Hanau, in Gau Hessen-Nassau-South, the district leader gathered his female supporters into an NSF group, slightly prematurely, in summer 1931.[170] But the hiatus between the July order and the formal inauguration of the NSF raised doubts in the minds of some who were poised to enlist new recruits and did not want to dampen their enthusiasm by delaying the founding of new groups until after October. In August 1931 the ever-energetic Lotte Rühlemann was asking Strasser to issue the new regulations as quickly as possible, so that groups 'on the new model' could be established in a number of local branches in Saxony where there was a demand.[171] Strasser was not giving anything away at this stage, however; he had already advised Lieselotte Pahl-Witzleben, of Siegen, Gau Ruhr, to form 'emergency groups' which could work on a provisional basis until the new forms were introduced.[172] The worsening effects of the Depression during 1931 meant that the Party's women had to be mobilised immediately to provide relief for needy families, whatever the organisational structure of their activity.

Because of Strasser's delay in issuing the new regulations, the transition to the new forms occurred amid some uncertainty, with local considerations paramount. But a major obstacle was removed when at its national congress at Potsdam on 6 September 1931 the DFO agreed to dissolve itself.[173] And in some Gaus the inauguration of the NSF took place smoothly and punctually on 1 October; the problems in Berlin ensured that the new order was implemented gratefully there as early as possible. On 24 September, an order announced the dissolution of all DFO and FAG groups in Gau Berlin, stating pointedly that 'all hitherto existing offices and functions have expired. All office-holders must therefore be appointed from scratch', and the nomination of 'a suitable woman leader' was placed firmly in the hands of the Party's political leadership.[174] In Saxony, Gauleiter Mutschmann, the bane of DFO local branch leaders,[175] followed Strasser's instructions to the letter, and installed Lotte Rühlemann as Gau NSF leader on 1 October.[176] But his assumption that action at Gau level would suffice to ensure the institution of the new order in the local branches was over-optimistic; in mid-October, the confused DFO leader in Misslareuth had yet to place her group under Party control, in the NSF.[177] And at the same time complaints reached Strasser from Chemnitz, where Hanna Schnabel's long illness at this time may have complicated matters, that local branch leaders were seizing DFO funds and dismissing leaders in the confusion resulting from the absence of specific regulations.[178]

For other Gauleiters besides Mutschmann the national dissolution of the DFO and the continuing uncertainty about the NSF provided a golden opportunity to take action against local DFO groups which they had long disliked. Adolf Wagner had been quick to ban the Munich DFO from making collections for the Party's funds,[179] and from the Breslau DFO leader Strasser received complaints that the Upper Silesian Party leadership had refused the DFO's proffered assistance in its 'interpretation . . . of the new organisation of the *Frauenorden*'.[180] On the other hand, while Gauleiter Robert Wagner of Baden resisted the change as long as he could, other DFO groups continued to exist and work beyond 1 October. In Trier, a group 30 or 40 strong did not dissolve itself until well into November, when 'the members were kept on in the [Party's] local branch . . . directly subordinate to the local branch leader, who used them for charitable ventures'.[181] According to the Halle-Merseburg Gau History, the DFO groups there did not join the NSF until the beginning of 1932.[182] In Dortmund, it was an FAG leader who was in doubt, feeling obliged to delay the implementation of the new order beyond the beginning of October until she was clearer about the details involved.[183]

The work of the NSF was to be divided into three categories, with training in both 'spiritual-cultural' matters and domestic management in a national context and, thirdly, charitable work.[184] The Organisation Plan issued on 1 October in Berlin gave one local interpretation of these activities. NSF members were to work in groups under a 'working group leader' subordinate to the NSF section leader; above her stood the district NSF leader and, in overall charge of NSF work in the Greater Berlin Gau, the Gau NSF leader (GNSFL). NSF members were expected to be active in Berlin, to visit Party members in prison or hospital, as charitable work, to staff kitchens and sewing rooms for the unemployed, to give clerical assistance in Party offices, or to prepare talks or articles on ideological or cultural subjects. Each member was to fill in a questionnaire so that the Gau NSF leadership could decide which of these activities she could most appropriately perform. For NSF members who were genuinely pressed for time or in poor health, the commuting of service into money payment or the provision of material goods to help the needy was permitted.[185] The new GNSFL, Frau von Gustedt, hoped that group leaders would be chosen and members allocated to their duties by mid-October, so that she could review the new system with her section leaders.[186]

Within a week of the founding of the NSF, Frau von Gustedt had issued detailed instructions for the establishment of canteens for the unemployed — the most pressing task in the grim Depression winter of 1931-2 — and sewing groups to gather, make and mend clothes for distribution to needy Party members, and she had also given detailed guidelines for the various kinds of charitable work envisaged. A systematic and uniform order in all these areas was to be established throughout the entire Gau.[187] At slightly greater leisure, she issued instructions about the adoption of a brown uniform which would bear words or symbols describing the 'working group' to which its wearer belonged, as well as the swastika badge. Unemployed women in the Party would be set to work to make the uniforms in three standard sizes, and the cost to the purchaser would be eight or nine marks.[188] Given the independent-minded tradition of the Berlin FAG, it is hardly surprising that the Berlin NSF should have proceeded so far before Strasser's final regulations were issued. They would confirm his earlier hints that the NSF was not a national organisation, but the women's branch of the Party performing its 'women's work' on a decentralised basis.

In fact, Strasser's conception of decentralisation went much further than the mere devolving of authority to the new GNSFLs. He was, on the contrary, at pains to curb their power at this stage, stipulating that GNSFLs had no authority to give orders to NSF leaders in the districts or local branches. But there were two concessions: first, a Gauleiter could permit a GNSFL the right of 'inspection' of a district or local NSF group, exceptionally, if malpractice were suspected; and the district Party leader was to consult the GNSFL about the appointment of a district NSF leader. But the local branch Party leader was not required to consult any NSF official before appointing the woman of his choice as his local NSF leader. No doubt this was to reinforce Strasser's insistence that the nature of the NSF's work – most immediately, in providing material assistance for SA and SS men and needy Party members – was axiomatically local.

At the centre, Strasser perhaps allowed Elsbeth Zander more apparent authority than he had suggested to Lotte Rühlemann, among others, that he would. She was to head a new Section for Women's Work in the Party's Organisation Office, with the task of advising Strasser on all policies affecting women which he might contemplate; she was also allowed to suggest policies, but had no independent decision-making power. One potentially troublesome provision was that a Gauleiter should consult Elsbeth Zander when choosing his GNSFL. In many cases, of course, appointments were already *faits accomplis*; and in other instances Gauleiters would disregard this rule, to Elsbeth Zander's irritation, but with apparent immunity. On the whole, then, Elsbeth Zander's function – like that of all NSF officers – was to find how best to implement the decisions of the Party's Leadership as they affected women, not to question them. Orders would be transmitted from Strasser's office to the Gauleiters, and then to the political leaders in the subordinate areas; they were to be responsible for ensuring that their NSF groups were put to work in the best interests of the Party. And so while the NSF began life with what looked from one angle like a national organisation with a chain of command from the centre to the local branches, from another point of view it appeared that some of the links were missing.

With hindsight, it is evident that this somewhat ambiguous arrangement would allow Strasser to choose, in time and as the Party's fortunes improved, either to accelerate or to inhibit the few centripetal tendencies which he had permitted at first. But from the standpoint of November 1931 it was in no sense inevitable that he would choose the former, far less that he would do so in a matter of months. Strasser's immediate objective was modest: to start afresh, with old grievances forgotten as far as possible. He thanked the members of the former groups warmly for their valuable work and stressed that dedicated workers would be unconditionally welcome, regardless of which group they had worked for in the past, since 'the women's work is work for the Party', and not for any sectional interest within it. Strasser was still undecided about some aspects of the new order. He had indicated privately already that he intended to change the character of the DFO's paper, the *Opfer-dienst*;[189] now he hinted that this would be considered, along with a change of name. And he also envisaged the creation of a fully professional Party nursing organisation which would bear the DFO's favoured designation 'Red Swastika'. In immediate terms, however, the local NSF groups were to devote themselves to charitable and welfare work. They would have to provide or collect the means for this themselves, but at least they had the initial benefit of taking over the property and premises of the dissolved women's groups in their area, although Strasser stressed that 'the *Frauenschaft* is in no sense the legal inheritor of the dissolved women's organisations, but constitutes a new, definite structure for bringing National Socialist women together'. The urgent priority in autumn 1931 was not so much the settling of organisational niceties as the immediate co-ordination of practical work at the local level, with 'winter aid action' for the needy as the Depression plumbed new depths and winter approached.[190] Frau von Gustedt in Berlin may have assumed more overall control than Strasser initially intended, but her energetic plans for speedy action were clearly on the right lines.

Notes

1. BDC, *Sammlung Schumacher* (hereafter *Slg. Sch.*), 211, circular from Gohdes to all officials of Party and State and to journalists, 30 January 1934.

2. Found in HA/13/254-6. The collection is not complete.

3. 'Nationalsozialistische Frauenarbeit', *Frauenkultur im Deutschen Frauenwerk* (hereafter *FK*), April 1937, pp. 6-9; 'Nationalsozialistische Frauenarbeit', *Nachrichtendienst der Reichsfrauenführerin*, April 1937, pp. 90-5 and May 1937, pp. 114-21; Reichsfrauenführung (ed.), *NS-Frauenschaft*, Berlin, 1937.

4. W.S. Allen, *The Nazi Seizure of Power: The Experience of a Single German Town 1930-35*, London, 1966, p. 75.

5. Cf. the hagiographical style of Lucy Middleton (ed.), *Women in the Labour*

Movement, London, 1977.

6. *FK*, op. cit., p. 6.

7. HA/13/254, Gau History (hereafter GH) Kurhessen, p. 1.

8. G. Franz-Willing, *Die Hitlerbewegung. Der Ursprung 1919-1922*, Hamburg, 1962, pp. 174-6; Werner Maser, *Die Frühgeschichte der NSDAP. Hitlers Weg bis 1924*, Frankfurt, 1965, pp. 319-20, 329; Hüttenberger, op. cit., pp. 9-11; Orlow I, pp. 11-55.

9. Peter Merkl, *Political Violence under the Swastika*, Princeton, 1975, pp. 122-36; HA/13/254, GH Halle-Merseburg, pp. 1-4, 12-13; Scholtz-Klink, op. cit., pp. 27-8, 516-19; the entire text of the latter is in HA/13/254, *Nationalsozialistische Partei-Korrespondenz*, 'Rede der Reichsfrauenführerin Gertrud Scholtz-Klink auf der Tagung der NS-Frauenschaft', at the 1936 Party Rally.

10. Reichsorganisationsleiter (ed.), *NSDAP Partei-Statistik*, Munich, 1935, vol. I, p. 30, gives the 1930 women's NSDAP membership (by the 1935 Gau boundaries): Greater Berlin, 917; Kurmark, 395; Saxony, 673; Munich/Upper Bavaria, 776; Bayerische Ostmark, 349; Franken, 404; and Schwaben only 83. Also: Düsseldorf, 121; Essen, 137; Koblenz-Trier, 63; Cologne/Aachen, 105; Palatinate, 65.

11. *FK*, loc. cit; HA/13/254, GH Halle-Merseburg, p. 3.

12. Ibid., GH Saxony, p. 4.

13. Franz-Willing, op. cit., p. 129.

14. Maser, op. cit., pp. 253-4.

15. IfZ, op. cit., p. 10, says three; Jeremy Noakes, *The Nazi Party in Lower Saxony 1921-1933*, Oxford, 1971, p. 17, says four.

16. HA/13/254, GH South Hanover-Brunswick, p. 1; presumably she was the 'sculptress' (Noakes, op. cit., p. 23).

17. HA/13/254, GH Saxony, p. 1; Geoffrey Pridham, *Hitler's Rise to Power. The Nazi Movement in Bavaria 1923-33*, London, 1973, p. 204.

18. *FK*, loc. cit.

19. HA/13/254, op. cit., pp. 5-6; GH South Hanover-Brunswick, pp. 3-8; Koonz, *Social Science Quarterly*, op. cit., p. 557.

20. HA/13/254, op. cit., pp. 1, 9-10; GH Halle-Merseburg, pp. 5, 8; GH Saxony, p. 1; HA/13/256, 'Frauengruppe Leipzig', letter from Goebbels, ? February 1927, and reply, 16 February 1927.

21. Bundesarchiv (hereafter BA), NS22/vorl. 349, Gau Mecklenburg/Lübeck, 'Satzung . . . ', 15 November 1924.

22. HA/13/255, 'Völkischer Frauenbund Nürnberg', pp. 1-5.

23. Guida Diehl, *Erlösung vom Wirrwahn*, Eisenach, 1931, p. 75.

24. F. von Gärtner, in Charlotte von Hadeln (ed.), *Deutsche Frauen-Deutsche Treue*, Berlin, 1935, pp. 316, 318.

25. On the *Schutz- und Trutzbund*, Orlow I, p. 14, and Merkl, op. cit., pp. 321, 353, 398-9.

26. HA/13/254, GH Saxony, p. 3.

27. The exact date of the DFO's founding is not clear. In BA, *Slg. Sch.*, 230, *Meyers Konversations-Lexikon*, 1932, 'Die National-Sozialistische-Frauenschaft (Deutscher Frauenorden)', September 1923 is given. But in HA, op. cit., p. 2, Hanna Schnabel is said to have founded the Chemnitz DFO in August 1923. Elsbeth Zander, born 17 October 1888, unmarried, joined the NSDAP on 1 April 1926, as number 33511; BDC, her Party membership cards.

28. BA, NS22/vorl. 349, letter from Hedwig Kruk to Elise Albrecht, 20 August 1924.

29. HA/13/254, GH South Hanover-Brunswick, letter from the NSF Gau Press Officer to NSDAP Hauptarchiv, 12 December 1935; BDC, Konrad Witzmann's file, letter from Thuringia Gau Leadership to NSDAP Reichsschatzmeister, 30 June 1938, and reply, 10 August 1938; BDC, *Partei-Kanzlei-Korrespondenz* (hereafter

PKK), letter to Gauschatzmeister, Berlin, 8 February 1941.
  30. BDC, Elsbeth Zander's Party membership cards.
  31. BA, op. cit. See also Orlow I, p. 50.
  32. *FK*, op. cit., p. 7.
  33. HA/13/255, op. cit., p. 2.
  34. BDC, *Slg. Sch.*, 230, letter from Elsbeth Zander to Streicher, 28 May 1926.
  35. Ibid., letter from Elsbeth Zander to Hitler, 19 May 1925.
  36. *FK*, loc. cit.
  37. HA, reel 89, cuttings from *Völkischer Beobachter* (hereafter *VB*): 7/8 November 1926; 9/10 and 25 October 1927.
  38. BDC, op. cit., letter from Elsbeth Zander to Hitler, 12 December 1927.
  39. BDC, *Slg. Sch.*, 230, *Meyers Konversations-Lexikon*, op. cit.
  40. Ibid., 'Richtlinien des Deutschen Frauenordens', n.d.
  41. BDC, op. cit., 'An die Mitglieder des Deutschen Frauen-Ordens', signed by Elsbeth Zander, 20 January 1929.
  42. HA/89, '*Auszug* aus den Mitteilungen Nr. 23 vom 1.12.30 des Polizeipräsidiums Berlin'.
  43. *Partei-Statistik*, loc. cit.
  44. E. Beckmann (ed.), *Des Lebens wie der Liebe Band*, Tübingen, 1956, letter from Gertrud Bäumer to Helene König, Berlin, 1934, pp. 63-4.
  45. HA/89, 'Aufgaben und Ziel des Deutschen Frauenordens', *VB*, 16/17 December 1928.
  46. See below, pp. 46-7.
  47. Orlow I, pp. 145-9.
  48. HA/13/254, GH Saxony, pp. 4-6; GH Halle Merseburg, pp. 6-8; GH South Hanover-Brunswick, pp. 5-8; HA/13/255, op. cit., pp. 3-5.
  49. Eberhard Schön, *Die Entstehung des Nationalsozialismus in Hessen*, Meisenheim am Glan, 1972, p. 100; Albert Krebs, *Tendenzen und Gestalten der NSDAP*, Stuttgart, 1959, pp. 56-7.
  50. HA/13/254, GH Halle-Merseburg, p. 5; GH South Hanover-Brunswick, pp. 8-9; GH Saxony, p. 3.
  51. Ibid., GH Bayerische Ostmark, p. 1.
  52. HA/13/255, op. cit.
  53. BA, NS22/vorl. 349, letters from Lotte Rühlemann to Klothilde Schütz, 23 November 1930, and 11 January 1931.
  54. HA/13/254, GH Saxony, p. 3.
  55. HA/13/256, 'Frauengruppe Leipzig', notice of 28 November 1926; circular signed by Lotte Rühlemann, 22 December 1926; 'Weihnachtsfeier', 4 January 1929; BA, loc. cit.
  56. HA/13/254, op. cit., p. 4.
  57. Ibid., 'Anschriftenverzeichnis. Stand: 1. Juni 1941'.
  58. HA/89, 'Vormerkung', 21 December 1930.
  59. HA/13/254, loc. cit.
  60. Ibid., GH South Hanover-Brunswick, p. 12.
  61. F.J. Heyen, *Nationalsozialismus im Alltag*, Boppard, 1967, reports of 12 August 1931, p. 58; 2 February 1932, p. 62; 2 February 1931, p. 68; 13 October 1931, p. 73.
  62. Lotte Rühlemann provides a good description of the various women's and girls' groups associated with the NSDAP in BA, op. cit., 'Die Organisation der Frau innerhalb der NSDAP' (accompanying letter to Gregor Strasser dated 8 August 1931).
  63. HA/13/257, 'Vorschläge der Reichsfrauenführung für die Ausstellung "Wille und Sieg des Nationalsozialismus" am 9. März 1943 in München'; HA/13/254, as note 48, above.

64. HA/89, 'Der Reichs-Vertretertag des Deutschen Frauenordens', *VB*, 25 October 1927, and *VB*, 16/17 December 1928, op. cit.

65. E.g., Irmgard Reichenau (ed.), *Deutsche Frauen an Adolf Hitler*, Leipzig, 1934.

66. E.H. Carr, *Socialism in One Country*, vol. 1, London, 1970, pp. 37-48.

67. BA, *Slg. Sch.*, 230, 'Grundsätze der Nationalsozialistischen Frauenschaft', n.d. (? 1931); Orlow I. p. 2 mentions 'the party's annual "German Christmas" parties'.

68. BDC, Lydia Gottschewski's NSF card, Charlotte Hauser's Party census form (1 July 1939), Friedrike Matthias's NSLB card (1 June 1939), Else Paul's NSF card, Gertrud Scholtz-Klink's NSF card, Paula Siber's information in a questionnaire.

69. W. Böhnke, *Die NSDAP im Ruhrgebiet 1920-1933*, Bonn-Bad Godesberg, 1974, pp. 143-54; Timothy W. Mason, *Sozialpolitik im Dritten Reich*, Opladen, 1977, pp. 55-6.

70. Ibid., p. 60; Werner Thönnessen, *Frauenemanzipation*, Frankfurt, 1969, pp. 161-62; Richard N. Hunt, *German Social Democracy 1918-1933*, Chicago, 1970, pp. 126-8.

71. HA/13/254, Hildegard Passow, 'Zur Chronik der N.S.-Frauenschaft', 1 July 1934, p. 1; ibid., GH South Hanover-Brunswick, p. 9.

72. Heyen, op. cit., p. 331 gives the age distribution of pre-1933 Party members. The conclusion is drawn from two limited samples: Merkl, op. cit., p. 121, and Lawrence D. Stokes, 'The Social Composition of the Nazi Party in Eutin, 1925-32', *International Review of Social History*, 1978, no. 1, p. 18; and from my general impression.

73. Conan Fischer and Carolyn Hicks, 'Statistics and the Historian. The SA's Rank and File 1929-1934', *Social History*, January 1980, pp. 131-8. E.G. Reiche, 'From "Spontaneous" to Legal Terror: SA, Police, and the Judiciary in Nürnberg, 1933-34', *European Studies Review*, April 1979, pp. 258-9.

74. Orlow I, pp. 133-51.

75. BA, NS22/vorl. 349, letters from Strasser to Klothilde Schütz, 6 May and 24 September 1929.

76. Dr Peter Stachura, Stirling University, is writing a biography of Gregor Strasser. The remarks here are impressions from the limited material which I have seen, but Dr Stachura has been kind enough to suggest that they are close to the mark.

77. BA, NS22/vorl. 348, 'Entwurf zur Führertagung', 22 June 1928, and 'Rundschreiben', 12 January 1929, both issued by Strasser.

78. BA, NS22/vorl. 349, letter from the Halle-Merseburg Gau leadership to the NSDAP Reichsleitung, 8 December 1930.

79. Ibid., letter of 20 August 1924, op. cit., and letter from Marie Martschenke and Hedwig Kruk to Strasser, 26 August 1931.

80. Ibid., letter from Klothilde Schütz to Strasser, 15 September, 1929.

81. Ibid., letter of 26 August 1931, op. cit.

82. HA/89, reports in *VB*, 8 January, 19 June, 3 July 1929; 16/17 February, 7 May, 15 October 1930.

83. Ibid., 'Zusammenkunft der "Arbeitsgemeinschaft nationalsozialistischer Frauen" am 6:5.30 im Gasthaus "Luisenquelle" '.

84. Ibid., 'Arbeitsgemeinschaft nationalsozialistischer deutscher Frauen', *VB*, 14 March 1931.

85. Pridham, op. cit., pp. 200, 341n 25.

86. HA/89, reports in *VB*, op. cit., and 'Vormerkung', 21 December 1930.

87. Ibid., 'Vormerkung', 4 November 1930.

88. BA, op. cit., letter from Rosa Stierhof-Schultes to Strasser, 7 April 1931.

89. BA, *Slg. Sch.* 230, 'Deutscher Frauenorden Gau Gross-München', circular

signed by Rosa Stierhof-Schultes, 29 June 1931.

90. BA, NS22/vorl. 349, letter from Rosa Stierhof-Schultes to Strasser, 17 September 1931.

91. Ibid., letter of 23 November 1930, op. cit.

92. Ibid., letter of 11 January, 1931, op. cit.

93. Ibid., letters from Strasser to Klothilde Schütz, 4 and 11 September 1931.

94. Ibid., letter from Elsbeth Zander to Strasser, 10 June 1931.

95. Ibid., letter of 8 December 1930, op. cit.

96. Ibid., letter from Frau von Glasow, Königsberg, to Strasser, 14 June 1931.

97. Orlow I, p. 208.

98. HA/13/254, op. cit., p. 13.

99. BA, NS22/1044, letter from Robert Wagner to Strasser, 29 July 1931.

100. See below, pp. 106-7, 112-14.

101. BA, NS22/vorl. 349, letter from Pastor Lossin to Strasser, 22 April 1931.

102. Ibid., letter from Edith Fischer-Defoy to the Newland Movement, 30 May 1931; HA/13/254, Hildegard Passow, 'Propagandistisch Erfassung der Frau', autumn 1931.

103. BA, op. cit., letter of 4 September 1931, op. cit.

104. Ibid., letter from Strasser to Lossin, 10 March 1931.

105. BA, NS22/vorl. 348, letters from Kurt Klare to Strasser, 6 October 1931, and from Strasser to Klare, 22 October 1931.

106. BA, NS22/vorl. 349, letter of 23 November 1930, op. cit.

107. Ibid., letter of 11 January 1931, op. cit. I am grateful to Dr Peter Stachura for information about Strasser's accident.

108. BA, op. cit., letter of 22 April 1931, op. cit.

109. Ibid., letter of 23 November 1931, op. cit.

110. Ibid., letter from Lossin to Reichsschatzmeister Schwarz, 19 February 1931.

111. Ibid., letter of 10 March 1931, op. cit.

112. Heyen, op. cit., report of 19 May 1930, p. 43.

113. BA, op. cit., letter from Lossin to Strasser, 6 May 1931.

114. BDC, *Slg. Sch.*, 230, report from Dr Conti to Goebbels, 3 June 1931; BA, op. cit., letters from Lossin to Strasser, 22 April, 6 May and 4 June 1931.

115. Ibid.

116. Ibid., letter from Strasser to Paul Schulz, 6 May 1931.

117. See below, pp. 50-2.

118. BA, op. cit., letter from Strasser to Elsbeth Zander, 11 June 1931.

119. Ibid., letter of 6 May 1931, op. cit.

120. Orlow I, pp. 210-20. Tyrell, op. cit., pp. 226-8, 314-16, 334-9, 341-3.

121. BDC, op. cit.

122. BA, op. cit., letter from Klothilde Schütz to Goebbels, 15 April 1931.

123. Ibid., file of complaints against the DFO's leadership, Berlin, August 1931.

124. Ibid., letter from Elsbeth Zander to Strasser, 6 June 1931.

125. Ibid., letter from Frau Grüder to Goebbels, 14 April 1931.

126. Ibid., covering letter with the file from Frau Grüder to Schulz dated 20 April 1931.

127. BDC, op. cit.

128. BA, *Slg. Sch.*, 230, letter from Goebbels to Strasser, 10 June 1931.

129. BDC, op. cit.

130. BA, op. cit.

131. Ibid., circular from Goebbels to the NSDAP Gau Berlin district leaders, 10 June 1931.

132. BA, NS22/vorl. 349, letter from Frau Sagawe to Strasser, 16 June 1931.

133. Ibid., letter from Lotte Rühlemann to Strasser, 27 August 1931.
134. BDC, op. cit.
135. Ibid., 'Anordnung', signed by Strasser, 6 July, 1931.
136. BA, op. cit., file of complaints, op. cit.
137. Ibid., statement signed by 44 complainants, 26 August, 1931.
138. Ibid., letter from the Berlin FAG to Strasser, 26 August 1931.
139. Ibid., statements in the file of complaints, op. cit.
140. Ibid., letter of 26 August 1931, op. cit.
141. Ibid., letter of 11 September 1931, op. cit.
142. Ibid., letter of 4 September 1931, op. cit.
143. BDC, op. cit.
144. BA, op. cit., letter from Schulz to Strasser, 30 April 1931.
145. Ibid., letters from Strasser to Frau von Glasow, 18 June 1931, and to Frau Göbel, Breslau, ? October 1931.
146. BDC, op. cit.
147. Ibid.
148. BA, op. cit., proposals made by the DFO Gau Ostmark leader, 14 August 1931; circular to all DFO members, 23 September 1931; letter from Ida Müssig, DFO leader in Schleiz, to Strasser, 17 July 1931.
149. Ibid., letter from Else Lauerbach, DFO Hamburg leader, to Strasser, 23 September 1931.
150. Ibid., letter from Schulz to Guida Diehl, 17 August 1931.
151. Ibid., letters from Lotte Rühlemann to Strasser, 8 and 27 August 1931.
152. Ibid., letter from Strasser to Frau Rendschmidt, Neustadt/Upper Silesia, 22 September 1931.
153. Ibid., letter from Strasser to Lotte Rühlemann, 2 September 1931.
154. HA/13/254, GH Saxony, pp. 2-3.
155. BA, NS22/1044, letter of 29 July 1931, op. cit.
156. Ibid., letter from Strasser to Wagner, 31 July 1931.
157. Ibid., letter from Walter Köhler to Strasser, 23 November 1931.
158. Ibid., letter from ROL to Gau Baden, 27 November 1931.
159. Ibid., 'Referenten der Gauleitung', 25 June 1931.
160. Ibid., letter of 29 July 1931, op. cit.
161. BA, NS22/vorl. 349, proposals of 14 August 1931, op. cit.
162. Ibid., letter of 8 August 1931, op. cit.
163. Ibid., letter from the Geislingen local branch leader to the NSDAP Reichsleitung, 29 July 1931.
164. Ibid., letter from the Dortmund FAG leader to Schwarz, 10 October 1931.
165. BA, *Slg. Sch.*, 230, 'Ausführungsbestimmungen . . . ', *Die Organisation der nationalsozialistischen Frauen in der Nationalsozialistischen Frauenschaft*, 1 November 1931.
166. BA, NS22/vorl. 349, proposals of 14 August 1931, op. cit.
167. Ibid., letter from A. Göbel, Breslau DFO leader, to Strasser, 6 October 1931.
168. Ibid., letter from the DFO local branch leader, Misslareuth, to Elsbeth Zander, 14 October 1931.
169. HA/13/254, GH Kurhessen, p. 1.
170. Ibid., GH Hessen-Nassau, p. 1.
171. BA, op. cit., letter of 27 August 1931, op. cit.
172. Ibid., letter from Strasser to Lieselotte Pahl-Witzleben, 28 July 1931.
173. Ibid., letters from Elsbeth Zander to Strasser and Schulz, 4 August 1931, and from Strasser to Elsbeth Zander, 7 August 1931.
174. BA, *Slg. Sch.*, 230, 'Rundschreiben Nr. 26', 24 September 1931.
175. BA, NS22/vorl. 349, letter from the DFO Gau Saxony to Strasser, 17

October 1931.
176. HA/13/254, GH Saxony, p. 4.
177. BA, op. cit., letter of 14 October 1931, op. cit.
178. Ibid., letter of 17 October 1931, op. cit.
179. Ibid., letter of 17 September 1931, op. cit.
180. Ibid., letter of 6 October 1931, op. cit.
181. Heyen, op. cit., reports of 13 October 1931, and 14 January 1932, pp. 73, 76.
182. HA/13/254, GH Halle-Merseburg, pp. 8-9.
183. BA, op. cit., letter of 10 October 1931, op. cit.
184. BDC, op. cit.
185. BA, *Slg. Sch.*, 230, 'Organisations-Plan für die Arbeit der Frauenschaft', 1 October 1931.
186. BDC, op. cit., 'Rundschreiben Nr. 1', 1 October 1931.
187. Ibid., 'Rundschreiben Nr. 2', 1 October 1931; BA, op. cit., 'Rundschreiben Nr. 3', 7 October 1931, and 'Rundschreiben Nr. 4', 7 October 1931.
188. Ibid., 'Rundschreiben Nr. 5', 22 October 1931.
189. BA, NS22/vorl. 348, letter of 22 October, op. cit.
190. BA, *Slg. Sch.*, 'Ausführungsbestimmungen . . . ', 1 November 1931, op. cit.

2 CENTRALISATION AND CONFLICTS OF INTEREST

Centripetal Forces and Local Initiatives

Within a year of its inauguration on 1 October 1931, the *NS-Frauen-schaft* had evolved, from being merely the collective body of women Party members working away in the local branches, to achieving a distinctly centralised identity and developing a variety of projects to be pursued on a nationwide basis with a fair degree of autonomy. Three major reforms, in April, June and September 1932, culminated in the elevation of Elsbeth Zander's Section for Women's Work to the status of a Main Department of the Party's Organisation Office (ROL) in October 1932. This development was certainly not implicit in Strasser's orders of July and November 1931, in which his overriding purpose had been to eliminate the damaging strife among the women's groups and to create a useful and stable women's auxiliary. But three factors seem to have persuaded him that the emphasis in the NSF should be shifted from the performance of purely local activities with little overall co-ordination of the women's work to the construction of a women's organisation as such, with its own central organisation and leadership corps. In the first place, this development was fully consistent with the general reorganisation of the Party structure which consumed much of Strasser's energy in summer 1932.[1] Further, the Party's disappointing impact on women voters in the almost continuous round of local, Land and national elections in 1932 demonstrated the unfavourable effect of much of the Party's propaganda about women's role and its value to the Nazis' opponents as electoral ammunition.[2] Strengthening the NSF, upgrading its status, and allowing it some independence were partly designed to combat this. And finally, Strasser seems to have been impressed by the energy and enthusiasm of the Gau NSF leaders, who assembled at two conferences in 1932, and to have been persuaded by them that the NSF should be brought more into the mainstream of Party activity.

As a result of the discussions at the first GNSFL conference in March 1932, Strasser issued an order in April which forged some of the links that were missing from the chain of command outlined in November 1931, with the effect that the GNSFLs' status was enhanced.

They became full members of their Gauleiter's staff with the power to issue orders to the district and local branch NSF leaders. The GNSFL was given discretion about the size and composition of her own staff and about the appointment and dismissal of district and local branch NSF leaders. Only in the event of disagreement between the GNSFL and the Party's district or local branch leader about any of these issues was the Gauleiter to intervene; but he had the final word, and his approval was required for appointments and dismissals to be valid. This accorded with the general access of domestic authority which Strasser confirmed to Gauleiters in summer 1932.[3] From April 1932, then, NSF leaders at every level of the Party's organisation remained directly subordinate to the political leader in their area, but now also took orders about their NSF work from their superior NSF leader, to promote uniformity throughout the NSF organisation in a Gau. NSF leaders in the districts and local branches had the responsibility of ensuring that their members' work was in line with the policies of both the Gau NSF leader and the Gauleiter.[4] Strasser's position as ultimate overlord of both the NSF and the Gauleiters was supposed to promote the necessary harmony between the two, but the increased autonomy which he gave to both the NSF's central office and the Gauleiters in the regions sometimes vitiated this aim. At least the new arrangements gave retrospective sanction to the authority which Frau von Gustedt had arrogated to herself — presumably with Goebbels's approval — in the highly organised Berlin Gau.[5]

In his April 1932 order Strasser exhorted Party officials to support the NSF's work at every opportunity;[6] but his words seem to have fallen on deaf ears. In August 1932 he felt compelled to write to the Gauleiters to remind them that they were responsible for ensuring that the NSF's resources were being fully utilised for the Party's benefit.[7] While some Gauleiters undoubtedly welcomed their women's activities and allowed their NSF leaders considerable scope, others neglected this aspect at what was, for the Party as a whole, a crucial period, with elections to fight, funds drying up, and the worst effects of the Depression on needy Party members to combat. Continued foot-dragging by the Party's local branch leaders, particularly, brought complaints from GNSFLs at their second national conference in September 1932. Apparently, some local branch leaders had refused to permit the appointment of local NSF leaders altogether; no doubt the memory of the troubles with the DFO was still vivid in many minds. Dr Rienhardt, now Strasser's adjutant in charge of NSF affairs, urged his chief to send yet another circular reiterating in the strongest terms that the NSF was to perform the specifically women's tasks of the movement, with the fullest support of the political leaders. There could, he added, be no question of local branch leaders dissolving NSF groups — as had been known to happen — since the NSF was not an organisation in its own right but was an integral part of the Nazi Party.[8]

While Strasser and Rienhardt were at pains to combat the obstructive male chauvinism of Party leaders at all levels, their purpose was primarily to create an impression which would attract women voters instead of alienating them. And yet, they seem to have genuinely believed that a well-ordered women's organisation could contribute valuably to the Party's struggle. Only Strasser's tolerance of a degree of feminist militancy could have permitted the issuing of 'Principles of the *NS-Frauenschaft*' which flamboyantly propagated the idea of a 'women's renewal movement' and demanded a prominent place for women of ability in Hitler's 'new Germany'.[9] Strasser himself could be found using the term 'women's movement' about the NSF,[10] a term favoured by a number of Nazi women[11] in spite of its obvious liberal and socialist connotations. No doubt this seemed to imply that only non-Nazi 'women's rightists' would be anathema in the Third Reich. Once the Party's leadership had captured political power, the militants in the women's organisation — like militants elsewhere in the NSDAP — would find that they were expendable. But as the political struggle intensified in 1931-2, with a successful dénouement apparently tantalisingly close, their enthusiasm was not to be checked; and their apparent naivety was encouraged by the sympathetic response of Strasser and Rienhardt. The latter clearly believed that his chief might agree to a suggestion by Elsbeth Zander, on behalf of the GNSFLs, that adopting women candidates for the local elections in autumn 1932 would be an effective antidote to opposition propaganda about the Nazis' intentions of depriving women of all political rights if they came to power.[12] But the reality of Nazi policy towards political participation by women at any level would be demonstrated yet again in a matter of months, with a directive to Gauleiters that in local elections women were not to be considered as candidates 'since the purely political struggle is the men's task'.[13] It was one of the more unalterable of Hitler's many 'unalterable decisions'.

In return for encouraging Party officials to work with the NSF and for enhancing the authority and status of the GNSFLs, Strasser expected every NSF member to be an activist. The Party's courts would be used to exclude identifiable dead wood, a tactic suggested to Strasser by Lotte Rühlemann.[14] On the other hand, there was a resolution of the problem of enthusiasts who could not afford a Party subscription, with the creation of the category of 'assistants'.[15] They were, however, expected to make a small contribution to the NSF, according to their means,[16] and this erosion of the original principle that the NSF should have no treasury of its own was compounded by the authorisation of 'welfare funds' in local NSF branches, to pay for the NSF's charitable work. The funds were to be generated by the energy and ingenuity of the NSF members themselves, further enhancing the small degree of autonomy which they were beginning to enjoy; but all NSF activities were subject to the approval of the Party's local branch leader, and NSF accounts were to be liable to scrutiny by the Party's finance officers.[17] No doubt this was a necessary safeguard: in 'Thalburg' it was alleged in 1932 that the Nazi women's leader 'had misused party money (in one case to buy herself stockings)'. The protection of the local branch leader saved her from her enemies in the NSF, for the time being,[18] but this was presumably not what Strasser had meant when he said in April 1932 that he was trying to make 'the women's work within the movement more than hitherto the concern of the responsible political leaders'.[19]

The April order began the process of emphasising the centripetal tendencies in the November 1931 regulations at the expense of the centrifugal ones which Strasser had originally stressed. Although it was still claimed in October 1932 that the NSF was essentially decentralised in nature and activity,[20] Strasser's Party reforms in summer 1932 had already strengthened its central office and given its staff, led by Elsbeth Zander, considerable authority over the NSF in the regions, contrary to his apparent intentions in 1931. In the first phase of the summer reforms, in June 1932, the Section for Women's Work was brought into the new Main Department III of the ROL, along with other 'offices which could not conveniently be fitted elsewhere',[21] under Rienhardt's supervision. Then, bringing the NSF even further into the mainstream of Party activity, it was agreed in September 1932 that women representatives should be appointed to other Main Departments in the ROL, those for education and health, agriculture, the NSBO (factory cell organisation), and civil servants.[22] This may have been partly an electioneering tactic, as voting patterns continued to show that the Nazis' rivals were far more skilled at appealing to women.[23] Orlow implies that this was the motive behind the elevation of Elsbeth Zander's office to the status of a Main Department, number VIII (HA VIII), on its own, in September 1932,[24] which at least gave the impression that the Nazi Party believed that its women were capable of exercising responsible control over their own affairs. In fact, Rienhardt in HA III continued to supervise the day-to-day business of HA VIII after its inauguration on 1 October 1932.[25]

Elsbeth Zander's office was a small concern at first; she was assisted by two secretaries and two full-time employees. One of these, Hildegard Passow, the daughter of Göttingen's pioneering Frau Passow,[26] had lost no time after the founding of the NSF, sending Strasser in autumn 1931 plans for 'attracting women through propaganda'.[27] Pointedly refusing to allow her to bypass Elsbeth Zander, as women's leader, Strasser sent the memorandum to her office.[28] Whether through Elsbeth Zander's or Strasser's choice, Hildegard Passow was regarded as an asset and installed in the Section for Women's Work as an 'assistant'. But it was Dr Käte Auerhahn from Heidelberg who carried the burden of the Section's organisational work. Elsbeth Zander was designated 'leader of the *Frauenschaft*',[29] and seems to have made many of the general policy decisions. But Strasser was probably determined that she should not control the detailed administration of the Section, after the disasters that had befallen the DFO as a result of her incompetence. Käte Auerhahn, created 'Reich Inspector' of the NSF, clearly was able to run the Section efficiently; but while she could work amicably with Elsbeth Zander — no mean achievement, on past form — it soon became clear that she had a genius for antagonising other NSF leaders. The intrusive degree of central authority which she tried to exert over Gau NSF affairs would alienate Gauleiters as well as GNSFLs, and help to terminate her short career in the NSF in 1933.

As part of the upgrading of the NSF in summer 1932, the new Nazi women's magazine, which Strasser had promised in November 1931, at last appeared. The first issue of this *NS-Frauenwarte* was published in July 1932.[30] But it, too, presented difficulties. Apart from its staff's accommodation problems, in an insect-infested room on the fifth floor of an already cramped building,[31] there was an intractable personality clash between the editor, Elsbeth Unverricht, and Hildegard Passow in the Section. This affected relations between the *NS-Frauenwarte*'s editorial board and the Section to the point where the magazine consistently failed to carry articles which the Section's staff regarded as important, and endeavoured to live, as Rienhardt complained to Strasser, 'a life of its own' although it was supposed to be the 'campaigning organ' of the NSF. Repeated exhortations to both sides to sink their differences for the common good were to no avail,[32] and the separation of the running of the paper from HA VIII resulted in the appearance in both the *Völkischer Beobachter* and the *NS-Frauenwarte* of a report of the GNSFLs' September meeting which had not been vetted by Elsbeth Zander's office.[33] Rienhardt now agreed to liaise between HA VIII and the editorial board to ensure that the NSF's material received approved coverage in what was, after all, supposed to be its own magazine.[34]

Strasser intended that his reorganisation of the Party's central administration in summer 1932 should be followed by 'the systematic buildup of a National Socialist proto-government within the Gau organisations'.[35] Accordingly, HA VIII was, like the other Main Departments, to be reproduced on a smaller scale in the Gau and district administrations, which *in toto* were to reflect the structure of Strasser's own office in the ROL. The Gau and district NSF leaders would therefore become the HA VIII leaders on the Gauleiter's or district leader's staff.[36] This prospect raised misgivings among some GNSFLs that the degree of independence which Strasser's April order seemed to guarantee them was now being withdrawn.[37] But Strasser's purpose was to try to create a balance across the country between the substantial amount of autonomy essential to a Gauleiter's effective control of his region and the kind of uniformity throughout the entire Party organisation which only his own office in the ROL could achieve through its authority over the Gauleiters. With the NSF there remained the special problem of hostility on the part of many political leaders to involving women in the Party's work even at this time of frenetic electioneering.[38] And so when the final phase of Strasser's reform of the NSF was unveiled on 1 October 1932, the machinery for keeping the ROL in direct contact with developments across the country was provided in the fashionable form of NSF area inspectors, whose ostensible task was to co-ordinate the work of the GNSFLs, but who were also empowered to report to the Land inspectors, the Gauleiters' superiors, any instances of 'difficulties, misunderstandings or a lack of interest, which had led to NSF leaders' being inhibited by a local political leader from contributing fully to the Party's struggle'.[39]

With the appointment of NSF area inspectors, who were full members of HA VIII, the size and competence of the NSF's central office grew markedly. From October 1932 it was divided into two sections; in the first of these Elsbeth Zander and Käte Auerhahn devised policy – within the confines of Party requirements and Strasser's approval – and they transmitted instructions to the GNSFLs in the regions and to the staff of the other section of HA VIII. This had two sub-divisions, for the area inspectors and for the leaders of the nine sub-departments which each represented an aspect of the practical work for which NSF groups throughout the country were to be responsible. These were: women's education, hygiene and occupational questions; welfare and youth; instruction about the national economy; and press, propaganda and information.[40] These divisions did not exactly match the 'organisation plan' which Gertrud Scholtz-Klink would develop during the 1930s, but they clearly formed the basis from which she proceeded. They were certainly intended to provide a long-term plan for NSF work, once there was a Nazi Government, since there is no mention of the activities that consumed the attention and energy of all National Socialists in 1932, helping needy Party members and their families in the Depression and supporting the SA, and collecting funds and recruiting members as part of the Party's election campaigns. These would all be obsolete functions once power was achieved.

There can be little doubt that in summer 1932 Strasser was consciously laying the basis for a new, Nazified society of the long-term, but near, future. The prominence given to the development of the women's organisation was bound to be partly for immediate electoral reasons, but it was also all of a piece with Strasser's intention to build a miniature model of his ideal society which would take over Germany once political power was achieved. It was perhaps odd that women should figure in his organisational scheme on a level with civil servants and disabled veterans, two other groups which received Main Department status in the second phase of the summer 1932 reforms.[41] But this categorisation of women as an interest group was the result of the Party's general insistence on keeping women out of political life, and therefore out of the essentially political mainstream activity of the NSDAP. And it also derived from the haphazard way in which women's Party activities had developed — itself a result of exclusion by the men — and the disastrous impasse to which this had led by 1931. If there were GNSFLs who were frustrated by the NSF's not being an autonomous Party affiliate[42] — analogous, presumably, to the Hitler Youth — the response of the more misogynist political leaders suggests that many of them would have been happy to see the DFO and the other groups of Nazi women wound up in 1931 without a substitute of any kind being devised. The peculiarity of Strasser's middle way, with women's interests being classed, by implication, as sectional, is comprehensible in the light of the NSF's development as an alliance of diverse groups of women, many of whom detested the NSF's leader; once the decision had been made in summer 1931 to have a Party women's group, it was essential to control it closely from within the ROL.

As well as regulating the NSF's organisation at the centre and in the larger territorial divisions of the Party, the ordinance introducing HA VIII also described the projected local organisation of the NSF from the local branch leader down into the smaller units of the cell and the block. The NSF local branch leader was empowered to appoint a 'cell wife' and a 'block mother' to supervise the detail of NSF work in the smallest possible units, and to propagate the National Socialist message as intensively as possible.[43] This chain of command would already be applicable in the Gaus whose districts had densely-populated local branches, in the larger cities of Gau Saxony, for example, and also in the sections of the mammoth Gaus of Berlin and Munich. But the very varying degree of Party, and therefore also NSF, development throughout Germany, with relatively little penetration of some rural areas and Roman Catholic bastions, as well as left-wing strongholds like the industrial Ruhr,[44] meant that this intricate organisational network would have only limited application across the country before 1933. But, again, Strasser had provided the framework which could be applied to the entire country once political power was achieved.

While the number of women Party members – from 1931 also automatically NSF members – increased over sevenfold, to 56,386, between September 1930 and the *Machtübernahme*,[45] this comprehended wide regional variations. In largely rural Hessen-Nassau-North, the first NSF groups were established in the Party's districts in 1931-2, although in 1932 the total number of women involved in the entire Gau was a mere 158. No methodical record of their activities was kept, but they did perform welfare work of the by now traditional kind, providing clothing for the needy, sustenance for the SA, and comfort for the families of political prisoners. In neighbouring Hessen-Nassau-South, the first women's group was formed in Hanau in July 1931 by nine women who spent their first meetings reading *Mein Kampf* and studying the Party Programme to familiarise themselves with National Socialist ideas. By autumn 1931 the group had expanded and was ready to open an SA canteen and to begin Christmas preparations for the enjoyment of the 88 SA and SS men and 23 Hitler Youth members in Hanau.[46] Gau Lower Franconia had as many as 389 NSF members in 1932, but they undertook no organised practical work until after the *Machtübernahme*.[47] And although there was an NSF local branch, under the leadership of a Protestant pastor's wife, in Bayreuth from 1931,[48] Gauleiter Hans Schemm waited until June 1932 before appointing his GNSFL, Thea Friedel, in Upper Franconia. This was in spite of the existence of seven FAGs in his Gau which should have provided a substantial basis for the NSF. But once development began in Upper Franconia it was rapid: whereas there were only ten local NSF branches in June 1932, by the end of the year there were 160. In this Gau the NSF concentrated on building up the organisational framework rather than launching into practical work.[49]

By contrast, where substantial women's groups were already well-established, the NSF's work could proceed more or less immediately after the reorganisation in 1931. Frau von Gustedt in Berlin had a head start on the rest, with the plans she issued during October 1931, and on 9 November — an auspicious date — she produced an ambitious programme for providing hot meals for standard-bearers and stewards before rallies as well as sufficient sandwiches for other SA and SS men on duty. Within this plan each of the Berlin NSF sections was given a specific task for the winter, 'since this kind of provision can no longer be left to chance'.[50] During the interminable round of elections in 1932, the demands on the Berlin NSF were heavy; on one occasion in the summer, Frau von Gustedt herself went 40 hours without sleep and three days without a hot meal while the NSF ministered to the needs of 10,000 Nazi men, in difficult circumstances.[51] The NSF's life was perhaps less hectic in Saxony than in the capital, but even so the Gau's several towns had severe unemployment, and Lotte Rühlemann's groups were kept busy providing food for the needy, making Party uniforms, and somehow 'procuring boots'. The heavy involvement of the Gau's male leaders with the political struggle allowed the women to work very independently, to their obvious satisfaction.[52]

The peaceful local branch of Göttingen, now elevated to a district, was particularly well organised in the last year before the *Machtübernahme*, with block NSF officials appointed in its thirteen local branches. Courses in ideological instruction, mothercare, domestic science and propaganda were started and co-operation between the branches — with joint meetings, for example — was encouraged.[53] By contrast, in Halle-Merseburg recruiting drives had a higher priority than organisational structuring or the mounting of courses, and it was only in 1932 that district NSF leaders were appointed outside Merseburg and Liebenwerda, the earliest organised NSF districts. Their first task was to establish local branches and then to concentrate on recruiting members since, as the GNSFL Eva Leistikow said, 'the first NSF groups were and wished to be nothing other than campaigning groups', completely absorbed in the 'stormy combat-heat of the present' with its 'full daily measure of demands'. While Eva Leistikow's personal memoir makes it clear that political battles with the Communists were the chief preoccupation of the Party's men and women alike, the excitement of the 'unforgettable' year 1932 was too much for the Gau historian who was incapable of coherently describing the NSF's activities at this time.[54]

Purely practical activity was to be expected above all in the Ruhr area, the part of Germany affected worst of all by the Depression and the scene of widespread KPD agitation and recruitment. To combat this, SA homes and canteens were opened all over the area, with the NSF active in raising the money to finance them.[55] In North Westphalia, 600 children from industrial areas were provided with holidays in the countryside by the NSF in 1932.[56] Remarkably, in the circumstances, Gau Düsseldorf was a model of organisational thoroughness, as well as winning Rienhardt's approval as an example to be emulated throughout the country for its conduct of welfare work.[57] The GNSFL, Paula Siber, who had joined the Party only in 1931,[58] quickly issued instructions for the 'spiritual', economic and charitable work to be performed by the NSF at every level of the Gau organisation. Strict uniformity was facilitated by the demand for regular reports from the local branches to the Gau NSF office, and by the stipulation that all speakers at local branch meetings must be authorised by the Gau NSF leadership. The hierarchical principle was exploited fully, with leaders at every level — down to the sectional leaders nominated by local branch NSF leaders for specific activities — given substantial authority and carrying full responsibility.

There was energetic practical work in Gau Düsseldorf of the customary varieties, but the 'educational' aspect of National Socialism was also given a prominent place, even at this busy time, with lectures and courses on racial policy, personal health and hygiene, the arts, legal rights, household management and consumer policy. All these activities were supervised by NSF officials at every level from the block upwards,[59] and the orderly conduct of both practical and theoretical work was clearly what brought Paula Siber notice in the Brown House, and encouraged her to aspire to office in HA VIII. But in spite of her manifest talents, Paula Siber, like many other ambitious Nazi women, would prove a liability in other ways. She stayed the course longer than most, but her eclipse in 1934 was already foreshadowed by Rienhardt's irritation in December 1932 at her insistent attempts to push herself forward: in a marginal note on one of her letters to the ROL his terse message was, 'personally gives an unpleasant impression — to be filed'.[60]

Personality Problems

The NSF's activities in the last months of the *Kampfzeit* clearly set the pattern for much of the 'women's work' of the Third Reich. The people who influenced its development in 1932 and into 1933 largely sank without trace after Gertrud Scholtz-Klink's appointment as NSF leader in February 1934. But in their separate ways a number of them – Käte Auerhahn, Paula Siber, Guida Diehl, as well as Elsbeth Zander – left a lasting mark on the NSF because of their formative influence. There were almost bound to be problems in the NSF's leadership because the legacy of bitterness from the old DFO days was too recent and too deep-rooted to be dissipated overnight, whatever pious hopes Strasser liked to express. In addition, the potential prestige of the NSF, as it grew and achieved improved status in 1932, and as the Party of which it was an integral part seemed poised to take over political power in Germany, proved magnetically attractive to women who had worked energetically in the regions and now saw the prospect of national fame and power within their grasp, if only they could gain access to the small but growing base in the ROL which became HA VIII. Not all GNSFLs were so ambitious: Lotte Rühlemann in Saxony, Eva Leistikow in Halle-Merseburg and Hedwig Schmalmack in Schleswig-Holstein, for example, were content as GNSFLs, and these three, among others, survived at their post into the war years.[61] But the more Strasser built up the Section for Women's Work, the more GNSFLs and others aspired to join its exclusive staff and, often, to replace Elsbeth Zander and Käte Auerhahn at its head.

The individual who left the most enduring mark on the NSF was its creator, Gregor Strasser. He had outlined its designated sphere of activity in November 1931, and he reiterated it in his April 1932 order. Auxiliary work with the SA continued to be a top priority during the *Kampfzeit*, although this ceased to be a function once the political struggle was won. But ideological training and 'national-economic' instruction would be NSF responsibilities in the Third Reich. It was Strasser who emphasised that housewives, the largest body of consumers, must be encouraged to spend in the national interest.[62] This theme of 'buying German' was a major concern in the Third Reich as the regime strove to promote autarky. In more detail, Paula Siber's wide-ranging projects in Düsseldorf put into effect Strasser's general plans more appropriately than was the case elsewhere. Of course, many GNSFLs must have felt, with Eva Leistikow, that this was a luxury they could not afford in the critical circumstances of 1932. But Frau von Gustedt, for example, was far from the mark in stressing the adoption of a brown uniform for the NSF,[63] something which people of as diverse opinions as Gauleiter Robert Wagner, Lotte Rühlemann and Strasser himself had long since dismissed as 'in bad taste' and redolent of 'uniformed Marxist women's groups . . . acting as unfavourable propaganda'.[64] No doubt the ill-repute of DFO 'sisters' in their brown uniforms only confirmed a foregone decision.

Starting in September 1932, Käte Auerhahn began to devise projects for the NSF on a nationwide basis, some of which were continued into the Third Reich while others increasingly came to fall within the sphere of competence of the Nazi welfare organisation, the NSV, which was founded in Berlin in winter 1931-2.[65] Käte Auerhahn's first priority was to instruct GNSFLs to stage training courses for district NSF leaders, to fit them to supervise NSF tasks in their area. The one or two-day courses were to be held as soon after 1 October 1932 as possible and conducted by 'experts' either in the Gaus or seconded from HA VIII.[66] Käte Auerhahn then produced a number of proposals which were approved by Strasser.[67] They show a preoccupation not only with usefully involving NSF members in Party work, but also with ensuring that in time of dire unemployment and stagnant business Party members aided or acted as clients of each other in a Nazi network. For example, the proposed 'NS Nursing Corps of the Red Swastika' could provide employment for trained nurses in the Party's ranks, particularly with the requirement that Nazi doctors use 'NS Sisters' in their consulting rooms. Nazi kindergartens could provide work for unemployed Nazi infant teachers. A 'railway station service' was to provide information and sustenance for young women Nazis when they travelled, and where they required accommodation it was to be found in hotels run by Party members. Nazi members of municipal councils were to help with finding suitable premises for both the kindergartens and the nursing homes of the 'NS Sisters'.[68] By autumn 1932 this was facilitated by the Nazis' takeover of some Land governments and a large number of municipal governments.[69]

Käte Auerhahn's remit was to produce plans for NSF work and to organise its operation. But others sought to draw Strasser's attention to themselves by making proposals for 'the women's work'. The failure rate among the ambitious was high, and Hildegard Passow was one of the few to achieve promotion through a direct approach to Strasser. By contrast, Hedwig Förster — rather later to find a comfortable niche in the Nazi system[70] — was sharply rebuked by Strasser when she complained that Elsbeth Zander had not replied to proposals she had made.[71] Both Hildegard Passow and Hedwig Förster were quicker off the mark than the new GNSFLs who had first to set their own house in order in autumn 1931. But even before the NSF had been created a much more influential figure had decided that the time had come to throw in her lot with the Nazis. Guida Diehl, founder and leader of the Newland Movement, joined the Nazi Party in August 1930, at the age of 62.[72] She shared in full measure the Nazis' anti-communism and anti-semitism, and was particularly concerned with stemming the tide of moral 'filth' including the campaign to legalise abortion.[73] It soon emerged that Guida Diehl had decided in summer 1931 not so much to join the new Nazi women's organisation as to take it over.

By this time, Guida Diehl had built up an impressive following among women who shared her prejudices; she was clearly an inspiring leader, talking and writing in mystical, para-religious terms, and from early spring until autumn 1931 the ROL received a steady stream of letters from her acolytes urging that she be welcomed by the NSDAP as a major asset, particularly because of her gifts as a speaker. Some suggested that she might be able to counteract the unfortunate impression given by the Party's apparent attitude to women,[74] and Guida Diehl herself was full of schemes for 'educating' and organising Nazi women. The Party Leadership recognised her potential value as one who — like Elsbeth Zander — personally commanded the allegiance of a substantial group of women who would unconditionally follow her lead if she pledged herself wholeheartedly to National Socialism. Strasser was clearly prepared to offer Guida Diehl a prominent place in the NSF, provided that she would collaborate with Elsbeth Zander, and he patiently told her supporters that she was to be brought into the NSF as expert adviser on cultural matters, under Elsbeth Zander's leadership.[75] But this was the problem; Guida Diehl reluctantly agreed to this arrangement, although she had no intention of accepting Elsbeth Zander's authority. Her view was that the DFO, under Elsbeth Zander, should be turned into an exclusively first-aid corps, while she herself would take over leadership of the NSF.[76] In this, she was encouraged — no doubt unknown to Strasser — by Paul Schulz, whose approach to Guida Diehl was nauseatingly sychophantic.[77]

Once she was installed as 'cultural adviser', from November 1931, Guida Diehl issued lengthy proposals for the ideological training of NSF members, particularly the schoolteachers among them, from her eyrie in the 'Newland House' in Gau Thuringia.[78] Her methods quickly brought her into conflict with Käte Auerhahn who, although not herself the soul of tact, had genuine cause for irritation with Guida

Diehl. First, Guida Diehl demanded to be able to work 'independently' within the NSF,[79] which in effect meant that she reserved the right to circulate material with proposals and instructions to the GNSFLs, without reference to the Section for Women's Work; she also refused to accept the authority of either Elsbeth Zander or Käte Auerhahn. This was completely anomalous, in view of the chain of command which Strasser had deliberately constructed. Further, while she expected to be involved in the NSF at the highest level, Guida Diehl had no intention either of leaving the Newland House or of abandoning her leadership of the Newland Movement and of the German Women's Campaigning Association, although the latter was affiliated to the *Bund Königin Luise* which was regarded by the Nazis as a hostile organisation.[80] Intensely irritated by this and by Guida Diehl's condescending manner, Käte Auerhahn asked Strasser that she be made to choose which organisation she was working for, and if it was to be the NSF, made to work within its prescribed framework.[81]

But Guida Diehl, too, was aggrieved not least at Elsbeth Zander's failure to respond to her repeated letters with proposals for the NSF's work. She was further frustrated by the cool reception which her ideas met at the March 1932 GNSFLs' meeting, and by the fact that she seemed not to be on the mailing list of the Section for Women's Work. She was offended by not being asked to speak in the early election campaigns of 1932, although GNSFLs had been invited, and claimed that the Nazi press had failed to report her activities. Most of all, she was angered by hostile remarks which Käte Auerhahn had made about her, 'which can obviously be traced back to Fräulein Zander', and outraged by the success that Käte Auerhahn had scored[82] in insisting that all her articles and letters for publication must first be vetted by the Section. In the end, she had no choice but to resign from her appointment as 'cultural adviser' in the NSF in October 1932; she would not give up her other involvements and she would not work within Strasser's system, as operated by Elsbeth Zander and Käte Auerhahn. She won some supporters within the NSF's ranks, but she antagonised more. The discussions at the GNSFLs' conference in September 1932 demonstrated this clearly enough, in spite of Paula Siber's attempts at conciliation. But Rienhardt showed here in public[83] the impatience with Guida Diehl which he had already intimated privately when he wrote in August 1932 of the 'necessity' of her being relieved of her position as 'cultural adviser'.[84]

The differences between Guida Diehl and the majority of NSF women were largely concerned with ambition and place-seeking, with resentment among those who had committed themselves to the Nazi cause in less propitious days at the takeover bid being lodged by a new-comer with intimations of divine right.[85] But detailed discussions at the September GNSFLs' meeting showed that Guida Diehl was also out of step with the policy ideas of the NSF leadership. She felt that her schemes for 'cultural training' were being wilfully spurned, for personal reasons, although current NSF policy was failing to score electoral success and clearly needed to be changed. But Hanna Schnabel from Chemnitz put the other side succinctly:

> In a state in which thousands are starving, the first duty is to give help of a practical nature. It would be no use at all if we went home from this meeting and brought our women these wonderful fine words, these ideas about a school to teach mothercraft. It isn't a matter to be abandoned altogether, but at the moment we must give our women something completely different. If we want to win over the simple, straightforward working-class woman, we must give practical social assistance – they won't have any sympathy for a Programme.

It was perhaps fitting that one of Elsbeth Zander's earliest associates should assert the primacy of the kind of practical work that the DFO had been involved in even before the Depression reduced many more Germans to misery. But Guida Diehl was closer to Hitler's long-term conception of political tactics in urging that greater attention be paid to winning over people's – in this case, ordinary women's – hearts and minds.[86]

Guida Diehl's plans for teaching NSF women to act as proselytisers of the Nazi view about the position of women in the community and in the family, questions of girls' education and careers for women, and women's responsibility for propagating German culture, formed the basis of the NSF's activities during the peacetime years of the Third Reich. As the leadership group among German women, the NSF was to ensure that its own members were thoroughly versed in the Nazi *Welt-anschauung* (complete view of life) so that they could then instruct German women at large about it and win their whole-hearted support for Hitler's regime. The kind of practical work proposed by Käte Auerhahn and favoured by most of the former DFO women would be performed in the Third Reich under the NSF's supervision, but – in theory, at least – actually by the mass of women who were not members of the leadership group. Elsbeth Zander herself claimed, with justification, that 'never in all my life have I thought of excluding the cultural aspect' from the women's organisation. But Hanna Schnabel's concern about the immediate practical needs of her members in industrial Chemnitz reflected the mood of the NSF's leadership in September 1932. Paula Siber, though, could see both sides of the argument. Coming from industrial Düsseldorf, she was well aware of the extent to which large-scale charitable work could impress a deprived urban population. But, she said, there was also an ideological battle to be fought with the many other women's organisations – 'from the anti-fascist women's league to the Luise league', across the political spectrum – in order to try to win recruits from their ranks. In challenging the Communist and Nationalist women's groups, particularly, she said, it was necessary to have a programme to make it clear to women voters what the National Socialist attitude towards women was.[87]

There was certainly a strong feeling in the NSF leadership that the Party was failing to appeal to women voters effectively, a diagnosis with which Strasser and Rienhardt agreed.[88] But they may all have overestimated the success of other groups in this respect. The KPD was indeed working hard to win women's votes, and yet it remained 'peculiarly unattractive to women'. The SPD believed that the middle-class women's movement was much more skilled than it at mobilising women's support, but members of the women's movement were depressed by the support which they divined among women for National Socialism. All that was clear was the preference of women voters for parties with strong clerical backing and, in the 1932 Presidential elections, for Hindenburg, the candidate of 'stability and order'. The Nazis fared reasonably well in attracting women's votes, whatever they said, and particularly the votes of younger women.[89] Their classification of the BKL as a hostile organisation is fully understandable – in spite of the degree of common ground between them – because the NSF was unlikely to win Catholic women from the Centre Party or committed socialists from the SPD or the KPD. The kind of women who would be attracted by Nazi ideas, particularly those about women and family life, were most likely to be in the Nationalist camp, with the BKL.

Guida Diehl, with a foot in that camp and with her strong emphasis on upholding Christian morality and opposition to socialism, could probably have appealed more effectively to this constituency than Elsbeth Zander, for example. But her ideas were rejected, partly for personal reasons, by the NSF leadership. War was declared on the BKL, with NSF women banned from membership of it,[90] and Guida Diehl resigned her office in the NSF, although she still campaigned for the

Nazi Party in the November 1932 election. At the same time, she submitted a formal complaint to Strasser, for adjudication in the Party's
court, detailing her many grudges against Elsbeth Zander as NSF
leader.[91] But although Rienhardt promised to look into it, in mid-
December, with Strasser departed,[92] it seems as if Guida Diehl's case
was shelved for good. Little more was heard of her; Kirkpatrick records
that in May 1933 it was announced that she was no longer authorised as
an official spokeswoman of the NSF,[93] but she continued to lead the
Newland Movement and was still able to publish her writings in 1936,
at least.[94] The influence of her ideas on the policies of the NSF after
1933 may have compensated for the slights which she felt that she had
suffered at the hands of Nazi women; but her name was never mentioned in connection with these policies.

Käte Auerhahn may have been victorious in engineering Guida Diehl's
exclusion from the NSF, but at the same time she sustained defeat in
trying to achieve the dismissal of one of Guida Diehl's supporters in the
NSF, the GNSFL in North Westphalia, Elisabeth Polster.[95] The strengthening of the Party apparatus at the centre in 1932 had given HA VIII
greater authority over the NSF throughout the country, but at the same
time Strasser had also greatly enhanced the Gauleiters' domestic power.
Strasser had promised to ensure harmony between the Party's political
leadership and the NSF's national leadership, but Käte Auerhahn saw
this relationship in one-dimensional terms, facilitating her own control
of Gau, district and local NSF affairs. Käte Auerhahn's attack on
Elisabeth Polster brought her into direct conflict with a determined and
energetic Gauleiter, Alfred Meyer, and demonstrated her lack of comprehension of the organisational network of the Party across the country
and the substantial power now held by Gauleiters as masters in their
own house. To her, the application of the leadership principle meant the
sanctioning of her control over NSF officials everywhere, but to Meyer
it meant confirmation of his unchallenged authority over all aspects of
Party activity in his Gau, including the women's work. In the industrial
Ruhr, with the Depression biting particularly hard and the struggle to
wrest support away from the left-wing parties increasingly intense,[96]
bureaucratic nit-picking by officials comfortably installed in Munich
must have seemed intolerable. Meyer stood his ground, and Käte
Auerhahn was doomed to failure.

Käte Auerhahn was irked by Meyer's appointment of Frau Polster
in the new Gau North Westphalia[97] without the stipulated consultation
with the Section for Women's Work. Her line of attack was to assert
that there was no record of Frau Polster's having joined the NSF, so

that she could not be an NSF official, and, further that she had shown a marked 'lack of discipline', speaking disrespectfully of Elsbeth Zander 'whom she does not recognise as leader of the NSF'. Käte Auerhahn told Meyer that she had hoped not to have to trouble him with this matter, imagining that Elisabeth Polster could be made to see reason and improve her conduct. But this had not happened, and now the Reich Inspector asked Meyer to persuade Frau Polster to resign, or else face *Uschla* proceedings.[98] Meyer replied politely but firmly that Frau Polster might be impetuous, but had done prodigious work in building up the NSF in his Gau; she certainly seems to have been an energetic leader.[99] Further, said Meyer – and this is the essential other side of the picture – she had been grievously hindered by some of her subordinates who had behaved in a way that was 'anything but National Socialist'. Alfred Meyer was willing to investigate the charges made against his GNSFL, but he made it clear that the ultimate decision about her fate lay with him.[100]

Although Käte Auerhahn pursued the matter[101] adopting a tone of authority which – as Meyer well knew – she had no power to exercise, she met firm resistance. Indeed Meyer speedily investigated the case, discovering immediately that Frau Polster had been a Party member since October 1931, and then finding that the charges against her rested on the 'evidence' of a disgruntled NSF district leader and little more.[102] Meyer wrote to Rienhardt to express his full confidence in Elisabeth Polster and to ask him to put pressure on Käte Auerhahn to desist from her vendetta. With limited grace, Käte Auerhahn accepted Meyer's decision, but two days later tried another tactic, sending Rienhardt a complaint from another district NSF leader about Frau Polster's conduct of a training course held in Buer in June 1932.[103] Elisabeth Polster was able to provide Rienhardt not only with a clear explanation of the somewhat trivial points which had been raised, but also with a testimonial to the success of the course from two GNSFLs, one of them the superior of the complaining district leader. Rienhardt intended to show this to Käte Auerhahn, but changed his mind.[104] There would have been little point in it.

Elisabeth Polster enjoyed a long period of office, still to be found as North Westphalian GNSFL in November 1937,[105] long after both Käte Auerhahn and Elsbeth Zander had faded into obscurity. Gauleiter Meyer's attitude and actions well illustrate how little power the NSF's national leadership had *vis-à-vis* the Party's political leaders, and also how dependent a GNSFL was on the goodwill of her Gauleiter. Like Gertrud Scholtz-Klink and Lotte Rühlemann, Elisabeth Polster was at a distinct advantage, even against her nominal superiors in HA VIII, because she enjoyed the confidence and protection of a powerful Gauleiter. Strasser may have given the NSF a central leadership, and gradually built up its authority over the NSF throughout the country, but he had in no way made it a match for a determined Gauleiter in any dispute between them. The primacy of the male political leadership in every sphere of the Nazi Party's activity prevailed, and would prevail throughout the Third Reich even as the organisation of Nazi women became more sophisticated and, at least apparently, more autonomous.

The End of the NSF's 'Girls' Groups'

The rationalisation of the Party's women's groups into the NSF in 1931 highlighted the confusion which had arisen over the organisation of Nazi girls, at the very time when the various Nazi boys' groups were being brought under the authority of a single *Reichsjugendführer* (Reich Youth Leader — RJF), Baldur von Schirach. The centralising trends evident in the creation of both the NSF and the Reich Youth Leadership (RJFg) suggested that a similar rationalisation of the girls' groups was not only desirable but probably also inevitable, and, at the same time, produced two contenders for control of any new Party monopoly girls' group which might emerge. As the ambitious Schirach took his title literally, using Hitler's dictum that 'the young must be led by the young'[106] to justify his claim to leadership of all youth groups associated with the Party, including those for girls, so there was tenacious resistance to his aspirations by the women and girls who, left to themselves, had organised Nazi girls' groups during the 1920s. One of the few points on which Elsbeth Zander and Lotte Rühlemann were agreed was that 'the girls belong with the women'.[107] There was a matter of principle, as well as vested interest, at stake here: the women not only resented the prospect of losing their girls' groups, but also genuinely believed in the Party's professed view that in organisational life the sexes should be segregated. The solution of the problems which had arisen by 1931 as a result of the haphazard development of different — and by now mutually hostile — Nazi girls' groups was urgently desired by most interested parties. From autumn 1931 Strasser was petitioned by representatives of both points of view to reach a speedy decision — in their favour[108] — and also by the leadership of one of the largest girls' groups, the NSSi (Nazi Schoolgirls' League), which had justifiable fears for its future existence in view of the trial of strength that was developing between the NSF and the RJFg for control of a new mono-poly Nazi girls' organisation.[109] Although Hitler himself gave a final decision in July 1932 in favour of the RJFg's candidate for this role, the *Bund deutscher Mädel* (League of German Girls – BdM),[110] NSF girls' groups continued to exist in some areas well into 1933, to the anger of Schirach and his staff.[111] The Party bosses' ultimate tactic was to replace Elsbeth Zander as leader of the NSF with the young woman who was already BdM leader, in April 1933,[112] in the hope that a single leader at the head of both organisations could enforce the harmony that had been so conspicuously lacking between them. While this achieved the aim of securing the BdM's monopoly status, it failed to eliminate the mutual acrimony between the two organisations, and demarcation disputes continued into the Second World War.[113]

The haphazard development of Nazi girls' groups in the 1920s resulted from the early indifference of the Party Leadership to organ-ising 'those who were too young to be Party members or voters',[114] compounded by the same explicit male chauvinism which had led to neglect of the orderly development of a Nazi women's organisation. While Kurt Gruber's Hitler Youth (HJ), recognised by Hitler as the Party's official youth organisation in July 1926, had a girls' section,[115] on the whole the initiative in bringing girls into Party activities was left to the women's groups, whether in DFO branches or FAGs. The *ad hoc* development of much of the women's group activity was matched by the evolution of girls' groups out of the gathering together of in-creasing numbers of daughters and younger sisters who were brought along to the women's meetings. When enough girls began to attend on a regular basis, volunteers from the women's group organised outdoor sports for them, gave them homecraft instruction, and familiarised them with basic National Socialist ideas. This experience reinforced the women's conviction that the young should learn from their mature elders, which was to be the NSF leaders' chief argument against the takeover of the girls' groups by the barely adult, immature leaders of Schirach's BdM. As with early Nazi development generally, there were wide regional variations in the growth and membership of the women's 'youth groups'; for example, sometimes it was found convenient to include pre-adolescent boys along with the girls, although this was by no means the rule.[116]

It was not always easy for the women to recruit enough girls to make a youth group viable in their local branch. In Kassel and Marburg, for example, the founding of girls' groups was announced but there was no response. The first real activity in Hessen came early in 1932 when

130 girls, in twelve groups, began to meet regularly, in Gau Hessen-Darmstadt.[117] The appointment as GNSFL there of the Baden leader, Gertrud Scholtz-Klink, with her interest in girls' 'educational work',[118] doubtless lay behind this growth. But elsewhere there were real difficulties, with one local branch leader in Thuringia telling how the leader of his girls' group had been obliged to disband it because of the 'open mutiny of the girls against her'.[119] In strongly Catholic areas the opposition of the clergy was a serious obstacle, not only before 1933 but also for years afterwards.[120] But, on the whole, where there was a robust Party organisation and a thriving women's group, progress was easier. A girls' group was founded by Frau Zideck in Hamburg in 1927, following the inauguration of a women's group there,[121] and around the same time one was started by Fräulein Zölffel in Göttingen.[122] Already there were active girls' groups attached to DFO branches, since Elsbeth Zander had stressed from the start the importance of 'educating' teenage girls in a *völkisch* manner, to make them aware of their responsibility to the nation and to alert them to the twin enemies of Jewry and 'Bolshevism' which conspired to deprave them. Soon after the founding of the DFO in 1923, girls' groups were begun in Berlin, Mecklenburg and East Prussia, and as the DFO spread across the country girls' groups were attached to each new branch as a matter of course.[123] By 1931, the women who had organised girls' groups had a lot to lose if these were taken away from them.

While the DFO and the FAGs in many parts of Germany founded and ran girls' groups as an integral part of their activities, there were also by 1931 two major Nazi girls' groups run by young people, as well as a motley collection of parochial, *völkisch* girls' groups which were increasingly turning to the NSDAP as its fortunes rose. Of the two main groups, the NSSi was the female counterpart of the NSS (Nazi Pupils' League), whose task was to recruit senior pupils, particularly, for the Nazi cause, since this group had been rather neglected by the Hitler Youth.[124] But this raised problems of class distinction; Lotte Rühlemann voiced anxiety about the segregation within the NSSi of middle-class, better-off girls from the 'simple and working girls' of the Leipzig *Frauengruppe*'s girls' group, which left the latter very short of suitable leadership material.[125] While the NSSi's leader, Annelies Mann, claimed that there were also girls who had left school in her organisation,[126] the relative exclusiveness of the NSSi attracted hostility from both Nazi women and the RJFg, and doomed it to extinction when it was absorbed into the BdM in summer 1932, shortly after the NSS had been absorbed into the HJ.[127]

Although there had been female members of the HJ more or less from its inception, it was not until June 1930 that the eventual winner in the contest to monopolise Nazi girls' activity, the BdM, was created, out of the *Schwesternschaft der HJ* (Sisterhood of the HJ) which, at the time of its founding in July 1929, had a select membership of 67. With the founding of several new local branches of the BdM in 1930 and 1931, including those of Magdeburg and Danzig, this figure rose to 1,711.[128] Hardly surprisingly, the women running well-established girls' groups resented the encroachment of this newcomer into their territory. Saxony was the storm centre, not least because Martha Assmann, the BdM's first national leader,[129] had changed her allegiance after having been entrusted in 1925 with the task of founding a DFO girls' group in Chemnitz. Hanna Schnabel became her sworn enemy once she began to recruit girls for a new BdM group in the same district.[130] From their different points of view, in 1931, both Hanna Schnabel and Lotte Rühlemann greatly resented the activities of the BdM in Saxony, which also happened to be the heartland of the NSSi. The severe competition between the various groups which were all trying to recruit from the same constituency, young and teenage girls, gave rise to a degree of friction which worried local Party leaders and representatives of the competing groups alike,[131] at a time when it was vital for all sections of the Party to work in harmony for the final political victory.

The development of Nazi girls' groups was also hindered by the various Land prohibitions imposed on HJ and NSS activity in the schools in the later 1920s and early 1930s, particularly in strongly Catholic areas, but also in predominantly Protestant Hessen, for example.[132] In some cases, the girls, like the boys, resorted to cover-organisations to keep a Nazi group alive during a ban. In Upper Bavaria, the *völkisch Deutscher Mädchen-Ring* (German Ring of Girls) had been founded for this purpose as early as 1924; when the Bavarian Land ban on HJ activity was lifted, on 1 April 1932, the *Mädchen-Ring* dissolved itself *de facto* by formally joining the BdM *en bloc*, its leader, Hilde Königsbauer, becoming Gau BdM leader.[133] But it was not until after the lifting of the national ban imposed by Groener on SA − and therefore also HJ and BdM − activity between April and June 1932 that the need to resort to various subterfuges to keep Nazi youth organisations alive was removed.[134] By this time, the BdM had been integrated into the HJ, subordinate to its leadership and therefore part of Schirach's empire. On the day of the NSF's inauguration, 1 October 1931, the BdM received the same territorial organisation as the HJ, and the BdM leader became a member of the HJ's national leadership. But the BdM retained considerable autonomy, with HJ leaders forbidden to interfere in the internal affairs of the BdM in their area.[135] Schirach was in a strong position to claim for the BdM a monopoly of Nazi girls' organisation, with the BdM now officially the girls' section of the Hitler Youth, which the *Führer* himself had recognised as the official Party youth organisation.

His success came soon after the lifting of the national ban on the HJ. Early in July 1932 Strasser and Schirach together issued an order to put into effect Hitler's personal decision that the BdM should be 'the only official Party organisation of National Socialist young woman-hood', and ordered the immediate dissolution of all other girls' groups associated with the Party. The members of the other groups were in-structed to join the BdM, and the pious hope was expressed that there would be 'comradely and confident co-operation' between the BdM and the NSF in all matters of mutual interest. At the same time, the BdM became fully independent of the HJ, with its own *Bundesführerin* (League Leader), Elisabeth Greiff-Walden, who would still be ulti-mately subordinate to Schirach as RJF, but otherwise autonomous.[136] Her jubilation at these provisions was obvious in the circular informing her members of the BdM's new status. No doubt her co-signatories from the RJFg ensured that magnanimous tribute was paid to the 'com-mendable accomplishments achieved' by the NSSi, and as tangible proof of the BdM's appreciation each Gau and local branch BdM leader was instructed to appoint an 'adviser on school problems' from among the former NSSi members. While NSSi girls were also to be asked to supply material for 'cultural' and ideological training, old anxieties about the NSSi's exclusiveness were evident in the warning that it must not be 'one-sided or too intellectual', since it was to appeal to all Nazi girls, not merely a well-educated minority.[137] The BdM's new regula-tions sought to allay a different kind of misgiving, stressing that while members should accept discipline and conduct themselves in an orderly fashion, the *Führer* did not want to see girls marching, since the Party categorically opposed any masculinisation of women.[138]

While the BdM showed some generosity in victory, the NSF was by no means prepared to accept defeat and give up its girls' groups. Al-though in Baden, once again, harmony seemed to prevail,[139] in a number of areas the political leaders had already expressed their preference for entrusting the leadership of Nazi girls to the NSF.[140] This probably stiffened the resolve of local NSF leaders and, more seriously, of the NSF's leadership in the Brown House to refuse to disband NSF girls' groups and to continue to argue their case with the Party Leadership. They may well have been encouraged by Strasser's apparently sympathetic attitude; Lotte Rühlemann had understood him to say at the 1930 Party Rally that the girls should be organised by the women.[141] And in December 1931 there were submissions from both Elsbeth Zander's office and Renteln of the HJ about the future organisation of Nazi girls, at Strasser's request.[142] But however much of an open mind he may have had, Strasser's loyalty to Hitler was unquestionable, and so from the moment of Hitler's personal decision to give the BdM a monopoly Strasser was committed to enforcing this policy. This was not understood by some of the NSF's leaders. Maria Meyer, the Hamburg GNSFL, clearly believed that there was some point in arguing about the decision with Strasser in September 1932.[143] And at HA VIII Käte Auerhahn, particularly, refused to accept that the matter was closed.

The intransigence of the NSF's leaders turned the rivalry between the NSF and the BdM into a running sore, and was a significant factor in consigning both Elsbeth Zander and Käte Auerhahn to political obscurity in spring 1933. While they had some reasonable points to make, they damned themselves by refusing to submit to Party discipline in a matter on which Hitler had pronounced. Rienhardt sympathised with them to some degree, reporting to Strasser that it was clear that a number of 10- to 18-year-old girls from Nazi families were not joining the BdM because their parents believed that the children should be supervised by adults; this substantiated the view consistently put forward by both the NSF leadership and some male political leaders. The problem with enforcing the BdM's monopoly was that these children were now being deprived of 'any National Socialist community', when, said Rienhardt, it would surely be preferable to allow them to attend groups run by the NSF.[144] But this special pleading had no effect, and Käte Auerhahn tried another line of attack, to break the spirit of the law while keeping to its letter, by proposing the creation within the NSF's central office of a section – not a separate organisation – to ensure that the interests of the NSF's youngest members were catered for.[145] Dr Glaser, acting for Strasser, was prudent to be cautious about this,[146] for it was soon reported by an angry Schirach that new 'NS Girls' Groups', while nominally for 18- to 22- or 23-year-old NSF members, were also recruiting girls under 18, to the detriment of the BdM.[147] To uphold the BdM's monopoly, Ley reiterated to the Gauleiters that there was a clear line of demarcation between the BdM and the NSF – the latter also enjoying a monopoly in its own area — and that it must be observed.

While Ley made it the responsibility of the Gauleiters to ensure that 'between the NSF and the BdM the kind of harmony prevails which is absolutely necessary in the interests of the common task and the goal to be achieved',[148] and while Rienhardt invited Elisabeth Greiff-Walden to discuss with him how closer co-operation between the BdM and the NSF could be achieved,[149] the matter remained unresolved. A week before Hitler's appointment as Chancellor, Schirach was again complaining to Ley about the continued existence of 'NS Girls' Groups' run by the NSF, and, as a counter-measure, proposing that the age of transfer from the BdM to the NSF be raised from 18 to 25, in order to remove once and for all any excuse the NSF might feel it had for organising its youngest members separately and then poaching on the BdM's territory.[150] The Gauleiters had clearly failed to obey Ley's order that the NSF's girls' groups must be disbanded. While this may have been partly because of the upheaval occasioned by Strasser's sudden resignation in December 1932, it must also have been largely because the Gauleiters had far more important preoccupations, with the last months of 1932 ones of severe economic depression as well as frenetic electoral activity. But there were also clear signs that in regions where the NSF and the BdM were at daggers-drawn, Gauleiters were often reluctant to enforce the decision in favour of the BdM.

The trouble was confined to a few Gaus, but there were enough of them, in different parts of Germany, for Schirach and the new *Bundesführerin*, Lydia Gottschewski, to feel that the BdM's monopoly status was far from secure. While Gaus as different as Baden and South Westphalia enjoyed the kind of harmony requested by the Party Leadership, others, equally diverse, like Essen,[151] South Hanover-Brunswick, Thuringia, Hessen-Nassau, Saxony and Schleswig-Holstein, were still problem areas, in the BdM's view, in the early months of 1933. In Thuringia publicity had been given in the Gau newspaper to the founding of a new NSF 'youth group'; its existence was said to be prejudicing the work of the BdM in the Gau, and Lydia Gottschewski claimed that here, as elsewhere, the NSF's campaign against the BdM was driving girls away from the Party altogether.[152] In Hessen-Nassau, not only had the NSF's girls' group not been dissolved as late as mid-April, but the Party's newspaper had failed to publish the order issued by Ley a fortnight earlier raising the age of transfer from the BdM to the NSF from 18 to 21.[153] The GNSFL said that she had been told by her national leadership to do nothing about altering the transfer age, and as a result of a phone call to Käte Auerhahn she had now, for the fourth time, put a notice in the Gau Party newspaper to this effect.[154] The Gau leadership in Schleswig-Holstein informed the BdM that it would not implement the new transfer age since it had not been confirmed by Hitler himself,[155] while in South Hanover-Brunswick the GNSFL simply stated that it would not apply in her Gau.[156] It was embarrassingly clear that a number of Gauleiters were on the NSF's side, but because the decision in the BdM's favour was Hitler's own, a way would have to be found of making them observe it, as soon as possible.

Even as these reports were coming in, Lydia Gottschewski and her staff were, slightly prematurely, celebrating the 'great victory' which they had won, thanks to Ley and the RJF, with the publication on 4 April of the order raising the transfer age to 21 and — yet again — demanding the dissolution of the 'NS Girls' Groups' of the NSF.[157] But, probably because of the continued evasion of Ley's latest order, Lydia Gottschewski personally won an even greater victory when, on 26 April 1933, it was announced that she had become the 'new leader of the NSF'. Schirach had been fully consulted, and had readily agreed since there was to be no question of merging the BdM and the NSF. The BdM would remain subordinate to the RJFg, while the NSF would continue to be under the direct authority of the Party Leadership. The new appointment was designed 'to give the entire women's movement [sic] a unified direction'.[158] In the end, it seemed to Ley and Schirach that the only way to force the NSF leadership to accept the BdM's monopoly, fully nine months after Hitler had decreed it, was to change that leadership, and, at least for a time, to have the same woman in charge of both organisations. With the NSF leadership's resistance broken, it was to be hoped that the GNSFLs and, behind them, the Gauleiters, would all at last fall into line and accept the BdM's monopoly of Party girls' group activity.

The settlement of the immediate points of contention between the BdM and the NSF was in fact the main achievement of Lydia Gottschewski's brief period as NSF leader, until September 1933.[159] The transfer age of 21 was confirmed and the remaining NSF girls' groups disappeared. There was a rearguard action in Gau Saxony early in 1934, with NSF officials alleging immoral behaviour between HJ and BdM members in an attempt to discredit the BdM: this was what happened, ran the message, when young people of both sexes were left to their own devices without adult supervision.[160] But the campaign blew over, and the new NSF leader, Gertrud Scholtz-Klink, in spite of her commitment to NSF involvement with the young, had many other problems to face in 1934 without pursuing an immediate vendetta against the BdM. The appointment of a standing liaison committee of representatives of both organisations in June 1934 was intended to ensure 'certainty of co-operation' between them,[161] and there were goodwill gestures, as when Frau Scholtz-Klink invited the BdM leader, Trude Bürkner, and her staff to take tea with her and her staff in October 1936.[162] But the NSF remained hostile to the BdM, and, once Gertrud Scholtz-Klink was established at its head, there began attempts to reverse the decision which had been enforced in 1933. As a start, the NSF won a victory over the RJFg when, at Gertrud Scholtz-Klink's request, it was assigned sole responsibility for organising six- to ten-year-olds of both sexes in 'children's groups' in March 1935; Hitler himself decided that the NSF and not the RJFg should assume this task.[163] The transfer age, however, was the major irritant,[164] and this became once more a matter of contention when the NSF formally created 'youth groups', for its members under 30, in 1936;[165] attempts to recruit 18-year-olds to these led Bormann to reiterate in August 1937 that the age of transfer from the BdM to the NSF was 21 and no earlier.[166] But two years later Schirach was prepared to enter an agreement with Gertrud Scholtz-Klink whereby 18-year-old BdM members could either volunteer to join the NSF's 'youth groups' or else remain in the BdM until they reached 21.[167] The choice, as Bormann emphasised,[168] was to lie with the young women themselves; but this was less to allow them genuine freedom of choice than to shift the initiative in recruitment from the two rival organisations, to try to neutralise their differences. The failure to do so was signalled by yet another order, in December 1941, which drew a different line of demarcation, making the BdM's *Glaube und Schönheit* section alone responsible for the recruitment and indoctrination of 18- to 21-year-old women, except for those who were married, who would transfer at once to the NSF. But to the NSF was assigned the conduct of 'the explicitly womanly educational tasks' of the *Glaube und Schönheit* members, in terms of providing the facilities and instructors for homecraft training, particularly. The by now customary insistence on 'comradely co-operation' between the two groups only emphasised the extent to which it had been lacking in the past.[169] Still in June 1942 a senior NSF official was referring in snide terms to the 'only scanty room for collaboration' which the women's organisation was allowed in *Glaube und Schönheit* activities, and exhorting GNSFLs and Gau 'youth group' officials to miss no opportunity to bring its members under NSF influence.[170] The differences between the two organisations continued virtually until the end of the war,[17] terminated only by the demise of both with Germany's defeat in May 1945.

Notes

1. Orlow I, pp. 258-65.
2. HA/89, 'Neuorganisation der nat.-soz. Frauenschaft', 1 April 1932; BA, NS22/vorl. 355, letter from A. Roth to Guida Diehl, 1 May 1932.
3. Orlow I, pp. 257, 273-4.
4. HA, op. cit.
5. See above, pp. 56-7.
6. HA, op. cit.
7. BA, *Slg. Sch.*, 230, order by Strasser to all Gau Leaderships, 31 August 1932.
8. BA, NS22/vorl. 355, report from Rienhardt to Strasser, 11 October 1932.
9. BA, *Slg. Sch.*, 230, 'Grundsätze der Nationalsozialistische Frauenschaft', op. cit.
10. HA, op. cit.; ibid., 'Die Deutsche Frauenbewegung', supplement to *VB*, 27-9 March, 1932.
11. HA/13/254, letter from a Berlin FAG leader to the *Reichsleitung*, 24 August 1931.
12. BA, NS22/vorl. 355, op. cit.
13. BA, NS25/75, 'Rundschreiben Nr. 6' from Fiehler to all Gauleiters, 14 February 1933. I am grateful to Dr Geoffrey Pridham for pointing out this document to me.
14. BA, NS22/vorl. 349, letter of 8 August 1931, op. cit.
15. HA/89, 1 April 1932, op. cit.
16. BA, NS22/vorl. 357, report by Gohdes, HA III, Gau Pommern, 7 October 1932.
17. HA, op.cit.
18. Allen, op. cit., pp. 237-8.
19. HA, op. cit.
20. BA, NS22/vorl. 355, op. cit.
21. Orlow I, p. 263.
22. BA, NS22/vorl. 348, memorandum from Ley to HA III, 8 September 1932.
23. BA, NS22/vorl. 355, transcript of a discussion at the GNSFLs' conference, 29-30 September 1932.
24. Orlow I, p. 274.
25. BA, op. cit., report of 11 October 1932, op. cit.
26. HA/13/254, GH South Hanover-Brunswick, pp. 13-14.
27. Ibid., Hildegard Passow, op. cit.
28. BA, NS22/vorl. 349, letter from Strasser to Hildegard Passow, 21 November 1931.
29. BA, NS22/vorl. 356, HA III, 'Angestellte der NSF (DFO), 8.8.32', and 'Personalstand am 1.9.32'.
30. BDC, *Slg. Sch.*, 230, 'Hauptabteilung VIII', 1 October 1932, p. 7.
31. BA, NS22/vorl. 357, letters from Rienhardt to Glaser, and vice-versa, 29 and 30 August 1932. BA, NSS22/vorl. 356, letter from Glasow to Rienhardt, 3 December 1932. C.f. Orlow's remarks on the Brown House, I, p. 264.
32. BA, NS22/vorl. 355, letters from Rienhardt to Elsbeth Unverricht, 12 August 1932, and to Elsbeth Zander's office, 6 September 1932.
33. Ibid., report of 11 October 1932, op. cit.

34. Ibid., directive from Rienhardt to HA VIII and the *NS-Frauenwarte*'s editorial board, 14 October 1932.

35. Orlow, I, p. 275.

36. BDC, op. cit., pp. 5-6.

37. BA, op. cit., letters from Maria Meyer to Strasser, 8 and 9 September 1932.

38. Ibid., report of 11 October 1932, op. cit.

39. BDC, op. cit., p. 2. On Strasser's inspectorate system, see Orlow I, pp. 259-60, Hüttenberger, op. cit., pp. 59-60, and Wolfgang Horn, *Führerideologie und Parteiorganisation in der NSDAP (1919-1933)*, Düsseldorf, 1972, pp. 381-3.

40. BDC, op. cit., p. 1.

41. Orlow I, p. 274.

42. BA, op. cit., letter from GNSFLs Hedwig Schmalmack and Maria Meyer to Strasser, 15 September 1932.

43. BDC, op. cit., pp. 4-5.

44. Thomas Childers, 'The Social Bases of the National Socialist Vote', *Journal of Contemporary History*, October 1976, pp. 17-42; Böhnke, op. cit., pp. 148, 174-93.

45. *Partei-Statistik*, loc. cit.

46. HA, op. cit., GH Kurhessen, pp. 1-4, GH Hessen-Nassau, pp. 1-3.

47. Ibid., GH Mainfranken, p. 1.

48. Pridham, op. cit., p. 171.

49. HA, op. cit., GH Bayerische Ostmark, p. 1.

50. BDC, *Slg. Sch.*, 230, 'Rundschreiben 6a', 9 November 1931.

51. BA, NS22/vorl. 357, letter from Frau von Gustedt to Strasser, 2 August 1932.

52. HA, op. cit., GH Saxony, pp. 7-8.

53. Ibid., GH South Hanover-Brunswick, p. 10.

54. Ibid., GH Halle-Merseburg, pp. 9-14.

55. Böhnke, op. cit., pp. 137-43, 154, 161; HA, op. cit. GH Düsseldorf, pp. 4-5.

56. BA, op. cit., 'Bericht 12.X.32', the judgment in the case between Käte Auerhahn and Elisabeth Polster.

57. HA, op. cit., pp. 1-7; BA, NS22/vorl. 355, memorandum from Rienhardt to Käte Auerhahn, 18 October 1932.

58. Paula Siber, born 1893, married an army Major. BDC, her Party membership card and 'Lebenslauf', 16 February 1938.

59. HA, op. cit.

60. BA, op. cit., letter from Paula Siber to Rienhardt, 26 November, 1932 (his scribbled note dated 14 December 1932).

61. HA/13/254, 'Anschriftenverzeichnis 1. Juni 1941', op. cit.

62. BA, *Slg. Sch.*, 230, 'Ausführungsbestimmungen . . .', op. cit.

63. See above, pp. 56-7.

64. BA, NS22/1044, letter from Wagner to the *Reichsleitung*, 26 September, 1928; ibid., letter from the ROL to Otto Wenzel, Heidelberg local branch leader, 2 April 1931. BA, NSS22/vorl. 349, letter of 8 August 1931, op. cit.

65. BA, NS22/vorl. 357, *NS Volkswohlfahrt e. V. Gross Berlin*, 'Bericht', 28 December 1932.

66. BA, NS22/vorl. 355, 'Anordnung' signed by Käte Auerhahn and Elsbeth Zander, 12 September 1932.

67. Ibid., report of 11 October 1932, op. cit.

68. Ibid., 'Errichtung nationalsozialistische Schwesternschaft vom Roten Hakenkreuz' and 'Errichtung eines Bahnhofsdienstes', both 28 September 1932.

69. Orlow I, p. 277.

70. Stephenson, op. cit., pp. 118, 160, 164-5.

71. BA, NS22/vorl. 349, letters from Hedwig Förster to Elsbeth Zander and

Strasser, both 12 December 1931, and from Strasser to Hedwig Förster, 15 December 1931.

72. Ibid., letter from a Newland member to Strasser, 27 October 1931, and note scribbled on letter from Rienhardt to Guida Diehl, 20 December 1932.

73. Ibid., letter from Guida Diehl to Strasser, 15 June 1931, and letter of 27 October 1931, op. cit.

74. Ibid., letter from 3 Newland members to Hitler, 27 March 1931; letter of 30 May 1931, op. cit.

75. Ibid., letters from the ROL to Lotte Fischer, Chemnitz, 22 April 1931, and to Martha Bröse, Mühlhausen, 1 August 1931.

76. Ibid., letter of 15 June 1931, op. cit.; letter from Guida Diehl to Strasser, 17 June 1931.

77. Ibid., letters from Schulz to Guida Diehl, 16 July and 17 August 1931.

78. Ibid., letters from Guida Diehl to Strasser, 20 November and 8 December 1931.

79. Op. cit.

80. BA, NS22/vorl. 355, letter from Käte Auerhahn to Strasser, 1 June 1932, and report of 11 October 1932, op. cit.

81. Ibid., letter of 1 June 1932, op. cit.

82. Ibid., 'Beschwerde' sent by Guida Diehl to Strasser, 7 November 1932; letter from Käte Auerhahn to Guida Diehl, 19 August 1932.

83. Ibid., transcript, 29-30 September 1932, op. cit.

84. BA, NS22/vorl. 357, memorandum from Rienhardt to Glaser, 18 August 1932.

85. BA, NS22/vorl. 349, letter of 17 July 1931, op. cit. BA, NS22/vorl. 355, letter of 1 June 1932, op. cit.

86. Mason, op. cit., Chapter 1, pp. 15-41.

87. BA, op. cit., transcript, op. cit.

88. HA/89, order of 1 April 1932, op. cit.; BA, loc. cit.; BA, op. cit., report of 11 October 1932, op. cit.

89. Richard J. Evans, 'German Women and the Triumph of Hitler', demand publication article, *Journal of Modern History*, March 1976, pp. 30-2; Stephenson, op. cit., pp. 20-1, 58-9; BA, R45II/64, DVP Reichsgeschäftsstelle; *Frauenrundschau*, 4 March 1932, 'Deutscher Frauenausschuss für die Hindenburgwahl', and 6 April 1932, 'Zur Hindenburgwahl am 10. April'.

90. BA, NS22/vorl. 355, op. cit.

91. Ibid., 'Beschwerde', 7 November 1932, op. cit.

92. Ibid., letter from Rienhardt to Guida Diehl, 20 December 1932.

93. Kirkpatrick, op. cit., p. 100.

94. Guida Diehl, *Erlösung vom Wirrwahn*, Eisenach, 1936 edition has an advertisement for the *Neulandblatt*, her magazine, which was still being published.

95. BA, op. cit., letter from Paula Siber to Strasser, 20 September 1932.

96. Böhnke, op. cit., pp. 137-43.

97. Ibid., pp. 147-8; Hüttenberger, op. cit., p. 49.

98. BDC, op. cit., letter from Käte Auerhahn to Alfred Meyer, 8 August 1932.

99. BA, op. cit., circular from Elisabeth Polster to NSF local branch leaders in Gau North Westphalia, 27 September 1932.

100. BDC, op. cit., letter from Meyer to Käte Auerhahn, 15 August 1932.

101. BA, op. cit., letters from Käte Auerhahn to Meyer, 22 August and 2 September 1932.

102. BDC, *PKK*, letter from the Gaugeschäftsführer, North Westphalia, to Käte Auerhahn, 27 August 1932; BA, NS22/vorl. 357, letter from Rienhardt to Meyer, and 'Bericht' both 12 October 1932.

103. Ibid., letter from the Gaugeschäftsführer, North Westphalia, to Rienhardt, 21 October 1932, with Käte Auerhahn's scribbled note, 'Kenntnis genommen', 9

November 1932; BA, NS22/vorl. 355, letter from Käte Auerhahn to Rienhardt, 11 November 1932.

104. BDC, *Slg. Sch.*, 230, letter from Elisabeth Polster to Rienhardt, 7 December 1932, with his noted 'Frau Auerhahn' crossed out.

105. BDC, *Slg. Sch.*, 230, 'Anschriftenverzeichnis der Gaufrauenschafts-leiterinnen. Stand vom 10.XI.1937'.

106. Peter D. Stachura, *Nazi Youth in the Weimar Republic*, Santa Barbara and Oxford, 1975, pp. 149-50, 162.

107. BA, NS22/vorl. 349, letter from Lotte Rühlemann to Strasser, 8 August 1931.

108. Ibid., letters to Strasser from the Gaugeschäftsführer Magdeburg-Anhalt, 8 August 1931; the Ostmark Gau DFO leader, 14 August 1931; Hanna Schnabel, Chemnitz, 26 November 1931; the Chemnitz NSDAP district leader, 3 December 1931; BA, *Slg. Sch.*, 251, report by Renteln of the HJ, 1 February 1932.

109. Ibid., letter from Annelies Mann, NSSi Saxony, to Strasser, 23 September 1931.

110. Ibid., 257, 'Anordnung', signed by Strasser and Schirach, 7 July 1932.

111. BA, NS22/342, letter from Schirach to Ley, 23 January 1933; ibid., letter from Lydia Gottschewski to Robert Wagner, 23 February 1933.

112. 'Neue Leiterin der NS-Frauenschaft', *Das Archiv*, 1933 I, 26 April 1933, p. 270.

113. I am grateful to Mrs Louise Willmot, Somerville College, Oxford, for information about this.

114. Noakes, op. cit., p. 190.

115. Stachura, op. cit., pp. 23-4.

116. HA/13/254, Hildegard Passow, 'Zur Chronik der NS-Frauenschaft', op. cit., p. 1. HA/13/255, op. cit., pp. 1-5. BA, *Slg. Sch.*, 257, 'Der Entwurf zur Neugestaltung der nat. soz. Jungmädchengruppen', Anna-Luise Kühn, 2 December 1931, p. 2.

117. Schön, op. cit., p. 101.

118. Scholtz-Klink, op. cit., pp. 28-9.

119. IfZ, MA 135, frame 136612, letter from Otto Witticke, NSDAP local branch leader Bad Liebenstein, to Sauckel, 15 November 1931.

120. Heyen, op. cit., pp. 259, 344.

121. Krebs, loc. cit.

122. HA/13/254, GH South Hanover-Brunswick, p. 6.

123. BA, op. cit., p. 3.

124. Noakes, op. cit., p. 193.

125. BA, NS22/vorl. 349, letter from Lotte Rühlemann to Strasser, 8 August 1931.

126. BA, *Slg. Sch*, 251, op. cit.

127. Pridham, op. cit., p. 208.

128. Mercedes Hilgenfeldt, 'So wurden wir', *Mädel Eure Welt*, 1940, pp. 8-9.

129. BA, *Slg. Sch.*, 257, 'Verfügung Nr. 6', *Kommandobrücke*, no. 3, 5 October 1931.

130. Ibid., 251, op. cit., pp. 3-4.

131. See note 108.

132. Schön, op. cit., pp. 102-3.

133. BA, op. cit., report by Hilde Königsbauer to the NSDAP, Gau München/Oberbayern, '23. Ostermonds 1933'.

134. Stachura, op. cit., pp. 157-64.

135. BA, op. cit., 257, op. cit., and 'Anweisung Nr. 14', op. cit.

136. Ibid., 'Anordnung', 7 July 1932, op. cit.; c.f. H.C. Brandenburg, *Die Geschichte der HJ*, Cologne, 1968, p. 52.

137. BA, op. cit., 251, 'Anweisung: Organisation 6/32 betr. Überführung des

NSSi', issued by the BdM, 10 August 1932.

138. Ibid., 'Richtlinien für den BdM', June 1932, p. 29.

139. BA, NS22/1044, report from Gau Baden to Strasser, 31 August 1931.

140. BA, NS22/vorl. 349, letter from the Gaugeschäftsführer Magdeburg-Anhalt to Strasser, 8 August 1931, and letter of 3 December 1931, op. cit.

141. Ibid., letter from Lotte Rühlemann to Strasser, 8 August 1931.

142. BA, *Slg. Sch.*, 257, 'Der Entwurf . . . ', 2 December 1931, op cit.; ibid., 251, report of 1 February 1932, op. cit.

143. BA, NS22/vorl. 355, letter from Maria Meyer to Strasser, 8 September 1932.

144. Ibid., report of 11 October 1932, op. cit.

145. Ibid., letter from Rienhardt to Glaser, 22 October 1932.

146. Ibid., letter from Glaser to HA III, 25 October 1932.

147. BA, *Slg. Sch.*, 230, letter from Schirach to Strasser, 8 November 1932.

148. BA, NS22/vorl. 355, circular from Ley to all Gau leaderships, 21 November 1932.

149. BA, NS22/vorl. 357, letter from Rienhardt to Elisabeth Greiff-Walden, 29 November 1932.

150. BA, NS22/342, letter of 23 January 1933, op. cit.

151. Ibid., letter from Marta Voss, BdM Gau South Westphalia, to Lydia Gottschewski, 22 February 1933.

152. Ibid., letter of 23 February 1933, op. cit.

153. 'Altersgrenze für den BDM', *Das Archiv* 1933 I, 4 April 1933, p. 267.

154. BA, op. cit., report from the BdM, Gau Hessen, 11 April 1933.

155. Ibid., report from the BdM leadership, Gau Schleswig-Holstein, to the BdM Bundesführung, April 1933 (exact date not given).

156. Ibid., report by Edith Schlarb, Gau South Hanover-Brunswick, 12 April 1933.

157. Ibid., letter from Lydia Gottschewski and Gertrud Marten to the Gau BdM leaders, 14 April 1933.

158. *Das Archiv*, p. 270, op. cit.

159. See below, pp. 98-9, 101-2.

160. BA, op. cit., copies of letters and statements marked 'Klage über HJ' and signed by NSF members in Gau Saxony, March 1934.

161. '5 Jahre Reichsfrauenführung', *FK*, February 1939, p. 3.

162. HA/13/254, Reichsfrauenführung Abt. Presse-Propaganda, report for October 1936, 29 October 1936.

163. Scholtz-Klink, op. cit., p. 152.

164. Ibid., pp. 145-6.

165. Stephenson 1978, pp. 201-2.

166. BA, *Slg. Sch.*, 251, 'Anordnung – A 48/40', signed by Bormann, 25 April 1940.

167. BDC, *Slg. Sch.*, 230, 'Anordnung Nr 2/39', signed by Gertrud Scholtz-Klink, 25 October 1939.

168. BA, loc. cit.

169. BA, NSD 3/5, *Verfügungen, Anordnungen, Bekanntgaben* (hereafter *V,A,B*), 1942, vol. 1, 'A 52/41 vom 6.12.41', pp. 617-22.

170. HA/13/253, 'Rundschreiben Nr. 132/42', 3 June 1942.

171. See below, p. 206.

3 STABILISING THE NSF WITH GERTRUD SCHOLTZ-KLINK

The Leadership Crisis in the NSF

For a party that was able to celebrate a major political victory at the end of January 1933, the NSDAP was in a remarkable state of internal turmoil consequent on Strasser's resignation and Hitler's vindictive determination to discredit him and his work. As Orlow says, Hitler and the men between whom he deliberately divided Strasser's former functions, Robert Ley and Rudolf Hess,[1] 'showed far more enthusiasm for destroying the old than for developing a new programmatic or organisational synthesis'.[2] This had its effect on the NSF which, like other branches of the Party, now had to find a role as the official women's organisation of the Third Reich, with the main tasks of the *Kampfzeit* obsolete. It was not unreasonable of the calendar of the 'women's work of the Third Reich' to take February 1934 as its starting point, with the appointment of Gertrud Scholtz-Klink as NSF leader;[3] in the year preceding that date, maladroit leadership by successive unwise appointees and bitter internecine strife consumed most of the organisation's energy. There were also problems caused by the claims of competing empire-builders to authority over the organisation of the mass of German women under the NSF's leadership, with Hess and Ley — whatever their mutual differences within the Party organisation[4] — at least at one in denying the right of the new Reich Minister of the Interior, Wilhelm Frick, to a share in this. Thus the NSF's own peculiar internal difficulties were severely aggravated both by the Party's confused condition after Strasser's resignation and by the aspirations of the new leaders of Party and State agencies now that Hitler's appointment had suddenly presented them with opportunities of which they had only dreamed for years.

This event did not itself finally settle the political issue in the Nazis' favour, but it allowed them to ensure that the result was not long delayed. At first, all the Party's resources were concentrated on winning the general election of 5 March 1933, intended to be the last of its kind.[5] Seasoned campaigners were in demand, and both Elsbeth Zander and Käte Auerhahn undertook numerous speaking engagements. Enthusiastic reports of enrolments of new recruits to the NSF in the wake of such events testified to their effectiveness.[6] Once the election was decided, more or less in the Nazis' favour, the Party and its affiliates began the *Gleichschaltung* of the vast number of heterogeneous organisations throughout the country, forcing the dissolution of the politically objectionable and purging the remainder, bringing them under 'politically reliable' leadership.[7] The women's conservative 'patriotic' groups were quick to pledge their loyalty to the new regime, rejoicing in its victory over the socialists and liberals who had put them on the defensive for years, but also anxious in case their claims to recognition in the 'national state' might be swept aside by the progress of the Nazi juggernaut.[8] While the early excesses of Party militants repelled such potential allies to the extent that Hitler announced on 6 July 1933, that 'we must not keep looking round to see what next to revolutionize',[9] there could be no doubt that the Nazification of loyal and enthusiastic non-Party groups was on the agenda.

The undoing of Strasser's work provided the opportunity for a reform of the NSF's leadership which had some of the elements of a purge. HA VIII became the Office of the *Frauenschaft*, and Strasser's most trusted staff — including Rienhardt — disappeared from the scene, to be replaced by men and women dependent on the new masters, Hess and Ley, including Erich Hilgenfeldt, who was the head of the new Office for the People's Welfare.[10] Their association with Strasser would alone have been enough to threaten Elsbeth Zander's and Käte Auerhahn's position, but other obvious factors, too, suggested that their days were numbered. The violent personal animosity which Elsbeth Zander had so often provoked, her indifferent health, and her administrative incompetence had already led Strasser to ensure that she was more a figurehead than an executive leader of the NSF. Her removal from office, after a decent interval for gratitude for her co-operation in the founding of the NSF had elapsed and her limited value had depreciated, was predictable under any circumstances. But Käte Auerhahn was different: in her early thirties in 1933, she had already emerged as a businesslike administrator; but this was a two-edged quality, her brusqueness provoking hostility. Worse, she had increasingly manifested that assertive independence which to the Nazi leadership spelled 'indiscipline', the cardinal sin. Above all, her obstructiveness over the dissolution of the NSF's girls' groups was intolerable. This issue was the occasion for the first change in the NSF's leadership, in April 1933, and Käte Auerhahn's role in it ensured that she was not Elsbeth Zander's successor, although she had begun to seem like the heir apparent. Instead, the appointment as NSF leader of the 26-year-old BdM leader, Lydia Gottschewski, was specifically intended to eliminate the damaging friction that had developed between the NSF and the BdM. But although she succeeded in solving the immediate problem of NSF intransigence over the 'girls' groups', her leadership raised other problems which were at least as serious. The solution of these, in turn, was the purpose for which her successor, a man called Krummacher, was chosen, in September 1933. But he, too, proved to be an unhappy choice, although he was unlucky to find himself in the middle of the jurisdictional conflict which had developed between the Party bosses and Frick. The resolution of this conflict was the necessary precondition of the creation of a stable and productive leadership for the NSF and the 'women's work' generally, and this consumed the early months of 1934, dragging on even beyond Gertrud Scholtz-Klink's appointment. Much of the blame for this can be attributed to Paula Siber, who relinquished her post as GNSFL in Düsseldorf in summer 1933 on promotion to a position in Frick's Interior Ministry which made her his candidate for the leadership of German women, and therefore an obstacle to the designs of the Party leaders. The implacable hostility which they visited on her might have seemed intolerable had she not given ample justification over months and even years of Rienhardt's early appraisal of her — ' personally gives an unpleasant impression'.[11]

During the year or more of the NSF's leadership crisis, a number of women who had seemed to enjoy Strasser's protection or had manifested excessive 'indiscipline' were removed from office in the NSF. The militants had served their purpose in the *Kampfzeit* but at the same time had had to be allowed some latitude to enable them to win adherents to the cause by any means. The preoccupation with combating the Party's anti-feminist image in the election campaigns of 1932 must have convinced some militants that National Socialism was not the irretrievably male chauvinist movement which it had in reality always been. But in the realm of women's rights, as everywhere else, the application of the leadership principle, which justified the demand for unquestioning obedience in the name of Party discipline, required that those who did not conform to the current orthodoxy as stated by the Party Leadership forfeit their right to a place in the chain of command. During 1933 and 1934 a number of GNSFLs who had questioned rather than implemented policies decreed from on high disappeared from their posts to be replaced by more amenable successors, just as the more biddable Gertrud Scholtz-Klink finally replaced the militants at the head of the NSF. The ambitious Frau von Gustedt of Berlin had already been replaced by Sofie Fikentscher who, like

Grete Blass – Paula Siber's successor in Düsseldorf – enjoyed a long term of office, no doubt testifying to an acceptable degree of docility in both cases. But while some of those who had been implicated in the resistance to the BdM's monopoly, like Maria Meyer of Hamburg and the GNSFLs of South Hanover-Brunswick and Essen, were removed, others similarly involved, like Hedwig Schmalmack of Schleswig-Holstein and Lotte Rühlemann in Saxony, survived unscathed, perhaps because of the protection of senior Gauleiters.[12]

Not all the losers were left without a consolation prize, although Käte Auerhahn's departure from office in 1933 marked the end of her career as more than an ordinary Party member, living for several years near Heidelberg as a 'housewife'.[13] After her removal from the NSF's leadership in September 1933, Lydia Gottschewski was employed in the Berlin NSF office, resigning to marry in March 1935.[14] Even Paula Siber eventually found a niche in the Reich Chamber of Culture for a while.[15] But Elsbeth Zander's work for the Party had won her a unique place in the official history, in which none of these others figured,[16] as well as earning her the Party's Gold Badge. From July 1934 she was employed in the Gauleiter's office in Kurmark,[17] and when in 1941 it was decided to award her an honorarium, Hess personally recommended that she also receive a monthly pension of three hundred marks, to 'be generous in this case'.[18] Elsbeth Zander had her limitations, but she was an old comrade who had campaigned alongside Hitler and Hess when the Party was struggling, and while she had become politically expendable, their gratitude ensured that she was pensioned off reasonably comfortably.

Elsbeth Zander was perhaps fortunate in being spared involvement in the jurisdictional conflict which flared up between the Party bosses and Frick over the conduct of the *Gleichschaltung* of the surviving non-Nazi women's groups, which were generally of a cultural, sporting, charitable, housewifely or 'patriotic' nature. Frick was of the view that his position as Minister of the Interior axiomatically entitled him to involvement in any domestic matter which was not a purely internal Party concern. The organisation of the non-Party women's groups seemed to him to fall into this category. By contrast, the Party bosses asserted that any matter involving the organisational life of the community was obviously the concern of the supreme organisation in the country, the NSDAP.[19] In summer 1933 the two sides embarked on a collision course, each delegating to a chosen woman leader the creation of an umbrella organisation which would bring together under unified – and Nazi – leadership all the non-Party women's organisations, to ensure that their activities were geared to the objectives of the new regime. Ley took the initiative, announcing in May 1933 the creation of a *Deutsche Frauenfront* – intended to be analogous to his new Labour Front[20] – under the direction of the new NSF leader, Lydia Gottschewski. Its relationship to the NSF was not defined.[21] A month later, Frick produced his counter-measure, a National Federation of German Women's Organisations, to be led by Paula Siber and subordinate to the Ministry of the Interior. Paula Siber had justified her selection by her ability as a GNSFL; she resigned this post on her appointment as 'adviser on women's affairs' to Frick in June 1933.[22] This promotion was also partly to reward the Sibers for the staunch work for the Party put in by Major Siber as well as his wife, at the cost of the temporary loss of his job when Severing dismissed him for 'his nationalist convictions'.[33]

While 'the unity of Party and State' remained a myth, and while 'the outstanding loser in the struggle for survival [between them] was the Party',[24] nevertheless the *Gleichschaltung* of the women's groups was not the only area in which Frick engaged in a trial of strength with the Party leaders and lost,[25] but in this case there was the complication of the assertive personalities of the women involved, whose feuds and arbitrary behaviour caused the Party Leadership acute embarrassment. After appointing Lydia Gottschewski as NSF leader in order to solve the differences between the NSF and the BdM, the Party leaders found that a rift had opened within the NSF itself, partly because of the animosity between Lydia Gottschewski and Paula Siber, and partly because of Lydia Gottschewski's open contempt for the older generation of NSF leaders. Bormann later admitted that Paula Siber and Lydia Gottschewski each had the support of about half of the GNSFLs, which made the position of both impossible in what was supposed to be a unified, monopoly organisation, and threatened to destroy the NSF.[26]

In the feud between these two, Paula Siber seemed to emerge the victor largely because Lydia Gottschewski was proving something of an embarrassment. Her arbitrary treatment of potential allies from the nationalist camp alienated them at a time when disarming them with conciliatory gestures was the regime's current tactic, while more objectionable adversaries were picked off individually in a policy of domestic *Blitzkrieg*. Particularly damaging was her treatment of the BKL, with its 150,000 members, whose leadership had thrown itself wholeheartedly behind Hitler after the *Machtübernahme*. This willing co-operation by an organisation which had been classed as 'hostile' in 1932 earned Frau von Hadeln, its leader, the deputy leadership of the new *Frauenfront*. But Lydia Gottschewski refused to work with her and behaved towards BKL members in a way which Walter Buch, the Chairman of the Party Court who had become involved peripherally and unwillingly in the problems of the NSF, found crass and insulting, as well as contrary to current Party policy. Her indiscipline won her Buch's intense displeasure after he had listened sympathetically to Frau von Hadeln's complaints, and did much to seal her fate as NSF leader. He had in any case, he said, had strong misgivings about putting such a 'young girl' in charge of the NSF — 'setting the daughter above the mother, as it were'.[27] Lydia Gottschewski had been useful to a limited extent, in ending the worst of the hostility between the BdM and the NSF and in stridently ridiculing the middle-class women's movement, and its leading figure, Gertrud Bäumer, in particular; but she had also criticised male chauvinist attitudes and sounded uncomfortably feminist at times.[28] Her militancy, her indiscipline, her ability to alienate allies and her limitations as executive leader of the NSF led to her being relieved of her positions in the NSF and the *Frauenfront* on 13 September 1933; she was succeeded in both of them by Dr Gottfried Adolf Krummacher,[29] who was left to pick up the pieces of 'so much shattered porcelain' caused by 'the arbitrary action of your predecessor', as Walter Buch informed him.[30]

Krummacher seemed to many a strange choice: a male executive leader of the women's organisations not only offended many NSF members but also seemed anomalous in a movement which laid such stress on keeping the sexes separate in organisational matters. But since the women had been making nothing but trouble for several months — in reality, since Strasser's strong hand had been removed — it was felt that perhaps a man could bring more authority and therefore more order to the NSF. Still, a local government official from Gummersbach, near Cologne, who had joined the Party in April 1930 and was a member of the Synod of the Evangelical Church hardly seemed the automatic choice as NSF leader. He was, in fact, the nominee of Ludwig Müller, leader of the 'German Christians',[31] and as one of the less radical members of this pro-Nazi religious group,[32] as a lawyer and a family man, and as a pillar of the local government establishment,[33] he was chosen as the antithesis to Lydia Gottschewski, to reassure alarmed conservative groups that her hostile, radical behaviour had been an aberration as far as the Party was concerned. His task was so to reconcile groups like the BKL and the social groups affiliated to the Evangelical Church to National Socialism that they would be prepared to sink their identities in a mammoth organisation embracing all 'desirable' elements in the women's community, under Nazi leadership. But he also faced an internal problem which would have to be solved before this could be effected: the existence of both the *Frauenfront* and Paula Siber's National Federation, resulting from the rivalry between the Party leaders and Frick, clearly demonstrated that there was no single leadership of women's affairs in the Third Reich.

The fruit of Krummacher's first fortnight in office was the dissolution of both the women's umbrella organisations and the creation out of their constituent member-groups of a single new combine, *Das Deutsche Frauenwerk* (DFW – German Women's Enterprise). The DFW was the result of a compromise to which both Frick and Hess agreed, and its leadership reflected this: Frick became the DFW's patron, while Krummacher was its leader and Paula Siber – at Frick's instigation – became its deputy leader.[34] Krummacher, at least, foresaw the problems which this division of authority over the DFW between the Party, represented by himself, and the State, through Frick and Paula Siber, would present. Further, the precise demarcation of the limits of authority between the two agencies was left vague, no doubt deliberately, since Hess and Frick each hoped to define them in his own favour at a later date. Krummacher has had rather a bad press,[35] but he was placed in an unenviable position as pig-in-the-middle while Frick claimed sole authority over the DFW, as its patron, and the Party leaders insisted that the DFW was, by its very nature, subordinate to them. His mounting frustration at being unable to achieve even the formal inauguration of the DFW, because of the need to obtain the agreement of both parties on a suitable date, and his anxiety not to be the cause of strife between them, led Krummacher to ask that they determine the 'limits of competence' for the DFW between themselves.[36]

Krummacher's difficulties did not end there. Frick had scored a victory in having the DFW's central office situated in Berlin, in Paula Siber's department in his Ministry. Krummacher's provincial responsibilities and his home were in Gummersbach, and it had been enough for him to travel regularly to Munich, to attend to the business of the NSF and the now-defunct *Frauenfront* there. The NSF itself needed urgent attention, and Krummacher was driven to compose a lengthy new arbitration and conciliation procedure because the 'innumerable dissensions which occur among the almost one million members of the *Frauenschaft* make [this] necessary as quickly as possible'.[37] In spite of his misgivings about the duality of control over the DFW, he felt obliged to delegate much of its early organisation to Paula Siber, as the person on the spot — and was rebuked by Ley for so doing. The arrangement did, however, suit Paula Siber admirably: she was able to operate virtually independently of Party control, appointing personnel to assist her without reference to the Brown House and asserting that she was responsible to Frick alone.[38] This meant, however, that once it became apparent, in January 1934, that the DFW was in such organisational and financial confusion that some of the groups were actually seceding from it, many associating themselves with the more effective NSV,[39] it was easy for Krummacher and his superiors to lay the blame squarely on Paula Siber.

While the division of authority over the DFW meant that there were bound to be difficulties with it, the personal animosity which flared up between Krummacher and Paula Siber in winter 1933-4 ensured that they would be insoluble. Paula Siber claimed that Krummacher had visited DFW headquarters only three or four times in as many months, and then had succeeded only in creating confusion by countermanding orders which he had already given. In a lengthy report in January 1934 she detailed instances of this with their effects, which included antagonising the very organisations — of a 'patriotic' and Evangelical nature — which he was supposed to conciliate. It had, she said, been impossible to begin any meaningful work, although the will was there, because of Krummacher's refusal to co-operate with her.[40] Krummacher's view of events, not surprisingly, was that Paula Siber had refused to co-operate with him, repeatedly deferring the date for the DFW's inauguration 'allegedly at the desire of the Minister', and that it became obvious that she 'had lost her mental balance and . . . was no longer equal to the task'. Accordingly, he and Ley agreed that the DFW's headquarters should be transferred to Munich, to enable him to supervise its work personally, although this would run the risk of provoking a confrontation between the Party leaders and Frick. Perhaps because Krummacher was unwilling to assume full responsibility for the decision,[41] he was relieved of his positions in the women's organisations at the end of January 1934, as a result of 'organisational blunders', according to Bormann. Once again, Paula Siber seemed to have prevailed over her rival. Her victory was short-lived. To the Party leaders, the division of authority over the DFW was 'an organisational nonsense',[42] and the involvement of Frick and Paula Siber in it had to be terminated.

Paula Siber was completely oblivious to the hostility with which the Party leaders regarded her, imagining that Krummacher's dismissal was a direct result of her revelations about the DFW's condition. No doubt Frick's role as her protector gave her a justifiable sense of security, but her behaviour during 1934 demonstrates the full extent of her naive self-confidence which cocooned her in a world of self-delusion. She clearly believed that she would ultimately emerge as the obvious choice as NSF leader, and her complaints against Lydia Gottschewski's and then Krummacher's conduct of NSF and, latterly, DFW business were transparently aimed at eliminating these rivals. She had some justification for her ambition: she had been an effective GNSFL and was now a senior figure in the NSF — although there was some dispute about whether the Frick-Hess compromise had actually designated her its deputy leader. She did not have the support of almost all the GNSFLs, as she imagined,[43] although Bormann conceded that about half of them were behind her.[44] But by attacking Krummacher in her report on the DFW she showed yet again that she was unable to work amicably with people chosen by the Party leaders; indeed, she seemed proud of having worked to oppose every nominee from Elsbeth Zander onwards.[45] In this and other respects she demonstrated that she had no comprehension of the extent of Party discipline required from officials; but most important of all, she was Frick's candidate. That her conceit blinded her to the way in which Frick was using her was irrelevant as far as Hess and Ley were concerned; even if she had been an attractive choice from other points of view, her function as Frick's protégée disqualified her from selection by them.

The choice of Krummacher as NSF leader, like Lydia Gottschewski before him, had been from the start a short-term manoeuvre to meet the needs of a particular crisis involving the NSF, in her case to solve the problem of the girls' groups, in his to reassure the conservative non-Nazi women's groups. But the major problem of the role which the NSF should play in the Third Reich and its relationship to the DFW, with its own inherent difficulties, not only remained unsolved by these appointments but was positively aggravated by them. The Party leaders were now determined to choose a new women's leader who would be their instrument in bringing order out of the dissensions in the NSF and also in bringing all women's organisational activity firmly under Party control. The experiment of having a man as executive leader of the NSF had been an unhappy one, and in February 1934 Ley agreed to meet the GNSFLs' request that Krummacher's successor should be a woman.[46] As an interim measure, he entrusted the day-to-day supervision of the NSF and the DFW to the tough, abrasive leader of the NSV, Erich Hilgenfeldt, who had been a member of the NSF's central office team for some months. While the women were to be allowed to have a female executive leader once again, Hilgenfeldt was appointed as head of their central office, so that a strong hand could be brought to bear on the strife-ridden organisation with immediate effect. Hilgenfeldt retained his position as administrative boss of the NSF for several years,[47] although his involvement in it diminished markedly once a reasonable degree of order had been achieved, during 1934.

Hilgenfeldt's brief was twofold. He had been made administrative chief of the NSF and the DFW to enable him to proceed quickly and, if necessary, ruthlessly against the trouble-makers who were at the root of the strife in the NSF. Once a woman leader had been appointed, his task was to ensure that all the GNSFLs, for a start, accepted the Party's choice and agreed to work amicably with her. At the same time, he was to find a way of removing Paula Siber, the source of much of the trouble, from a position of influence in the women's organisations. This was in itself a difficult proposition, primarily because Frick could be expected to try to defend her — and thus his own position — strenuously; in addition, her supporters among the GNSFLs might prove troublesome to a new leader if Paula Siber were removed. On the other hand, if Paula Siber were not removed, she would — especially with the support she enjoyed — be a constant threat to the position of a new leader and to harmony within the NSF. For both organisational and personal reasons, Paula Siber had become a menace to the peaceful ordering of the women's organisations. Hilgenfeldt's advantage was that her over-confident and high-handed manner had made her a number of enemies who were prepared to collaborate with him in a plan to discredit her to such an extent that neither Frick nor her supporters in the NSF could defend her position. Hilgenfeldt's methods were completely unscrupulous, but to the Party leaders they were fully justified by the result. Paula Siber was the most obvious casualty of Hilgenfeldt's spring offensive in 1934, but Frick was the most significant.

Hilgenfeldt began by announcing that the DFW's office would be transferred to Munich and its organisation altered. To try to resist both these moves, Paula Siber canvassed the leaders of the DFW's member-organisations for support.[48] But her activities were cut short when the Party leaders floated Gertrud Scholtz-Klink's nomination as leader of both the NSF and the DFW as a possibility in mid-February 1934. Not least because she imagined that she would be preferred by most GNSFLs, Paula Siber urgently intimated to Hilgenfeldt her own misgivings about 'burdening' with these commitments the woman who had recently been appointed leader of the Women's Labour Service.

She also represented to Hilgenfeldt the feelings of the majority of GNSFLs as being of 'the greatest dismay' at the proposal.[49] Her predictable reaction confirmed Hilgenfeldt's view that Paula Siber would be a constant source of unrest in the women's organisation unless she were removed completely from it. It can hardly have been a coincidence that a former subordinate of his, who had worked in the DFW and now harboured a personal grudge against Paula Siber, laid charges amounting to 'indiscipline' against Paula Siber a week after the announcement of Gertrud Scholtz-Klink's appointment on 24 February. More seriously, this Charlotte Hauser suggested to one of the auditors in Party Treasurer Schwarz's office — Hermann Ried, who had clashed with Paula Siber over her plans for a magazine for the DFW[50] — that he scrutinise the DFW's finances, which had been under Paula Siber's control.[51]

Ried's preliminary investigation revealed discrepancies in the DFW's accounts which seemed to give substance to Charlotte Hauser's charge that Paula Siber had embezzled money to finance her own publications. On 13 March 1934, Hilgenfeldt informed Major Siber of this, and suggested that his wife might wish to resign from Frick's Ministry until the matter was clarified. But she refused to do this, undertaking only to abstain from public speaking engagements for the time being.[52] Hilgenfeldt then resorted to threats, warning Paula Siber that he would bring other charges against her if she did not resign her position voluntarily.[53] Since she would not, he wrote to Frick to explain the charges against her; but Frick responded calmly, suspending Paula Siber while he undertook an investigation of his own into the DFW's affairs. This he completed in two months, and, as he wrote to Hilgenfeldt, he discovered nothing that suggested any kind of dishonourable conduct on Paula Siber's part. Accordingly, he was reinstating her as his 'adviser on women's affairs'. He conceded that she might have made errors through inexperience, but emphasised that there could be no doubt about her industry and enthusiasm.[54] Regarding this as a complete vindication, Paula Siber now began to write a veritable flood of letters, to Hilgenfeldt, to Gertrud Scholtz-Klink, to Bormann, among others, demanding that she be once more admitted to a position in the women's organisations, as demonstrable proof of her innocence.[55]

Unable to retreat from the course of action on which he had embarked in attempting to discredit Paula Siber, Hilgenfeldt was left with little choice but to manufacture new charges against her. His most urgent concern was to persuade the GNSFLs — conveniently gathered for a meeting in Coburg at the end of May 1934 — that Paula Siber was indeed guilty of embezzlement, and that there was no question of her being admitted in the future to the work of either the NSF or the DFW. His task was the less easy because Paula Siber had already informed the GNSFL of Pomerania, Charlotte Wigant, of Frick's finding; Hilgenfeldt was reduced to telling the GNSFLs that 'a rehabilitation of a kind' had taken place, but that one had only to read between the lines of Frick's letter to see that there were even stronger reasons for not accepting Paula Siber back. Gertrud Scholtz-Klink expressed the hope that Paula Siber would 'have the sense to let things rest now' so that there would be no need to resort to a court case. But she was aware of the precariousness of her own position, since some of the GNSFLs, she said, did not trust her. Between them, Hilgenfeldt and Gertrud Scholtz-Klink managed to disarm the GNSFLs who had taken Paula Siber's part − including Lotte Rühlemann of Saxony and Elisabeth Polster of North Westphalia − to the extent that they wrote regretfully to her to say that after what had been said they felt that they could press her case for reinstatement no further.[56]

In vain did Paula Siber write to all the GNSFLs indignantly with a copy of Frick's letter to Hilgenfeldt which cleared her as far as he was concerned.[57] Bormann had already submitted the four letters which she had recently written to him to the Party's Court,[58] and the laying by her of a formal, eleven-page long, indictment against Hilgenfeldt on 2 June[59] meant that the entire matter was now *sub judice*. Hilgenfeldt sent a message to the GNSFLs to point out that there could, therefore, be no discussion whatsoever about his 'dispute with Frau Siber'; to be on the safe side, he requested written acknowledgment of this ban from each of them.[60] Bormann further asked for a ruling from the Court that while the case was pending Paula Siber be ordered to refrain from making any statement about it, 'in particular, to desist from sending round circulars to the Gau NSF leaders'.[61] These measures, and the continuing ban on Paula Siber from speaking in public which Bormann reiterated,[62] resulted in her being effectively muzzled and isolated from potential allies during the critical months when Gertrud Scholtz-Klink was, with Hilgenfeldt's authority behind her, establishing herself in control of the NSF and the DFW. Further, since she was barred from playing an active part in the women's organisations, Paula Siber's value to Frick plummeted; he saw no alternative to asking her to resign from her position in the Ministry of the Interior as from 30 June 1934.[63]

The achievement of Paula Siber's resignation, the goal which they had sought from the start, was the end of the matter as far as the Party leaders were concerned. Paula Siber, however, persisted with her case against Hilgenfeldt, believing that he had waged a personal vendetta against her for his own ambitious reasons. She had no inkling of the issues involved, nor of the attitude of some of the people she importuned with requests for help in rehabilitating herself in the NSF. She had been treated brutally, with her enforced silence preventing her from explaining the circumstances of her resignation from Frick's Ministry. As her husband was to say, there were all sorts of rumours about her fate, with some people saying that she had fled abroad, others that she had run away from him, and the more morbid suggesting that she had fallen victim to that more notorious event of 30 June 1934, the purge of the SA.[64] But as far as the Party was concerned, Hilgenfeldt's purpose had been achieved. When her case against him was heard, beginning in October 1934, the cards were stacked heavily against her. She did at least obtain a full retraction from Hilgenfeldt of all the accusations which he had made against her, from embezzlement to indiscipline, from consorting with Gertrud Bäumer to having a close association with the disgraced Gregor Strasser.[65] But this was of little value when she was forbidden to publicise it. The Court's Chairman, Walter Buch, who had formerly been sympathetic towards Paula Siber, was informed of the real issues in the case by Bormann and by Hilgenfeldt. Two days before the Court ruled that Paula Siber had in no way behaved 'dishonourably', Hilgenfeldt explained utterly frankly to Buch that

> the Siber affair, in which I had to be involved, to prevent the dissipation of the energy of the women's movement, is immaterial as far as I am concerned. It's not about a person but about a cause.[66]

To a great extent, this was true: unifying the leadership of women's organisational life was the absolute priority. But by late 1934 Paula Siber's personality had been paraded in all its facets in a repetitive way before a number of Party notables, with the letters which she turned out industriously to complain, beg, accuse, cajole impressing the recipients more with her tiresome self-centredness than with her injured innocence. Bormann gave the Party leaders' view confidentially in a tactful and balanced way to Buch, his father-in-law, near the start of the proceedings:

> the exclusion of Frau Sieber [sic] from the handling of women's affairs lay completely within the policy of the Party leadership, since the effect of Frau Sieber as adviser on women's questions in

the Reich Ministry of the Interior led to constant unrest.[67]

Paula Siber was so far out of touch with reality that she expected to be reinstated in NSF and DFW work once she had won a full retraction from Hilgenfeldt — although she had been obliged to declare her acceptance that he had acted in good faith in laying accusations against her.[68] Hilgenfeldt warned Gertrud Scholtz-Klink that Paula Siber and her husband would campaign tirelessly to win a position for her, as indeed they did throughout 1935,[69] in order to prove to the wider circle of NSF and DFW members that she had not been guilty of any offence whatsoever. No doubt primed by Hilgenfeldt, Gertrud Scholtz-Klink, now bearing the title *Reichfrauenführerin* (RFF — National Women's Leader), pre-empted the issue by writing to Hess to refuse to accept Paula Siber either as an official in the NSF or the DFW or as a journalist on their magazines. She had, she said, a responsible organisation which operated in an honest and disciplined way, but if the Party Leadership chose to instal Paula Siber somewhere in it, she would have to ask to be relieved of her own position.[70] Bormann transmitted this to Buch with the message that the RFF, 'like other leaders of organisations, should not be forced to accept someone as a colleague, since she carries the responsibility'.[71] How wrong Paula Siber was to insist that 'between Frau Scholtz-Klink and me there has never been the slightest disagreement'![72] After rehearsing their tales of sterling service to the Party in the *Kampfzeit* several times, the Sibers eventually accepted that the battle for her reinstatement was lost. The Party bureaucrats had become increasingly irritated by the Sibers by the end of 1935, and decided that

> in spite of their indisputable earlier contributions, it is imperative that the . . . unjustified petitions with which they are gradually pestering all the higher offices of the Party be refused.[73]

Frick had been unable to help her in her overriding ambition, but when Paula Siber lowered her sights and applied to Hinkel at the Propaganda Ministry, with whom she had worked before, and he expressed readiness to employ her as an 'adviser' in the Reich Chamber of Culture,[74] Frick provided a glowing reference, regretting the termination of her work for him as a result of 'special circumstances' and admitting to having been 'extremely satisfied' with her work for him.[75] Hess, Bormann and Ley, to say nothing of Hilgenfeldt, could hardly have envisaged the nuisance-value that Paula Siber was able to generate on her own account. Admittedly, she was no threat once Frick had asked for her resignation, but even so the lengths to which the Party leaders, through the agency of the Party Court, were prepared to go to enforce her silence on the entire matter even after the end of her case against Hilgenfeldt[76] gives an interesting indication of their fear of the kind of damage which her garrulousness might do. There were undoubtedly personality problems and mutterings of discontent within the NSF long after Paula Siber's connection with it had been severed, but the knowledge of these was kept within a close circle and Party discipline ensured that the NSF's new image of harmony and homogeneity was the one consistently presented in public. With Paula Siber, there could never be any guarantee that Gertrud Scholtz-Klink's leadership would at least seem to have unanimous support, nor that an embarrassing scandal of some kind would not break unexpectedly. When Hilgenfeldt brought a Party Court case against Schirach in summer 1934 for saying that he was a homosexual and everyone knew it, it transpired that this allegation arose from rumours which seemed to have their source in Paula Siber's resentful utterances about Hilgenfeldt at that time.[77] But Paula Siber had a good run for her money: as Frick's protégée she could never be acceptable to the Party leaders, and Hilgenfeldt's assertion in the Party Court that he had originally contemplated appointing her to Frau Scholtz-Klink's staff[78] was transparently false. She sank into virtual obscurity after having to abandon her ambition of playing a leading role in the Nazi organisation of women; but for someone who had occasioned the Party leaders so much effort and irritation she was probably fortunate to emerge from the protracted 'Siber affair' otherwise unscathed.

Gertrud Scholtz-Klink, National Women's Leader

While Paula Siber was fighting for reinstatement in the women's organisations, Gertrud Scholtz-Klink was consolidating her position at their head. She was helped by the determined support of the Party Leadership, with Hilgenfeldt's obtrusive presence as head of the Office of the *Frauenschaft* — where she became his deputy — ensuring that as long as she remained in favour she would be protected. There was also a barrage of propaganda attacking 'false reports in the press [which have] persistently disrupted the current reconstruction of both the German women's organisations and the women's work'. This implausible story, with strict censorship by now in force, can have convinced few NSF members that the problems of the past year or so were merely the mischievous invention of journalists, but it set the tone for the public reporting of NSF and DFW affairs throughout the Third Reich. Further, NSF leaders at every level were forbidden to make public statements about the women's organisations and the relationship between the NSF, the DFW and the Women's Labour Service (WLS) – all now led by Gertrud Scholtz-Klink – until Hilgenfeldt issued the authorised version.[79]   And this was where Gertrud Scholtz-Klink's great value to the Party lay: while there were squabbles and more serious differences beneath the calm surface of her organisations until their demise, she demonstrated time and again that she accepted unquestioningly the Party's insistence on maintaining a public image of unity and uniformity; even in retrospect she has deviated from this line to only the smallest, most occasional degree.[80]

Public announcement of her appointment was deferred until 2 March 1934, when a brief, factual statement appeared in the *Völkischer Beobachter*.[81] This low-key treatment was indicative of the initial insecurity of her position, with the recent frequent turnover of NSF leaders demonstrating that there was nothing sacrosanct about the office or its incumbent. Paula Siber probably exaggerated the 'dismay' with which the appointment was received by the GNSFLs,[82] but even so Gertrud Scholtz-Klink was far from being the obvious choice. It was true that she had made her mark in south-western Germany, delighting Robert Wagner as GNSFL in Baden and, on his recommendation, being invited to become GNSFL in Hessen-Darmstadt in addition in autumn 1931.[83] And Wagner's own advancing career undoubtedly benefited her; his brief period as leader of the Party's personnel office, between December 1932 and April 1933,[84] enabled him to introduce her to Ley, who invited her to assist Lydia Gottschewski in planning the NSF's work.[85] And once Wagner was appointed *Reichsstatthalter* (Reich Governor) of Baden in May 1933,[86] he appointed her 'women's adviser' in the Baden Ministry of the Interior. From this base she drew up plans for a Women's Labour Service, and was allowed to implement them in a large area, taking in the Palatinate and Württemberg as well as Baden.[87] She also assumed the leadership of all women's organisational life in Baden, dissolving the liberal feminists' organisation[88] and then endeavouring to 'win the trust and readiness' of the politically unobjectionable groups which survived the new regime's purges;[89] her euphemistic cliché does not disguise the narrowness of the options left open to the groups – submit or dissolve.

With her new authority in south-western Germany, Gertrud Scholtz-

Klink's ambitions soared. Like many Nazis, she hoped that the *Macht-übernahme* would bring her into an inheritance richer than the relatively parochial responsibilties of the *Kampfzeit*. But she did not leave it to fate and Robert Wagner. She worked energetically in each new office, and worked also to undermine the positions of the new front-runners who had emerged in the women's organisation. She sought out Paula Siber, in her new office in Berlin, partly to complain about Lydia Gottschewski's incompetence but also to ask to be consulted about Paula Siber's plans for the 'women's work'. Having established a contact in the Ministry of the Interior, she sent Frick himself proposals for a Women's Labour Service and a request for an interview to discuss them. To her chagrin, Frick passed her memorandum to Paula Siber who, pleased no doubt to be able to exercise a degree of patronage, undertook to press Gertrud Scholtz-Klink's candidacy for leadership of the existing WLS, which was in a piecemeal, rudimentary condition. Here she met opposition, with Krummacher taking over leadership of the WLS as an interim measure in autumn 1933 and the Labour Service chief, Hierl, unwilling to appoint a woman as WLS leader. Nevertheless, whether or not as a result of Paula Siber's exertions, Hierl eventually agreed to accept Gertrud Scholtz-Klink's nomination, announcing that from New Year 1934 a new German Women's Labour Service would be led by Frau Scholtz-Klink from Karlsruhe.[90] The *Völkischer Beobachter* gave prompt publicity to this appointment.[91]

Why Gertrud Scholtz-Klink emerged within weeks as the Party bosses' choice as leader of the NSF and the DFW as well is not clear. It was true that she had, in a short time, made a decisive start in reorganising the WLS,[92] and she had apparently fully accepted the political leadership's authority and manifested no signs of feminism or indiscipline. She had presumably impressed Ley in his brief dealings with her in 1933. By February 1934, the Party leaders may not have known exactly which qualities they required in a women's leader, but recent experience had forcefully demonstrated which characteristics were intolerable. Paula Siber embodied most of them; Gertrud Scholtz-Klink seemed remarkably unsullied. She may well, then, have been chosen as much for negative as for positive reasons. She had impressed a few influential people, and had been careful to antagonise no one who mattered. She had worked single-mindedly for her own advancement, but had not pushed herself forward obnoxiously, as others had done. For a woman who is generally dismissed as rather simple and unimaginative,[93] she had shown considerable political astuteness where her own career was concerned. She was still young — a year younger than

Käte Auerhahn, at 32 when she was appointed — and was therefore able to appeal to the younger generation of Nazi women supporters; but she was not a militant who despised the older generation, like Lydia Gottschewski. Gertrud Scholtz-Klink was, in addition, the mother of a large family, and therefore apparently experienced and responsible enough to appeal to the older generation of 'German wives and mothers' too. As she was aware,[94] the feminist women's organisations of the 1920s had suffered from a 'generation problem', with younger women reluctant to join them when they were dominated by middle-aged women with long memories.[95] Gertrud Scholtz-Klink could perhaps bridge that gulf, being neither too fuddy-duddy for active young women nor too inexperienced or irresponsible for sedate matrons.

Gertrud Scholtz-Klink also had considerable value to a regime obsessed by population policy and the need to raise the German birth-rate: her three marriages produced altogether eleven children, some of whom did not survive childhood. Although she had four young children when her first husband died in 1930,[96] she threw herself into work for the Nazi Party in Baden. Her continuing political activity after a new marriage led to allegations that she neglected her family while 'persuading other women to devote themselves to their families', as Kirkpatrick observed.[97] Paula Siber argued rather that a woman with several children would not be able to devote the necessary time to the women's organisations,[98] and accusations about her neglect of her work — not least when she was adding to her family — were made from time to time.[99] Her marital affairs were the subject of interest and speculation for another reason, too: early in her period as RFF there was gossip about her alleged 'liaison of several years' with Erich Hilgenfeldt.[100] It was natural that the relationship between a woman in her early thirties and a man five years older who had to work together should be the subject of rumours, but there seems to have been some substance to them. While the NSF and the NSV were supposed to collaborate closely, there was mounting resentment at NSV headquarters in 1935 because 'the influence of the *Frauenschaft* in NSV concerns was too great'. This was articulated by the organisation leader of the NSV's nursing corps, Helmut Lemme, who was heard to complain about the 'influence of political petticoats', which his audience assumed referred to the personal influence wielded by Gertrud Scholtz-Klink over Hilgenfeldt. Lemme was alleged to have said that while she was on the verge of deserting her husband, Hilgenfeldt's wife was reduced to abject misery, and both marriages were well on the way to ruin.[101]

Hilgenfeldt acted with characteristic forcefulness, bringing a Party Court case against Lemme in 1936, but Lemme's allegations were partially corroborated by witnesses,[102] and he was let off with a warning.[103] Even so, Hilgenfeldt persuaded Hess to dismiss him since 'his continued presence in the office is impossible'.[104] In fact, Hilgenfeldt had separated from his wife in 1932 or 1933, and they were divorced in 1940 under the 'irretrievable breakdown' provision of the new marriage law,[105] to enable him to remarry. This he did on 7 December, 1940[106] — the day after Gertrud Scholtz-Klink married her third husband, senior SS officer Heissmeyer.[107]

Whatever the truth about the personal relationship between Hilgenfeldt and Gertrud Scholtz-Klink was, she undoubtedly benefited from his protection in the first months after her appointment. He admitted privately that his at times savage behaviour in the 'Siber affair' was designed to prevent Paula Siber from undermining the new leader's position, as her activities in 1934 threatened to do.[108] Hilgenfeldt's role here may have helped to convince observers that the RFF was merely a figurehead whose token presence at the head of the women's organisations was used by the Party Leadership to keep women controlled and docile in the Third Reich. Indeed she maintained an image of obedience which was entirely in keeping with her own conception of 'Party discipline'; her inclination was to promote the duties and responsibilities of women as wives and mothers above all, whatever sympathy she might claim, forty years later, to have had for feminists and their aims. Her words and deeds at the time clearly give the lie to this.[109] Kirkpatrick presents a shrewd contemporary portrait of her, emphasising her appeal as a public speaker and as the kind of woman — with little formal education but with experience as a wife and mother — with whom substantial numbers of ordinary women could identify.[110] She was certainly unsophisticated, in spite of her political acumen, and was able, in her simple and direct way, to appeal to women like herself. But, even so, as a lower middle-class wife and mother the circle of women to whom she could appeal was limited. During the 1930s it would emerge that her persona and her ideas about the 'women's work' had less attraction for working-class women on the one hand and for better-educated middle-class women on the other. To some extent, her appointment was a victory for the old DFO and the simple practical work which had characterised its efforts, and indeed her own in Baden.

Some critics have dismissed Gertrud Scholtz-Klink as being not only compliant and unoriginal but selfish, lazy and greedy as well.[111] One of her own staff certainly complained about this to one of Himmler's subordinates in 1942, in a conversation which revealed frustration with other aspects of the NSF's role in wartime as well.[112] How widespread discontent with the RFF was is not clear, but there were certainly also women in the NSF and on her staff who were unquestioningly, even fanatically, loyal to her. And there were times when she seemed to be a diligent leader, interminably making formal visits, delivering speeches and receiving honoured guests.[113] The public image presented of her was of an assiduous, dedicated leader who demanded of her subordinates a standard as high as that which she maintained. But it is clear that − like Hitler − she spent little time on desk-work; her intellectual and administrative shortcomings[114] were, however, compensated for by the abilities of the women whom she chose as her 'closest collaborators'. There is no reason to defend Gertrud Scholtz-Klink; she was an enthusiastic Nazi who propagated all aspects of the Nazi creed, and who followed her *Führer* to the end. In retrospect, when the full horrors of the Third Reich are common knowledge, she has offered no apology and shown no remorse.[115] But she was not merely a cardboard cut-out used by the Party to pretend that the women's organisations had a woman leader, even if there were times when she was obviously used as a 'token' woman. Once she was consolidated at the head of the NSF and the DFW, she periodically asserted herself in a way that demonstrates that she was not a full-time toady to the masters of the 'master race'. She was prepared to put in a good word for the old liberal feminist Gertrud Bäumer, when there was a move to prevent her from working as a journalist in the later 1930s.[116] And by January 1938 she was prepared to make a lengthy complaint to Bormann which derived immediately from a case of discrimination against a woman astronomer,[117] but which also expressed more general anxiety about 'the increasing tendency to deny advancement in their work to gifted, capable women and not to reward their achievements simply because they are accomplished by a woman'.[118] Once, in autumn 1937, Ley, at least, felt that she had gone too far, and lodged a formal complaint with Hess about Frau Scholtz-Klink's pursuit of 'women's emancipation'. Here, as in other similar instances, she undoubtedly benefited from the mutual antagonism between Hess and Ley.[119]

The duality of control over the NSF, with Ley still involved after Hess had won a decisive shift in the balance of authority in his favour by the end of 1934,[120] gave Gertrud Scholtz-Klink some room for manoeuvre; it is too much to say that she played Hess and Ley off against each other, but it seems clear that when she had one of her periodic differences with Ley, Hess was ready to take her side against his rival. Hess and Bormann no doubt used her in their trial of strength with Ley,[121] but this meant that they also had to uphold her position. To a great degree, she was allowed to be mistress in her own house; Hilgenfeldt, as the Party Leadership's representative, was explicitly authorised 'to protect the women's work and to decide its political direction',[122] but, otherwise, Gertrud Scholtz-Klink had executive power over her organisations, segregated as they were as exclusively women's organisations from the mainstream of male Party activity. Although she was bound to be on trial at first, the conferring on her of the title *Reichsfrauenführerin* in November 1934 signalled the end of her period of probation, and even before this date the Party leaders had begun to show that this time they would at least behave as if they had, at last, made the right choice. Accordingly, the RFF was assigned the authority for administering the work of her organisations from her central office in Berlin which was dignified with the title *Reichsfrauenführung* (RFFg – National Women's Leadership) in June 1936.[123]

From the time of her appointment in February 1934, Gertrud Scholtz-Klink held the positions of leader of the NSF and the DFW, retaining also her leadership of the WLS. Her connection with the WLS was terminated in 1936 when Hierl reorganised the entire Labour Service, making the 'National Labour Service for Young Women' an integral part of his own organisation.[124] But by this time the RFF had amassed other offices and titles, some functional and many more purely decorative, in different areas of Party and national activity. At the beginning of June 1934 she became leader of the new, co-ordinated Women's Association of the German Red Cross,[125] and in the following month Ley appointed her head of his new Women's Office of the Labour Front,[126] possibly to try to exert direct control over her in his capacity as Labour Front leader, as part of his contest with Hess.[127] In August 1934 Gertrud Scholtz-Klink was nominated 'adviser for the protection of women at work' on a committee of the NSBO, although by this time she was prepared to see 'a fully reliable woman Party member' appointed in her place; in the end, she accepted the position herself.[128] Other nominations included those to Frick's Council of Experts on Population and Racial Policy, in March 1935, and, appropriately, to the Honorary Leadership Circle of the League of Large Families in May 1936.[129] Frau Scholtz-Klink was honoured in 1936 by being appointed to the Academy of German Law, and also by being awarded the Party's Gold Badge – at the same time as Hilgenfeldt – at the commemoration service for the 'martyrs' of 1923 in November

1936.[130] From time to time, Hess formally and publicly expressed 'the *Führer*'s gratitude' for the RFF's work so far,[131] and although she remained officially Hilgenfeldt's deputy in the Party's *Frauenschaft* office, which became a Main Department of the Party again in 1934, Bormann sent round a circular in October 1937 to emphasise that 'at the *Führer*'s order' Gertrud Scholtz-Klink held the rank of Leader of a Main Department, and must be treated at Party functions accordingly.[132] In reality, Hitler's lack of interest in the women's organisations — as in many aspects of internal policy — was summed up by the RFF in January 1938 when she told Bormann that she had 'not yet once had the chance to discuss women's affairs with the *Führer* personally'.[133] But Hitler was as conscious as anyone of the need to project a public image of the women's organisations and of their leader which reflected their alleged value and contribution to the movement, as he demonstrated in his fulsome references to them in speeches at the annual Party Rally and elsewhere.[134]

The RFF herself was frequently invited to make speeches — which tended to be limited to a small number of predictable themes — to groups outside her own organisation. In October 1934 she spoke at a Gauleiters' conference in Dresden,[135] and Alfred Rosenberg issued regular invitations to her to participate in functions organised by his office.[136] She also addressed groups of visitors from abroad and, occasionally, spoke in public when she herself visited a foreign country.[137] In 1938 she played an active part in the plebiscite campaigns in Austria and the Sudetenland,[138] although the plebiscite was not, in fact, held in the latter case.[139] But her journey may not have been in vain, since some 300,000 women from the Sudetenland joined her organisations in 1938, along with the 470,000 recruits from Austria,[140] where there had been an active NSF group since 1931.[141] Gertrud Scholtz-Klink was also regarded as a useful source of patronage. Rosenberg's secretary, Thilo von Trotha, asked her to spare the time to speak with his mother, an NSF district leader in Stettin, when she visited Pomerania in April 1935, since Frau von Trotha had 'not insignificant things to tell her' about circumstances there.[142] Rosenberg himself more than once asked the RFF to try to find ways of employing writers whom he regarded as worthy but who had fallen on hard times.[143]

But while Gertrud Scholtz-Klink became fully acceptable to senior Party members and was on cordial terms with some of them,[144] at the time of her appointment she had been neither well-known nationally nor particularly popular with the GNSFLs who were acquainted with her. Her defensive response was to build up a personal staff in her

Berlin headquarters as far as possible from people whom she already felt she could trust. On the whole, this ruled out promotion for GNSFLs, although many of them were clearly content to remain women's leader in a region. The RFF did have to accept as associates a number of women who were nominated by the Party Leadership along with her own appointees, but Hess had already made it clear that she would not be forced to take on women with whom she felt she could not work.[145] After the troubles of 1933-4, this was a prudent decision. But her desire for security in her personal office was demonstrated by her choice as her administrative deputy of Else Paul, who had joined the Party in February 1930 and who had been her deputy when she was GNSFL in Baden. Else Paul was 'deputy RFF' until the end of the Third Reich,[146] but remained in the obscurity of her Berlin office, rarely emerging into the limelight of publicity in the way that a number of other 'advisers' on Gertrud Scholtz-Klink's staff did, although she occasionally attended NSF functions in the regions as a representative of the RFFg.[147] Else Paul's value lay not merely in her loyalty to her chief, but also in the extent to which she dealt with a heavy weight of administrative business[148] of the kind with which Gertrud Scholtz-Klink either could not or would not cope.

The remarkable continuity of personnel at the RFFg testifies to the trust placed by Gertrud Scholtz-Klink in her closest colleagues, and the extent to which she felt it was justified. That the harmony was at times broken by criticism both of members of this staff and of the RFF herself is hardly surprising and does not detract from the atmosphere of quiet collaboration which generally prevailed. The purge of the NSF in 1933-4 affected its central office as well as the GNSFLs, and removed many of those whose appointment Strasser had approved. But two typists who had been in their posts in 1932, Ellen Semmelroth and Rosel Kohnle, survived to be promoted to senior positions in the RFFg, the former as editor of the *NS-Frauenwarte*, replacing the abrasive Elsbeth Unverricht, and the latter as leader of two sections, those for Auxiliary Service and Organisation/Personnel. Some of the new officials, appointed after 1934, were young single women who married during their service at the RFFg, like Erna Röpke, leader of the Mothers' Service Section, and Erika Kirmsse who headed the section for Press and Propaganda.[149] Some were Hilgenfeldt's nominees, like Meta Bottke, the leader of the NSF's first 'political education' college who had been entrusted with the task of preventing the GNSFLs from spreading Paula Siber's side of her case against Hilgenfeldt.[150] Another of his appointments was Dr Ilse Eben-Servaes, an experienced lawyer who became legal adviser in the RFFg in 1934, although she had joined the Party only after the *Machtübernahme*. In terms of public status and exposure, Ilse Eben-Servaes was second only to Gertrud Scholtz-Klink until she went into semi-retirement in 1942.[151] But however reliable and capable the RFFg's staff were, past experience with financial mismanagement – under Elsbeth Zander and, to some extent, Paula Siber – ensured that Party Treasurer Schwarz would reserve the right to nominate the RFFg's accountant; the long-serving Hans Wolff was the only man on the staff of the RFFg.[152]

In spite of the Party's general anti-intellectualism and its insistence that the Nazi women's organisations were for the mass of 'Aryan' German women, not for a class-based or well-educated elite, Gertrud Scholtz-Klink found herself using graduates and professionally-qualified women in the senior positions of her organisation from the start. It was perhaps a strange contradiction at a time when the Party's attitude to higher education and professional employment for women seemed to be less than favourable.[153] Ilse Eben-Servaes was by no means the only doctoral graduate on the RFFg's staff. The leader of the Border and Foreign Department, Martha Unger, and the leader and deputy leader of the section for National Economy/Domestic Economy, Else Vorwerck and Aenne Sprengel each had a doctoral degree. In addition, the RFF gathered around her a group of professional advisers from among the women who acted as 'female adviser' in the Nazi professional associations. Dr Auguste Reber-Gruber, who was appointed to a senior position in Rust's new Ministry of Education in 1936, had been leader of the section for girls' education in the Nazi Teachers' League since 1934.[154] Another adviser in the same association, Friedrike Matthias, had been a senior schoolteacher in Kiel and was leader of the National Association of German Women Graduates; she became a sectional leader in the NSF in October 1934.[155] Dora Hein, a career civil servant who had joined the Party as early as May 1925, became leader of a section in the Nazified Civil Servants' Association in October 1934,[156] and Dr Lea Thimm was leader of the Society of German Women Doctors. They, too, became advisers on matters concerning their profession the RFFg.[157]

As the Nazi Party theoretically at least, opposed intellectual pursuits for women, so it was similarly opposed to the employment of married women. But apart from Gertrud Scholtz-Klink herself and those women who married while working in the RFFg there were also others who contradicted this principle, including Auguste Reber-Gruber and Ilse Eben-Servaes. There was even an association of married women teachers affiliated to the DFW.[158] With the National Women's Leader setting this kind of example − and being allowed by the Party leaders to set it − it looked as if the Party did not after all take seriously some of the harsher policies concerning women which it had formulated before 1933, in spite of some of the new Government's early measures.[159] Similarly, the very act of creating a Women's Section in the German Labour Front suggested that women were not after all to be driven out of industry and business in the way that many Party propagandists had threatened in the darkest days of the Depression. Gertrud Scholtz-Klink remained nominally the leader of the Women's Section and steadfastly maintained the fiction that it was under the 'spiritual leadership' of the NSF. Women's Section officials belonged to the staff of the relevant NSF territorial leader as well as to that of the relevant Labour Front territorial leader, and the RFF from time to time put her name to orders concerning the Women's Section.[160] But in reality she had no influence over the Labour Front's policies towards women, and the closest that the women's organisations came to affecting the work of the Women's Section was in providing domestic science courses for working women at their place of work[161] and small numbers of NSF members and female students to work voluntarily to afford women workers some extra paid holiday.[162]

Gertrud Scholtz-Klink's lack of influence in the powerful Labour Front, and, further, the lack of influence which the NSF and the DFW were able to exert over the female population at large, are adduced as evidence of her failure as a leader of women and of women's organisations, her inability to promote the interests of the women whom she was supposed to represent, and the contempt with which the Party's male leadership could treat the mass of German women with impunity.[163] Unlike the leaders of other Party affiliates, however, the RFF was working against very heavy odds in trying to build up a mass membership in the DFW, the organisation which was supposed to embrace all 'valuable' German women who did not have the credentials required for membership of the elite NSF. It was one thing for the leader of the Civil Servants' Association or the Nazi Teachers' League to require all civil servants or all schoolteachers to join his organisation, to achieve as near a 100 per cent membership as was humanly possible. It was quite another for Gertrud Scholtz-Klink to try to persuade all German 'Aryan' women to join the DFW. Professional employees who refused to join the relevant professional association and industrial workers who refused to join the Labour Front − men and women alike − could be dismissed, and this was a palpable threat especially while there was still serious unemployment in many sectors of the economy until 1936. But the women in Frau Scholtz-Klink's constituency, a substantial proportion of whom, as the ideal non-employed 'German wife and mother', in town and country, had no other organisation of specific relevance, had no job to be dismissed from, and virtually no sanction which could be used against them for not joining the DFW. They could hardly, as 'valuable' wives and mothers, be physically threatened or denied family allowances, since such tactics would have conflicted with the regime's population policies, which had far greater priority than recruitment to the women's organisation. In any case, the use of force in this context ran directly counter to the Party's aim of winning consent by persuasion and propaganda. The Government and the Party were unable to persuade women in this same constituency to go out to work to assist the war-effort in the early 1940s;[164] small wonder, then, that Gertrud Scholtz-Klink could not force them to join the DFW. The resistance of the majority of German women to being organised by the RFF for the Party's purpose condemned the DFW to insignificance, deprived the NSF of any political clout, and left the National Women's Leadership as an increasingly sophisticated bureaucratic machine with just about as much to administer in its own office as in the country at large.

The *Reichsfrauenführung* seems to have become almost an end in itself, with the continuous expansion and embellishment of its structure as a magnificent edifice of main sections, sub-sections, auxiliary offices, subject areas, and so on, each with its leader and back-up staff, from which representatives were chosen to sit on a multiplicity of committees in other Party agencies and Government bodies. Much of the energy of the RFFg's staff was inevitably expended in creating this increasingly intricate network. Gertrud Scholtz-Klink had started in a small way in 1934, with an office in the building in east Berlin which accommodated the NSV's central administration, no doubt partly for Hilgenfeldt's convenience. While the removal of the RFFg to new premises at 21 Derfflinger Street in west Berlin in July 1936[165] probably eased the tension that had developed between the NSV and Gertrud Scholtz-Klink over her alleged affair with Hilgenfeldt, it was also warranted by the substantial growth of her administration in two years. Further expansion necessitated the farming out of two main sections to an annexe round the corner from the main office, and the RFFg also used a number of other buildings in Berlin as guest-houses for foreign visitors, training centres for DFW officials and premises for the practical instruction of DFW members.[166] By 1937 it was possible to issue the first 'organisation plan' of the RFFg, with its work divided into nine sections. Four of these were largely administrative, but they also provided services for the other five 'working sections', which were in effect the central offices in which the DFW's work across the country was devised and from which uniform instructions were issued to try to ensure that a co-ordinated programme of work was being followed in all DFW branches.

Of the four business sections, the treasury issued DFW membership cards and supervised the finances of both the DFW and the RFFg; the administrative section dealt with the general internal running of the RFFg; the organisation section gathered statistics, supervised the running of the 'political education' colleges, and acted as a personnel office; and the press and propaganda section prepared press releases, the RFFg's contributions to radio programmes, exhibitions of the 'women's work', and posters, films, slides and leaflets for the working sections. The five working sections which had evolved by 1937 were the Mothers' Service, National Economy/Domestic Economy, Border and Foreign Affairs, and, most recently, Auxiliary Service and Culture/Education/Training, and there were, in addition, embryonic 'youth groups' for the youngest NSF and DFW members and 'children's groups' for those too young to join the Hitler Youth. The work of these sections will be discussed in the last part of Chapter 4; suffice it to say here that new sections and parts of sections were added to the RFFg year by year, so that the 1941 'organisation plan' had eleven main sections, each with a variety of subdivisions.[167] In the optimistically-styled 'peacetime plan', approved in April 1941, twelve 'offices' – formerly Main Departments – were envisaged, with finance removed to the direct jurisdiction of the Party Treasury and two completely new offices, Law and Arbitration and the Munich Office, joining the existing main divisions of the RFFg's labour. Provision was made for there to be, after the war, a full-time staff of 580 administrators, instructors, secretarial staff, manual staff and chauffeurs.[168] But this expansive dispensation had to be revised when the war began to go badly for Germany, and in April 1943 Ley was obliged to authorise a drastically slimmed down 'wartime plan' instead for the immediate future.[169]

The *Reichsfrauenführung*, as an administrative office and not an organisation, was ultimately responsible for directing all the specifically female organisational activity in the Third Reich, from the earliest days of Gertrud Scholtz-Klink's tenure of office. It supervised and planned the work of the DFW, but the actual performance of the work took place at the local level, increasingly under the authority of NSF officials. But while the DFW was subordinate to the RFFg, and the

RFFg was subordinate to the Party Leadership, the NSF had no direct relationship with the RFFg beyond the fact that its leader was the National Women's Leader. The NSF had been a Party affiliate and in March 1935 it became a member-organisation of the Party, subordinate to the authority and control of its leadership alone.[170] This untidy arrangement was perhaps characteristic of the NSDAP's methods, but in this case it seems to have presented few real problems, no doubt because of the constantly growing involvement of NSF leaders in the DFW's work and Gertrud Scholtz-Klink's undisputed authority in all the women's organisational work. When she came to the conclusion, in 1941, that it would be more convenient to merge the NSF and the DFW, under her leadership, it was less for the administrative reasons that she adduced[171] than because of the embarrassingly low membership which the DFW had been able to muster.

Expecting to be able to organise all German women, under one leadership, in officially-sponsored activities, was wholly presumptuous, unrealistic and appalling in its totalitarian ambition. In the first place, it assumed as a precondition the segregation of the sexes based on a firm belief in the fundamental differences of their interests and abilities which is nothing short of offensive to-day. But it was also based on the demands of the regime. Men and women were to be organised separately in much the way that they had been in the *Kampfzeit*, with the 'fighting menfolk' doing heavy work and being trained for the armed forces, and with Germany's wives and mothers, actual and potential, being trained to bring up their children to be healthy and National Socialist and to order their domestic duties to accord with the regime's overall political and economic policies. Women were also to provide the kind of auxiliary welfare assistance which Nazi women had afforded the Party's men in the *Kampfzeit*; and now the provision of 'volunteers' for welfare work would save the Government money which it would rather spend on its foreign policy. Presumably there were to be no mixed doubles in sports, and all-male orchestras and all-female choirs would be the result of enforcing segregation in cultural life. The images to be conjured up from this dogmatic and unimaginative policy are at once horrifying and absurd, and the degree of resistance to this organisational apartheid — by the passive refusal to be organised — was yet another factor in the many which contributed to the DFW's remaining a minority concern. But the petty-bureaucratic Nazi mentality demanded that this kind of uniformity be imposed as a means of social control and as an attempt to guide German women towards activities which would, in however indirect a way, serve the power-political desires of the ruling elite and condition the female population to accept and applaud these desires.

Notes

1. Tyrell, op. cit., pp. 369-70. Horn, op. cit., pp. 384-6.
2. Orlow II, p. 22.
3. *FK*, April 1937, op. cit., p. 8; February 1939, loc. cit.
4. Orlow II, pp. 14-16.
5. 'The Cabinet Meeting of 31 January, 1933', in Jeremy Noakes and Geoffrey Pridham (eds.), *Documents on Nazism 1919-1945*, London, 1974, p. 159.
6. HA/13/254, 'Ausschnitte aus der Wahlarbeit', *Informationsdienst der N.S. Frauenschaft (Deutscher Frauenorden)*, 24 February 1933.
7. Karl Dietrich Bracher, 'Stufen der Machtergreifung' in K.D. Bracher, Wolfgang Sauer, Gerhard Schulz, *Die Nationalsozialistische Machtergreifung*, Cologne and Opladen, 1960, pp. 175-205. Martin Broszat, *Der Staat Hitlers*, Munich, 1969, pp. 105-29, 173-218, 230-46.
8. Stephenson, *Women in Nazi Society*, pp. 27-30.
9. 'Hitler on the conclusion of the revolution, 6 July 1933', in Noakes and Pridham, op. cit., p. 204; Broszat, op. cit., pp. 244-52.
10. Erich Stockhorst, *Fünftausend Köpfe*, Bruchsal, 1967, p. 198; BDC, Hilgenfeldt's Party membership card.
11. See Chapter 2, note 60.
12. HA/13/254, 'Anschriftenverzeichnis . . . 1. Juni 1941', op. cit.
13. BDC, Käte Auerhahn's Party membership card, and letter from Gauschatz-meister Baden to Party HQ membership section, 12 December 1940.
14. Ibid., Lydia Gottschewski's Party membership card.
15. Ibid., Paula Siber's file, 'Lebenslauf', 16 February 1938.
16. *FK*, April 1937, op. cit.
17. BDC, Elsbeth Zander's Party membership cards.
18. BA, *Slg. Sch.*, 368, *PKK*, 'Vorlage an den Stabsleiter', 18 April 1941.
19. BDC, AOPG 2684/34, submission by Bormann to the Party's High Court, 30 May 1934.
20. Dörte Winkler, op. cit., p. 39.
21. 'Eine deutsche Frauenfront', *Das Archiv*, 9 May 1933, p. 430.
22. 'Referentin für Frauenfragen im Reichsinnenministerium', ibid., 21 June 1933, p. 498.
23. BDC, op. cit., letters from Frick to Major Siber, 7 May 1930, and 7 February, 21 June, 18 October 1932; letter from Gauleiter Florian to Goering, 4 February 1933.
24. Schoenbaum, op. cit., p. 221.
25. See, e.g., Jill Stephenson, ' "Reichsbund der Kinderreichen": the League of Large Families in the Population Policy of Nazi Germany', *European Studies Review*, July 1979, pp. 350-75.
26. BDC, op. cit., Bormann's submission, op. cit.
27. BDC, op. cit., report from Buch to Krummacher, 20 September 1933.
28. Lydia Gottschewski: *Die Frauenbewegung und Wir*, n.p., n.d. (? 1932); 'Zur Einführung!', *Die Deutsche Frauenfront*, August 1933; *Männerbund und Frauenfrage*, Munich, 1934, pp. 13-32.
29. BDC, op. cit., Bormann's submission, op. cit.; 'Dr. Krummacher Leiter der NS-Frauenschaft', *Das Archiv*, 13 September 1933, p. 854.
30. BDC, op. cit., report from Buch to Krummacher, op. cit.

31. Ibid.

32. On the German Christians, see J.R.C. Wright, *'Above Parties': The Political Attitudes of the German Protestant Church Leadership 1918-1933*, Oxford, 1974, pp. 91-8, 110-11, 117-42, and J.S. Conway, *The Nazi Persecution of the Churches*, London, 1968, pp. 12-13, 41-59.

33. Stockhorst, op. cit., p. 254; BDC, Krummacher's Party membership card.

34. 'Zusammenfassung der Deutschen Frauenverbände', *Das Archiv*, 28 September 1933.

35. Kirkpatrick, op. cit., pp. 60-1.

36. BDC, AOPG, letter from Krummacher to Frick, 25 April 1934.

37. BA, *Slg. Sch.*, 230, letter from Krummacher to Buch, 22 December 1933.

38. BDC, op. cit.

39. Ibid., report from Paula Siber to Frick, 15 January 1934.

40. Ibid.

41. Ibid., letter of 25 April 1934, op. cit.

42. Ibid., Bormann's submission, op. cit.

43. Ibid., report of 15 January 1934, op. cit.; letter of 25 April 1934, op. cit.; letter from Paula Siber to Gertrud Scholtz-Klink, 21 May 1934.

44. Ibid., Bormann's submission, op. cit.

45. Ibid., letter of 21 May 1934, op. cit.; letter from Paula Siber to Hilgenfeldt, 14 January 1935.

46. Ibid., letter of 21 May 1934, op. cit.

47. BDC, Hilgenfeldt's Party membership card; *PKK*, letter from Schwarz to Hilgenfeldt, 12 October 1936.

48. BDC, AOPG , letter from Charlotte Hauser to Paula Siber, 4 March 1934; letter from Hilgenfeldt to Bormann, 2 June 1934.

49. Ibid., letter of 21 May 1934, op. cit.

50. Ibid., statement by Paula Siber n.d. (?October 1933).

51. Ibid., letter of 4 March 1933, op. cit.; letter from Paula Siber to Hilgenfeldt, 6 March 1934; letter from Hilgenfeldt to Major Siber, 14 March 1934.

52. Ibid., op. cit.; letter from Hilgenfeldt to Paula Siber, 14 March 1934.

53. Ibid., letter from Paula Siber to Bormann, 22 May 1934.

54. Ibid., letter from Frick to Hilgenfeldt, 12 May 1934.

55. Ibid., e.g., letter of 21 May 1934, op. cit., and letters to Bormann, 21, 22, 23, and 28 May 1934.

56. Ibid., letter from 7 GNSFLs to Paula Siber, 30 May 1934.

57. Ibid., letter from Paula Siber to a GNSFL, 2 June 1934.

58. Ibid., letter from Bormann to Paula Siber, 30 May 1934.

59. Ibid., 'Anklage gegen Amtsleiter Hilgenfeldt', 2 June 1934.

60. Ibid., letter from Hilgenfeldt to Meta Bottke, 5 June 1934.

61. Ibid., letter from Bormann to the Party's High Court, 14 June 1934.

62. Ibid., letter of 30 May 1934, op. cit.

63. Ibid., letter from Hilgenfeldt to Bormann, 2 June 1934.

64. Ibid., Major Siber's submission, 27 January 1935.

65. Ibid., letter of 2 June 1934, op. cit.; Paula Siber's submission, 6 October 1934; statement by Hilgenfeldt, 5 December 1934.

66. Ibid., letter from Hilgenfeldt to Buch (with copies to Hess and Ley), 3 November 1934.

67. Ibid., Bormann's submission, op. cit.

68. Ibid., Paula Siber's statement, 5 December 1934.

69. Ibid., e.g., letters from Paula Siber to Hilgenfeldt, 14 January 1935, to Frick, 2 February 1935; letters from Major Siber to Hitler, 5 August 1935, to Hess, 6 August 1935.

70. Ibid., letter from Gertrud Scholtz-Klink to Hess, 20 December 1934.

71. Ibid., letter from Bormann to Buch, 11 January 1935.

72. Ibid., letter of 14 January 1935, op. cit.

73. Ibid., letter from Knop, at the Party's High Court, to Hitler's adjutant, 14 December 1935.

74. BDC, Paula Siber's file, letter to Hinkel, 5 September 1935; letter from Metzner at the Ministry of the Interior to Hinkel, 28 January 1936.

75. Ibid.

76. BDC, AOPG, letter from Knop to Hilgenfeldt, 12 January 1935.

77. BDC, AOPG 581, letter from Hilgenfeldt to Walter Buch, 13 August 1934.

78. BDC, AOPG 2684/34, Hilgenfeldt's submission, 1 October 1934.

79. BA, op. cit., 'Gau Verordnungsblatt 2/34', NSF Schleswig-Holstein, 1 March 1934.

80. Scholtz-Klink, op. cit., pp. 45 and 145-6, mentions the confusion in the NSF in 1933 and the differences with the BdM.

81. Report in *VB*, 2 March 1934.

82. BDC, op. cit., letter from Paula Siber to Gertrud Scholtz-Klink, 21 May 1934.

83. Scholtz-Klink, op. cit., pp. 28-9; Wiener Library Personality File G15, cutting from *Der Neue Tag*, Prague, no. 93, 3 April 1941.

84. Tyrell, op. cit., p. 370.

85. BDC, op. cit.

86. Hüttenberger, op. cit., pp. 79, 81-2.

87. Scholtz-Klink, op. cit., p. 30; Wiener Library, op. cit.

88. Richard J. Evans, *The Feminist Movement in Germany 1894-1933*, London, 1976, pp. 256-7.

89. Scholtz-Klink, op. cit., pp. 29-30.

90. BA, *Slg. Sch.*, 262, 'Neuordnung des weiblichen Arbeitsdienstes', *Deutscher Arbeitsdienst*, 23 January 1934, p. 54.

91. Report in *VB*, 3 January 1934.

92. BA, op. cit.

93. Kirkpatrick, op. cit., pp. 63-4. Winkler, op. cit., p. 40.

94. Scholtz-Klink, op. cit., p. 145.

95. Stephenson, op. cit., p. 26.

96. Scholtz-Klink, op. cit., p. 28.

97. Kirkpatrick, op. cit., p. 26.

98. BDC, op. cit.

99. Winkler, loc. cit.; IfZ, MA 341, fr. 2-667390-94, report from Berger to Himmler, 2 April 1942.

100. Winkler, op. cit., p. 212n11.

101. BDC, AOPG 736/1936, submissions by Walter Dressler and Heinz Wendland, 3 April, 1936, and Wendland's evidence to the Party's High Court, 8 July 1936.

102. Ibid., op. cit.; and evidence by Erna Mach, 19 August 1936.

103. Ibid., the judgment, 22 September 1936.

104. Ibid., letter from Hilgenfeldt to the Party's High Court, 29 October 1936; letter from Volkmann at the Party's High Court to Gau Berlin District court no. 5, 2 February 1937.

105. Stephenson, op. cit., pp. 42-3.

106. BDC, Hilgenfeldt's SS file.

107. Ibid., Gertrud Scholtz-Klink's NSF card.

108. Ibid., AOPG 2684/34, letter from Hilgenfeldt to Metzner, 7 June 1934.

109. Interview with Gertrud Scholtz-Klink in Christian Zentner (ed.), *Das Dritte Reich*, vol. 1, Hamburg 1975, pp. 218-20, 262-4.

110. Kirkpatrick, op. cit., pp. 63-5.

111. Winkler, op. cit., p. 40; Koonz, *Becoming Visible*, op. cit., p. 469.

112. IfZ, op. cit.
113. *FK*, February 1939, op. cit.; HA/13/254, reports from the RFFg, Press and Propaganda section to the Party Archive, October and November 1936.
114. Kirkpatrick, loc. cit.
115. Scholtz-Klink, op. cit., pp. 32-3, 53-4, 479-84; *Das Dritte Reich*, loc. cit.
116. BDC, Gertrud Bäumer's file, 'Aktenvermerk' signed by Metzner, 27 December 1937.
117. Stephenson, op. cit., pp. 173-4.
118. BA, R43II/427, letter from Gertrud Scholtz-Klink to Bormann, 24 January 1938.
119. I am extremely grateful to Dr Gisela Miller, Hochschule der Bundeswehr, Hamburg, for information about this.
120. Orlow II, p. 110; Diehl-Thiele, op. cit., pp. 210-12.
121. As note 119.
122. 'Das Deutsche Frauenwerk über die Eingliederung der Verbände', *Die Frau*, April 1934, p. 506.
123. *FK*, op. cit., p. 4.
124. Hanna Röbke, 'Arbeitsdienst für die weibliche Jugend', *Jahrbuch des Reichsarbeitsdienstes*, 1936, pp. 46-9; Konstantin Hierl, *Im Dienst für Deutschland 1918-1945*, Heidelberg, 1954, p. 95.
125. 'Zusammenschluss der Frauenvereine im Roten Kreuz', *Das Archiv*, 1934/5 I, 15 and 30 May 1934, p. 244.
126. *FK*, op. cit., p. 3.
127. Winkler, op. cit., pp. 39-40.
128. BDC, *PKK*, correspondence between the NSBO and Gertrud Scholtz-Klink, 20 July, 11 and 28 August 1934.
129. *FK*, op. cit., pp. 3-4.
130. HA/13/254, op. cit. Hilgenfeldt had his badge sent to him because he was ill at the time of the presentation. BDC, letter from the Party Chancellery to Hilgenfeldt, 17 November 1936.
131. *FK*, op. cit., pp. 3, 5.
132. BDC, *PKK*, 'Rundschreiben Nr 128/37' signed by Bormann, 6 October 1937.
133. BA, op. cit.
134. Max Domarus, *Hitler, Reden und Proklamationen 1932-1945*, vol. I, Würzburg, 1962, pp. 449-52, 530-2, 640, 721.
135. *FK*, op. cit., p. 3.
136. IfZ, MA 253, Rosenberg-Akten, frames 667, 683, 692, 696, letters from Rosenberg to Gertrud Scholtz-Klink, respectively 9 May 1939; 1 June 1937; 28 May and 22 December 1936.
137. Scholtz-Klink, op. cit., pp. 519-27; 'Nachrichten aus der Reichsfrauenführung. Januar-März 1939'; *FK*, May 1939, inside cover.
138. *FK*, February 1939, op. cit., p. 5.
139. Alan Bullock, *Hitler, a Study in Tyranny*, London, 1962, p. 469.
140. BA, *Slg. Sch.*, 230, *Reichsfrauenführung Jahresbericht 1938*, p. 15.
141. There is material on this in HA/13/257.
142. IfZ, op. cit., frame 723, letter from Thilo von Trotha to Gertrud Scholtz-Klink, 28 March 1935.
143. Ibid., frame 712, letter of 11 November 1935; frames 662-3, letter of 13 November, 1939.
144. Ibid., frames 671, 670, 661, birthday and Christmas greetings exchanged by Rosenberg and Gertrud Scholtz-Klink; BDC, letter from Daluege to Gertrud Scholtz-Klink, 7 January, 1937.
145. Ibid., AOPG, letter from Bormann to Buch, 11 January 1935.
146. Ibid., Party Chancellery form, 14 April 1945.

147. 'Nachrichten aus der Reichsfrauenführung April-Juni 1939', *FK*, August 1939, inside cover; IfZ, MA 130, letter from the Gau Baden Youth Group leader to district leader Bickler, 30 October 1942.

148. BA, NS22/vorl. 318, *Reichsfrauenführung* 'Nr. St', 25 July 1940, describes the varied and wide-ranging duties of the deputy RFF.

149. BA, NS22/vorl, 356, HA III, 'NSF (DFO)', 8 August 1932, and 'Personalstand am 1.9.32'; BDC, *Slg. Sch.*, 392, 'Anschriftenverzeichnis der NSDAP', 3rd edition, 1937, pp. 53-4, and 4th edition, 1941, pp. 45-6.

150. Ibid., AOPG, letter from Hilgenfeldt to Meta Bottke, 5 June 1934.

151. Ibid., Ilse Eben-Servaes's file, letters of 31 May and 14 June 1935.

152. Ibid., *Slg. Sch.*, 392, op. cit.

153. Stephenson, op. cit., pp. 130-5, 152, 155-60.

154. BA, *Slg. Sch.*, 230, 'Stab des Hauptamtes NS-F und DFW', n.d.; Stephenson, op. cit., p. 164; BDC, letter from Hess's office to Auguste Reber-Gruber, 9 October 1936.

155. Ibid., Friedrike Matthias's NSLB card; Stephenson, op. cit., p. 167.

156. BDC, 'Parteistatistische Erhebung 1939, Nr. 59951', and 'Antrag... Nr. 136846', 28 July 1939.

157. BA, op. cit., *Reichsfrauenführung Jahresbericht 1938*, p. IV.

158. Ibid.

159. Stephenson, op. cit., pp. 88-9, 158-9; Winkler, op. cit., pp. 42-5.

160. BA, op. cit., 'Frauenamt der DAF und NS-Frauenschaft. Anordnung 9/35', 17 August 1935.

161. Winkler, op. cit., p. 77.

162. Stephenson, op. cit., p. 96.

163. Winkler, op. cit., pp. 40-2; Koonz, op. cit., pp. 459-60.

164. Stephenson, op. cit., pp. 109-10; IfZ, MA 441/8, frames 2-759517-18, 'Lücken in der Verordnung über die Meldung von Männern und Frauen für Aufgaben der Reichsverteidigung vom 27.1.1943', n.d.

165. *FK*, February 1939, op. cit., p. 4.

166. HA/13/254, 'Anschriftenverzeichnis . . . ', op. cit.

167. *FK*, April 1937, op. cit., p. 9; 'Organisationsplan der Reichsfrauenführung', *Deutsches Frauenschaffen im Kriege*, 1941 (reproduced on p. 223).

168. BA, NS22/vorl.318, 'Antrag der beantragten Planstellen und beantragte hauptamtliche friedensmässige Besetzung für: Reichsfrauenführung . . . geprüft München 4. April 1941'.

169. BA, NS22/2008, 'Anordnung 3/43' signed by Ley.

170. *FK*, February 1939, op. cit., p. 3.

171. BA, *Slg. Sch.*, 230, letter from Schwarz to Ley, 2 April 1942.

4 THE WOMEN'S ORGANISATIONS IN THE THIRD REICH

Co-ordination and the *Deutsches Frauenwerk*

Gregor Strasser's careful construction of the Nazi Party's apparatus, at the centre and across the country, with an array of affiliates corresponding to the various social and professional group interests in Germany, was designed to enable the Party to take over the leadership of the State and society once the political struggle was won.[1] But the anathematising of all his works on the eve of Hitler's appointment as Chancellor, along with the blurred division of his former authority between Hess and Ley, and, further, the revelation in 1933 that Hitler did not propose to permit the Party to take over the State, resulted in there being no coherent strategy for Nazifying Germany. Destroying the aspects of Weimar political life which most offended the Party was easy enough, and was the one area in which there appeared to be a genuine sense of direction. Constructing the living 'people's community' (*Volksgemeinschaft*) which had been promised remained an aim, but not one which was unequivocally delegated to the Party in the new State, as Frick's pretensions demonstrated; nor was there much agreement at Party headquarters as to how to set about it.[2] While the Party's ambitions were explicitly monopolistic, the reality of trying to take control of the entire population of a sophisticated and industrially-advanced country, when only a minority had given the NSDAP its support, combined with the Party's internal problems to produce strange ambiguities, not least in the women's organisation. Under the faltering direction of the NSF, hamstrung by its leadership crisis and compromised by Paula Siber's appointment in Frick's Ministry, a hybrid solution emerged to the problem of reconstructing German women's organisational life in the Third Reich whose evolution during the 1930s from a federal to a centralised system only thinly disguised its origins.

The way in which the new forms developed owed more to the existing structure of German women's organised social life, and to the way in which the aspects of that structure which were most objectionable to the NSDAP were destroyed, than to any positive scheme conceived by the Party or the NSF. The irony was that the Party's obsession with eliminating its political enemies, particularly on the left, made it the prisoner of traditions it claimed to have come to power to break. The priority given to removing all vestiges of socialist, communist and trade union institutions in the first half of 1933 confirmed the separation of the organised working class, men and women alike, from the rest of the community; the formation of Ley's German Labour Front in May underscored this segregation which immediately contradicted the regime's stated aim of 'national unity'. The creation in July 1934 of a Women's Office in the Labour Front, under Gertrud Scholtz-Klink's nominal leadership, not only signalled the regime's acceptance of women in industry but also gave employed working-class women a substitute for an organisation, through which Ley was able to apply his concept of 'taking care' (*Betreuung*)[3] of working women. Gertrud Scholtz-Klink insisted that the four million or so women in the Labour Front were a part of her women's organisation, being 'daily under the influence of the leadership of the *NS-Frauenschaft*'.[4] It was an idle boast. The Women's Office was expected to co-operate with the RFFg, and its officials were expected to be NSF members,[5] but it remained an integral part of the Labour Front, committed to its policies of trying to reconcile the industrial working class to National Socialism through propaganda and social welfare.[6]

The elimination of the political parties, and of the array of social and charitable associations connected with the SPD and the KPD, particularly,[7] and the segregation of working women in their own occupational group, was an essential element of the *Gleichschaltung* policy, but was a negative one which automatically vitiated its positive purpose. After the destruction and dissolution of unacceptable groups there was to be the reorientation of the activities of all surviving groups to accord with the regime's power-political aims, under 'politically reliable' – which increasingly meant Nazi – leadership. With the women's organisations, this meant bringing a vast number of groups with markedly differing interests – 'patriotic' associations and sports clubs, sewing circles and music groups, for example – under the leadership and direction of the NSF. But since the social groups which had attracted working-class women had largely been associated with the outlawed political parties, and had therefore perished, the surviving groups were overwhelmingly middle-class in membership, disposition and, especially, leadership. Nazi-led social life for women was inevitably middle-class in character because it was built upon the remnants of women's organised social life which had not been sufficiently objectionable to be purged, and therefore had not been associated with the organisations which had catered for the interests of those working-class women – a distinct minority of them – who had joined social groups. The major exceptions to this were the organisations associated with the Churches, which attracted some women of all classes, which were allowed to survive for a time, and which provided the only tangible resistance to the monopolist demands of the NSF for the leadership of all women's group activity – and then only at parochial level.

The aim of creating a mass organsation of German women, under NSF leadership, which was vaguely formulated in the confusion of 1933 and positively espoused by Gertrud Scholtz-Klink, was thus vitiated from the start and for ever. Vast numbers of urban and rural working-class women had no tradition of joining organisations at all; the heavy demands which work and family made on farmers' wives prevented their having much social life and rather made nonsense of the disputes between the *Reichsnährstand* (Reich Food Estate) and the NSF over which of them should recruit rural housewives.[8] And women in rural areas were more likely to be influenced by their Church than by a Party agency in any case.[9] Women working in factories and offices, which meant some middle-class women and substantial numbers of working-class women,[10] had little choice but to join the Labour Front; although it was always intended by the RFF that the women supervised during working hours by the Women's Office of the Labour Front should participate in her organisations in their leisure time, the Labour Front itself provided competition with its 'Strength Through Joy' programme. If working women were reluctant to avail themselves of its facilities,[11] they were hardly likely to volunteer to join in the activities of a women's organisation constructed from the remnants of groups which they had on the whole not chosen to join in the past. There were, of course, employed women who were members of groups which survived and who were brought into the *Deutsches Frauenwerk* eventually, under NSF leadershp; but they were very largely middle-class women and not women from the manual working class.

In the early months of the Third Reich the regime's priority of destroying left-wing organisations, particularly, allowed a variety of non-Nazi women's groups to survive. A degree of expediency was involved, too: at a time when the anti-socialist sentiments of the Churches were being exploited to win their support for Hitler's Government, the federations of Evangelical and Catholic women's associations were not to be antagonised. And the many middle-class women's organisations, a substantial number of which were gathered in the League of German Women's Associations (BDF), a combine founded in 1894 to spearhead the liberal feminists' campaigns before 1914, had increasingly adopted a conservative stance[12] which disposed them to be sympathetic towards National Socialism, and which equally rendered them desirable as short-term allies. The BDF itself, however, as a large federation, was unacceptable to the Nazis, both as an outworn symbol of the feminism and internationalism which they deplored and as a rival focus of loyalty. With a number of its constituent groups, including the professional ones, already dissolved, and weakened by secessions, the BDF was dissolved by its own leadership in May 1933, a week after the founding of Lydia Gottschewski's *Frauenfront*, to enable the remaining member-organisations 'to decide for themselves in which form they want to continue to exist'.[13] It was an anti-climactic end to the German women's movement. Some of the BDF's groups now joined more extreme 'patriotic' bodies, like the BKL, in the *Frauenfront*, while others joined Paula Siber's National Federation; others still continued to exist independently, surviving in some cases into 1934 because of the uncertainty prevailing in the NSF.

The extent to which *Gleichschaltung* was applied seems largely to have depended on the energy of local initiatives, since many organisations were regional rather than national in character. The thoroughness of the process in 'Thalburg'[14] was matched elsewhere, but was not typical of the country as a whole. For one thing, in strongly Catholic areas the Concordat of July 1933 seemed to give protection to non-political Church associations − although there were violations, as the Vatican complained[15] − and the Catholic women's groups felt no urgency about joining the *Frauenfront* or the National Federation. Nevertheless, sometimes co-operation was forthcoming at the local level: in Gau Bayerische Ostmark, some branches of the Catholic Women's League worked amicably with the local NSF, although the League's national leadership held aloof from the NSF and the new combines because of its faith in the protection afforded by the Concordat.[16] One of Paula Siber's last efforts for the DFW was to try, in February 1934, to enlist Vice-Chancellor von Papen's aid in persuading the Catholic women's organisations to join it.[17] A number of the women's groups attached to the Evangelical Church did join the DFW,[18] but there were also reports, from Göttingen and Gau Saxony, for example, of hostility towards the NSF on the part of Evangelical women's groups into 1934.[19] And in one parish in Neuwied, near Koblenz, the overwhelming strength of the Evangelical women's guild had made it impossible even to found an NSF branch up to the end of 1935.[20] But many of the national leaders of the Evangelical women's organisations supported the general objectives of the 'national movement', even if they felt misgivings about some aspects of National Socialism.[21]

While some groups were quick to join the *Frauenfront* or the National Federation to try to buy their continued existence with compliance, others were slower to respond because they believed that sinking their identity in a large combine might be the prelude to dissolution. But the BKL's future seemed assured when its leader was made deputy leader of the *Frauenfront*. Its complacency was rudely shaken by Lydia Gottschewski's crass behaviour towards Frau von Hadeln,[22] and also by the continuing animosity manifested towards BKL branches by the NSF at the local level.[23] But Lydia Gottschewski's dismissal and Walter Buch's sympathetic attitude towards Frau von Hadeln[24] reassured the BKL for the time being, and the division of authority, between Party and State, for the *Deutsches Frauenwerk* which succeeded both the *Frauenfront* and the National Federation in September 1933, created the kind of uncertainty which enabled the BKL to continue to exist relatively independently, until it was undermined from within early in 1934. The stability which Gertrud Scholtz-Klink's appointment brought to the NSF ended the BKL's temporary immunity; resignations and the dissolution of local BKL branches, with many former members joining the NSF, led Charlotte von Hadeln to announce in March 1934 that the BKL would dissolve itself as from 1 April 1934.[25] For other groups, however, the uncertainty in the NSF and the DFW was either irritating or positively threatening. The NSF's magazine, *NS-Frauenwarte*, carried a notice in November 1933 ordering the dissolution of newly-founded local branches of the Evangelical Women's Aid, which led the Evangelical women's groups in the DFW to intimate their withdrawal from it. The leader of one of the large housewives' organisations also seems to have carried out her threat to take her members out of the DFW, because of the pointlessness of being in it.[26]

The groups which remained in the DFW in spite of the failure in winter 1933-4 to find any role for it beyond ensuring, through the provincial leaders' supervision, that the member-organisations behaved in a 'politically reliable' way,[27] were presumably content to pay one pfennig per member of their organisation to the DFW's central office[28] while the DFW remained inactive and they were able to conduct their affairs with reasonable latitude. But in mid-February 1934, at the time of Hilgenfeldt's appointment as NSF overlord, it was announced in the *Völkischer Beobachter* that a reorganisation of the DFW was imminent.

This raised fears in the affiliated groups that they would lose their separate identities in a mass organisation, or else that the DFW would be dissolved, and its constituent groups with it.[29] Paula Siber was convinced that the co-operation of the non-Party women's groups, and particularly the confessional ones, could best be assured by maintaining the DFW as a loose federation of organisations with a central office and NSF influence wielded by the GNSFLs as its provincial leaders. In particular, she maintained that the fears of these groups would be allayed by retaining the DFW's character as an institution of the State as well as the Party, since giving the Party full authority over the DFW would lead to friction with the confessional groups.[30] Had there been no other reason for removing Paula Siber from office, her encouragement to the leaders of the DFW's member-organisations to resist any change in its form[31] would have constituted sufficient indiscipline to warrant it.

Bringing the DFW under Party control and under the leadership of Gertrud Scholtz-Klink, as NSF leader, was the logical step for the leaders of a Party which aspired to totalitarian control because it meant that 'the entire German women's work will in future be under unified leadership'. The DFW's central staff was to include a representative of each of 'the great women's associations', while the smaller groups would be invited to send a delegate for discussions at central office from time to time. There was little change in the arrangement that the GNSFLs would replace the former provincial leaders of the DFW since most of these had already been drawn from the GNSFLs' ranks, but formalising this was intended to ensure that the work of the DFW's constituent groups would be conducted under the 'spiritual leadership' of the NSF. And a GNSFL was made explicitly responsible for all DFW work in her Gau, and was instructed to hold frequent meetings with the organisations' representatives there. The groups themselves were allowed some room for manoeuvre, as yet, with the order that in no territorial unit of the NSF's organisation should the NSF leader be directly in charge of the day-to-day running of all the working organisations.[32] These 'guidelines for German women's work', issued three weeks after Gertrud Scholtz-Klink's appointment,[33] indicated that the activities of the women's groups which had been allowed to survive were no longer to be performed in an individual, idiosyncratic way. The small degree of NSF control exerted at the local level was perhaps not sufficient to guarantee uniformity, but it was intended to ensure that social, charitable, cultural or sporting activities owed their character increasingly less to the nature of an affiliated group — whether it was Catholic or Evangelical or secular, for example – than to the developing demands of the new regime.

Nevertheless, the Nazi assumption of control of the 'women's work' at national and Gau level primarily affected its leadership, and meant that its nature continued to be determined by tradition rather than by Nazi innovation. After the elimination of left-wing, feminist and pacifist organisations, the remaining women's groups were brought into the DFW as corporate members, although some small and relatively insignificant ones were allowed to exist outside it until the later 1930s.[34] Although it was probably never intended that the groups which were allowed to survive the purging process should retain their identity for any length of time, they clearly provided the RFF with a convenient base, a ready-made non-Party women's organisation most of whose constituent groups represented areas deemed suitable in the Nazi view for German women's organisational life. More, the groups provided individuals experienced in certain skills or adept at devising propaganda for a cause, as well as premises, equipment and magazines. All of these were used to promote the work of the DFW, and to propagate it as a unified scheme which was the product of willing co-operation by former group leaders and members who welcomed the direction given by Gertrud Scholtz-Klink and her staff and the dedication of NSF activists.[35] This public image was projected to try to dispel suspicions that the DFW was merely the result of the forced nationalisation of existing groups – as indeed it was. In reality, but probably unconsciously, the DFW's leadership was instrumental in limiting the organisation's appeal; the way in which the RFFg was built up as a massive edifice for the direction of a mass organisation suggests that this was certainly not deliberate. But the way in which the DFW was constructed severely restricted the constituency among German women from which it could hope to attract recruits.

The months after Gertrud Scholtz-Klink's appointment saw increasing pressure being put on groups still outside the DFW to affiliate, since the monopoly delegated to it in January 1934[36] was to be enforced. Some of the pressure was counterproductive, leading to the voluntary dissolution of groups whose members were unwilling to distort their activities to suit the DFW's leadership. Allen describes how in 'Thalburg'

> often people simply stopped coming together. Either there was no more club, or the attractiveness of the club had been destroyed by *Gleichschaltung*, or people no longer had the leisure or the desire to

continue with their club.[37]

No doubt numerous women's local groups ceased to exist in this way. For groups which did affiliate to the DFW, a ban was placed on the founding of new branches and on the admission of new members to existing branches for the second half of 1934,[38] to give Hilgenfeldt and Gertrud Scholtz-Klink a breathing-space in which to take stock of their new resources and devise an organisation plan for the DFW to exploit them most effectively. Already in May 1934, on Mothers' Day, the RFF had announced the creation of a 'National Mothers' Service' (RMD), to train young women in all aspects of mothercare and to provide welfare for needy mothers and children.[39] While this suited Gertrud Scholtz-Klink's own disposition, and served the permanent population policy concern of the Party, it was conveniently constructed from the start on the mothers' welfare organisations which had for some time been run by the confessional women's groups, especially, as earnest of their concern for sound family life and their abhorrence of 'Bolshevist' 'new morality' as exemplified by recent legislation in the Soviet Union.[40]

Following on this, with the moratorium on the development of the constituent groups in force, the RFF began to build the DFW up as a monolithic structure to replace its initial federal nature with a system of sections and sub-departments which would be given overall direction by trusted officials in her Berlin office. The founding of the 'Abroad' section in July 1934, however, was above all in bitter response to the threat of a boycott of German goods by foreigners who asserted that German women were heavily oppressed by the new regime, in contrast with their alleged emancipation under Weimar. This new section, extended two years later as the 'Border and Foreign' section (GA), began as a propaganda agency to allay foreigners' misgivings about the position of women in Nazi Germany through literature, visits abroad, and hospitality to foreign visitors, to show them the 'reality' of women's life in Germany.[41] Again, there was a useful ancestry for the immediate and future activities of the GA in the various 'patriotic', colonial and German cultural groups which had been co-ordinated into the DFW.[42] And forming a third section alongside the RMD and the GA there was, from September 1934, the major concern of 'National Economy/Domestic Economy' (Vw/Hw).[43] While this owed its rationale to Strasser's strongly-held view that women, as consumers, should be encouraged to 'buy German', its practical basis was the large housewives' organisations whose origins lay in the Imperial period; these had done much to give the BDF its increasingly conservative aspect, and then, in 1932, had seriously weakened the BDF by seceding from it.[44]

Two large combines of housewives' organisations had amalgamated in March 1934 to form the National Association of German Housewives (RDH), possibly in the hope of resisting pressure to affiliate to the DFW from a position of strength.[45] But six months later, when the Vw/Hw section was created, the RDH agreed to join the DFW, and along with an odd assortment of smaller groups[46] it provided an invaluable basis for the new section. After another year, in September 1935, however, the section's work was sufficiently advanced for the RDH to have become superfluous, and even dangerous; with its huge size − perhaps a quarter of a million members[47] − it was the dominant element in the Vw/Hw, and this in itself was enough of a threat to thorough NSF influence to warrant its dissolution. Its magazine was conveniently adopted as the official organ of the Vw/Hw,[48] and it seems to have retained a substantial proportion of its readership in spite of the change-over.[49] The RFFg's account of the DFW's development paid handsome tribute to the 'valuable work' previously performed by the RDH and clearly implied that its dissolution was voluntary, with its former members happy to continue their work, as members of the Vw/Hw.[50] But some of them did not take kindly to the new order. From Hamburg it was reported in February 1936 that it had been necessary to prohibit former RDH members from meeting together for 'coffee mornings' or 'merry afternoons' as a substitute for their previous group activity.[51] Even informal association of this kind was regarded as a threat to the DFW's monopoly.

The creation of the sections, with two more 'working sections', 'Auxiliary Service' and 'Culture/Education/Training' joining the existing three in 1936 and 1937 respectively,[52] did not at first sight threaten the existence of the affiliated groups. In fact, groups which could be plausibly accommodated in a section may have felt that they were guaranteed continued existence, if at the price of further erosion of their independence, with the increasing degree of centralisation of authority in the RFFg. In the Vw/Hw, for example, there were, besides the housewives, organisations which had run private domestic science schools, in addition to the women's group of the Association against Alcoholism. The GA brought together groups which had long worked to maintain the interest of Germans abroad in the mother country as well as patently anti-Versailles organisations like the German Women's Navy League and the women's branch of the German Colonial Society.[53] But groups which could not be conveniently fitted into a section were the first to be at risk; having lost their *raison d'être*, and being of no further use, two old conservative women's groups, the Union of German Women and the women's association of the nationalist paramilitary *Stahlhelm*, were dissolved in autumn 1935,[54] at the time of the formal dissolution of the *Stahlhelm* itself.[55] The German Women's Navy League was dissolved a year later, its members expected to continue working in the GA section. At this time, too, the corporate membership of the Evangelical Women's groups was revoked;[56] with increasing attacks on the Protestant as well as the Catholic Church from within the Party,[57] there could no longer be a place for a sub-section for 'church work' in the DFW, while the 'mothercare work' of the Evangelical and Catholic groups had by now been fully integrated into the RMD section of the DFW.

By 1935 the total membership of the DFW's constituent groups was 2.7 million,[58] a figure which had risen to 'around four million' in the Greater German Reich at the end of 1938.[59] In the intervening period, the number of affiliated groups had, however, been drastically reduced. Of the 87 groups listed in 1935, all the Evangelical and all but one of the Catholic women's groups had disappeared by March 1938. It is true that most of the professional, occupational and welfare groups listed in 1935 − as up to a fifth of the total of 87 − continued to exist, although only four of them appeared in the severely truncated list of thirteen affiliated groups given in March 1938. There were also two new groups, two sporting and two cultural groups, and the Union of Blind Women of Germany and the anti-alcoholic women's group.[60] All the other social, cultural, sporting and charitable groups, as well as those connected with a variety of hobbies, had simply disappeared, their members gathered into the appropriate section of the DFW or else, in resisting this course, left without any organised social life. The only other group activity permitted was equally under the aegis of an organisation connected with the NSDAP, like the NSV or a co-ordinated occupational group, although it proved almost impossible to close down the church women's guilds altogether. Even if these were banned, priests and parsons could evade the prohibition if they were determined; for example, in summer 1938 it was reported that a priest in Saarburg had revived the former Catholic Women's Union there, under an alternative name.[61]

To emphasise the trend towards increasing centralisation of the DFW's activities, Gertrud Scholtz-Klink proposed in summer 1935 the drafting of a formal constitution for it. But both Hess's office and Ley had doubts about the detailed proposals she presented, and several months of deliberation followed to try to draft something that was both satisfactory and realistic. While Sommer, acting for Hess, proposed that the DFW

> should be the comprehensive women's organisation. To this end, the opportunity must be created to include or affiliate other women's associations, or else to dissolve them in the interests of the unified construction of the DFW.[62]

Ley pointed out that there were women involved in other organisations — the Party, the Labour Front, the Reich Food Estate, for example — who equally deserved the description of 'German women who are ready to collaborate in the *Führer*'s work of construction'. He also objected to suggestions that the DFW should either become an affiliated organisation of the Nazi Party or be designated a 'National Socialist Community'. The appropriate relationship between the Party and the DFW did not warrant the former, he said, while

> the description 'Community' is only to be applied to an association of persons from all sections of the population. The organisation of persons of one sex can therefore not be termed a community.[63]

Ley's objections were in the end overruled by Hess, and from January 1936 the DFW became a 'registered organisation',[64] with the status of an affiliated organisation of the Nazi Party. Its aim was 'the organisational combination of those German women who are ready to collaborate in the *Führer*'s work of construction, under the leadership of the *NS-Frauenschaft*'.[65]

But to give the DFW an enforceable monopoly a law had to be passed, and in September 1936 Bormann at last produced a draft law to this effect.[66] The response to it by Frick's junior Minister, Wilhelm Stuckart,[67] was one of detailed criticism, first of its lack of clarity and bad style, but more importantly of its content. For one thing, Stuckart was concerned — even if Bormann was not — about the violation of the Concordat with the Vatican that was involved in giving the DFW a legal monopoly of women's organisational life. And the threat of imposing a penalty of imprisonment or a fine on any who founded new organisations 'which pursue wholly worthy aims' and refused to dissolve them or affiliate to the DFW deeply offended him.[68] There is no record of this law's being passed, but for practical purposes it was not really necessary; it had already been possible to put sufficient pressure on a large variety of groups either to affiliate or dissolve — and in some cases to affiliate and then, after an interval, dissolve. It was bound to irritate Bormann, Ley and Gertrud Scholtz-Klink, with their blinkered obsession with uniformity, if the odd unimportant group continued to exist outside the Party's affiliated organisation for the mass of German women. But after 1936 there were few of these, and the real problem for the DFW was first its failure to attract a substantial number of new, hitherto unorganised women, to make it a genuinely mass organisation, and secondly demarcation disputes, with the Labour Front, the Food Estate and other groups which were within the Party's structure,[69] and upon whom pressure ought to have been able to be exerted to prevent their weakening the DFW's monopoly and, no doubt, also its credibility.

Gertrud Scholtz-Klink's desire to provide the DFW with a constitution reflected her undimmed ambition to expand its membership to a mammoth size. In February 1936, with the DFW newly-established as a 'registered organisation', the new category of individual membership was introduced, to compensate women who had aspired to join the NSF and now, with the imposition of a moratorium on admission to it, had to be disappointed.[70] This gave the RFF the opportunity to try to tap the large reserve of unorganised women of all classes who had so far not been accessible through a group that could be co-ordinated. In 1937, particularly, there was an energetic recruiting drive[71] which bore some fruit. From a figure of 23,000 individual members in mid-1936 there was a steady growth to almost one million two years later,[72] and at the end of 1938, with an influx of over 400,000 new members from the annexed Austrian Gaus, the total stood at a million and a half. Austrian women showed particular enthusiasm for the DFW with Gau Vienna alone providing 124,000 individual members; in fact, four of the seven Austrian Gaus were among the seven contributing most members to the DFW. In the 'old Reich', only huge Saxony and the border Gaus of Silesia and East Prussia compared with them. Together, these three German and four Austrian Gaus provided almost 40 per cent of the DFW's individual membership, while by contrast Franconia, Mecklenburg, Swabia and Hanover-East each contributed less than one per cent of it. There was enthusiasm in the Sudetenland, too, with 300,000 new DFW members from this area by early 1939.[73] But there was foot-dragging in the 'old Reich', and even complaints that NSF officials were overreaching themselves by trying to compel local authority officials to see that their wives joined the DFW.[74] This zeal on the part of NSF leaders was no doubt geared towards achieving a more impressive individual membership for the DFW than the six per cent of women over 20 in the 'old Reich' registered on the first day of 1939.[75]

From 1936, when the DFW became an organisation open to every 'Aryan' German women (provided that, if she was married, her husband, too, was 'Aryan'),[76] there was a determined effort to recruit as many members as possible. Drawing up a constitution and devising a badge for the DFW were intended to raise its status above that of the *ad hoc* combine which it had initially been. Building up the sections and bringing their work closely under the leadership of the NSF's territorial officials sealed the fate of most of the affiliated groups, and effected a Nazification of women's social life – in so far as they chose to engage in one, as was carefully pointed out[77] – to complete the nationalisation process. Members of the dissolved groups could continue to work in the section to which their group had belonged, or could join another section; how many actually resigned because they felt no allegiance to the combine which had swallowed up their own chosen group is not clear, although there was a steady trickle of resignations. But this was of minimal proportions: in 1938, 38,000 women left both the NSF and the DFW – as a mere one per cent of their combined individual membership – while almost 600,000 joined, in the 'old Reich'.[78] Nevertheless, allowing for the propaganda in favour of the DFW and the fact that no other purely social women's group activity was permitted, it is clear that the aim of creating a mass organisation of German women had not been achieved by the time the war broke out, five years after Gertrud Scholtz-Klink's appointment. The propaganda and the empty boasts about the DFW's strength, and its position as 'the largest women's organisation in the world',[79] for what that was worth, could not conceal the self-inflicted nature of its lack of appeal for the vast majority of German women. Because of the way in which it had evolved, and because of the regime's fears about the spread of socialism or communism among women workers as well as men,[80] the DFW had first been cut off from those working-class women who were in a position to be organised, as they were gathered into the Labour Front, and then had built its structure on the remaining essentially middle-class base in such a way that Labour Front women and, above all, the great mass of working-class women with no tradition of joining organisations, found it positively unattractive. There were plenty of middle-class women, too, especially those who were better-off and better-educated, who did not wish to have their social life organised for them, who resisted appeals to join the DFW. But it was the limit which the DFW's leadership, under Gertrud Scholtz-Klink, had to set on its horizons as a result of the negative aspects of *Gleichschaltung* which restricted from the start its potential for growth and deprived it of even the chance to become the mass organisation which its leadership had envisaged.

The *NS-Frauenschaft* and 'Political Education'

The structural fault which restricted the DFW's appeal from its inception was to only a limited degree the responsibility of the NSF, but it ensured that the NSF itself remained politically insignificant and increasingly found itself either acting as an agency for other, more powerful organisations – like the NSV, for example – or else operating in a backwater. Even if the NSF, and its leadership in particular, had not been in disarray during the critical *Gleichschaltung* period, the outcome might have been no different; on the other hand, purposeful canvassing by a united NSF during the heady days of 1933 when other women's organisations were being destroyed or were paralysed by uncertainty might have facilitated the creation of a more impressive women's organisation than the DFW turned out to be. Gertrud Scholtz-Klink has been blamed for the failure of the women's organisations in the Third Reich to achieve significance, but what she inherited in February 1934 was already a *fait accompli* – or, rather, an opportunity missed. This was in spite of the energetic work of individual GNSFLs – like Gertrud Scholtz-Klink herself – in bringing the non-Party groups in their region under NSF leadership.[81] But the GNSFLs had to operate without any effective overall direction for a year or so after the *Machtübernahme*, and, for a time, with the complication of the conflicting claims of Lydia Gottschewski's and Paula Siber's new combines.

There were also difficulties caused by changes in Gau boundaries, in some cases,[82] and by changes in personnel. This immediately meant that there was interregional diversity within the NSF of a kind which was implied by Strasser's original creation of it as the Party's women's auxiliary but which was also increasingly unsuitable for the women's branch of the official Party in the new State, with uniformity the desideratum. There were attempts to achieve unified practice with orders emanating from the centre and, in return, reports from the Gaus to the Office of the *Frauenschaft*. And the central office could dictate membership criteria and – a perennial problem – lines of demarcation between the NSF and other Party affiliates. But the access of domestic power to Gauleiters as a deliberate tactic by Hitler after Strasser's resignation ensured that they were 'the backbone of the Party organisation, so that Hitler — strictly speaking — had not *one* NSDAP, but 32 political Gau organisations at his disposal'.[83] Circumscribed by the limits set on the Party's own function and by the admission to affiliated organisations of large numbers of non-Party members who were not strictly under a Gauleiter's jurisdiction, the Gauleiters nevertheless benefited from the rivalry between Hess, with Bormann, and Ley which enabled them to retain considerable autonomy from Party headquarters in dealing with their Gau.[84] The extent to which a Gau NSF organisation was able to function productively was therefore at least partly dependent on the degree to which Gauleiters were prepared to involve the NSF in the Party's work; the unwillingness of some of them to do this, in spite of Strasser's exhortations, in 1932,[85] meant that in some cases the NSF would be restricted to supervising the DFW's activities, although in others — Baden, North Westphalia, Saxony, for example — the NSF's contribution to the Party's work had already been welcomed before 1933. Other Gauleiters besides Robert Wagner, Meyer and Mutschmann paid sufficient attention to their NSF to be aware of its work, and it was at their instigation that GNSFLs like Thea Friedel in Bayerische Ostmark, Else Faber in Pomerania, Eva Leistikow in Halle-Merseburg and Ida Günther in Danzig received the Party's Gold Badge, before the war. Gauleiter Forster gave Ida Günther a particularly glowing testimonial for this purpose.[86] Ley certainly encouraged the political leaders to make the best use of their NSF branch, in the belief that at the local level, particularly, a woman had far more influence, through her contact with other women in the daily round, than men.[87]

Potential for conflict still existed, however, with the GNSFL owing allegiance to two superiors, to Gertrud Scholtz-Klink and her growing central organisation, and to her own Gauleiter. Once the NSF became a member-organisation of the Party, in March 1935,[88] it ceased to be, formally, merely the Gau and local branch women's auxiliary and became finally an organisation in its own right, completing the tendency which Strasser had encouraged in contradiction of his own earliest intentions. This strengthened the chain of command within the NSF from Gertrud Scholtz-Klink down to the cell and the block, and enhanced the status of the GNSFL within her own organisation. But the insignificance in which the NSF remained meant that this was of limited effect outside a restricted circle of enthusiasts. And it did little to change the relationship between the Gauleiter and the GNSFL, particularly in the 17 (out of 32) Gaus where the GNSFLs who were in office by the end of 1934 retained their post until well into the war.[89]

The marked absence of conflict between the *Reichsfrauenführung* and the Gauleiters suggests that, above all, the NSF was not important enough for Gauleiters to quarrel about it, that an assertive Gauleiter who was prepared to use his NSF could do so without being challenged from the centre about his methods, that an ineffective or uninterested Gauleiter could leave his NSF to its own devices if he chose, and that Gertrud Scholtz-Klink's control over the NSF was more formal than effective. Typical of the *ad hoc* way in which Nazi policy developed, this state of affairs had been neither intended nor predicted. In spite of the confusion which consumed the NSF in 1933, there had been a realisation that it – like the Party as a whole – would have to find a new role now that the gruelling campaigning tasks of the *Kampfzeit* were suddenly obsolete. The role now assigned to the NSF was that of the 'political education' of the mass of German women – who would ideally be gathered together in the DFW for the purpose – to convince them that every act of policy devised by the regime, and every demand made of German women, was genuinely for the benefit of the nation as a whole, and therefore ultimately for their own benefit. The terms 'spiritual leadership', 'ideological training' and 'political education' were all used to describe this massive task of indoctrinating the good, German, 'Aryan' woman to reject previous allegiances – above all, Marxism and 'political Catholicism' – and to accept the need for hard work and sacrifice[90] in the national interest, as it was defined by Hitler and his closest associates.

The apparent contradiction between the Party's consistent anathematising of conventional political activity by women and its unceasing anxiety from 1933 about making women 'politically conscious' led to the development of a new definition of 'politicisation'. Writers pointed out that although the housewife's 'choice is decisive in the balance of fate' in many aspects of daily life, 'all too many women . . . are still not conscious of their responsibility' in this respect.[91] To remedy this,

> we claim no rights for our sex such as that woman politician [Rosa Luxemburg] demanded . . . rather we want to fulfil the tasks which the nation sets us as women . . . What we are striving for to-day is a completely different kind of politicisation of women, it is the dedication of women to the nation and therefore to the state, which is organically constructed upon the reality of race and nation'.[92]

The female support which the NSDAP had won in Weimar elections had been drawn largely from women who disliked female political activists and 'women's rightists'; now that these activists – inside as well as outside the Party – had been silenced, the women of Germany over-whelmingly subsided into yawning political apathy. This did not nec-essarily mean that they were discontented; often it was quite the reverse, with the satisfactory outcome of Hitler's appointment, fol-lowed by his neutralising of Nazi radicals, removing the motive for vigilance or interest in political affairs. But the Nazis always feared that where there was no show of support there might lurk opposition. Visible discomfort was manifested at the realisation that the Party's projected ideal women, the housewife and mother, 'is basically unpol-itical'. The nature of German politics in the 'liberal period' had been such that women had, understandably, it was said, 'stayed as remote from the political hurly-burly as possible'. But now there was a need for 'political education',

> to instil a particular attitude, an attitude which, from inner com-pulsion, approves official measures and applies these in daily life . . . so that in the enthusiasm of women for the nation's fate – that is, their politicisation – Germany will stand at the head of all nations.[93]

This enormous confidence trick involved two-tier exploitation: Hitler and the select group around him – and not, as propaganda had it, the NSDAP – would decide policies which suited their purposes, and would exploit idealistic, unpaid NSF officials and members who would verse themselves in the official view of all aspects of domestic and foreign policy and then indoctrinate ordinary German women to try to make them accept their role as tools of Hitler's designs.

But it was only after the completion of the initial *Gleichschaltung* process and the resolution of the NSF's leadership problems that it be-came fully apparent that the NSF needed this new role because it had lost many of its former functions. It was probably fortunate in having its association with the SA terminated with the need no longer to render assistance to the 'fighting menfolk' of the *Kampfzeit*; at least the women's organisation was not implicated in the Röhm purge. Also, apart from trying to arouse enthusiasm for Hitler's plebiscites, the NSF's electioneering activities were obsolete. And 1933-4 saw the drawing of lines of demarcation to define the activities of Party affili-ates which were almost exclusively to the NSF's disadvantage. Although the NSF and the DFW were given monopolies of women's Party and non-Party social organisation, respectively,[94] women were still able to join other organisations along with men, and were virtually obliged to join any relevant occupational group. The BdM's monopoly, painfully enforced in 1933, was still resented. And then in May 1933 Hitler decreed that the NSV should have a monopoly of responsibility for social welfare organisation.[95] As some Gau Histories pointed out, this meant the takeover by the NSV of much of the NSF's traditional work; but the continuing economic crisis in 1933-4 demanded action, not dispute, and the NSF in Göttingen district and in Gaus Saxony and Bayerische Ostmark, at least, threw itself into auxiliary work with the NSV, collecting money and clothes for the Winter Aid scheme.[96]

The NSV was also assigned the sole right to organise a Party nursing corps, after Hess's announcement early in 1934 that all Nazi nursing groups, including the NSF's, were to be dissolved. The formation of groups of 'brown sisters' or of 'the red swastika' — redolent of Elsbeth Zander's notorious bands — was explicitly banned.[97] Further, in 1936 Hilgenfeldt, as NSV leader was made responsible for every welfare project envisaged by any of the Party's affiliates.[98] NSF members were encouraged to work with the NSV, particularly during the war, but the NSF was allowed no independent welfare function of its own. It is hardly surprising that, in addition to the undercurrent of rivalry between the NSF and the BdM which persisted into the war,[99] there should also have been friction between the NSF and the NSV. The complaints made by Helmut Lemme[100] were one manifestation of this; the hostile reception by NSV officials of a speech made in April 1939 by Gertrud Scholtz-Klink[101] was another. And yet, the NSF was expected to work amicably with both the BdM and the NSV, in spite of having lost important functions to each of them. As Lydia Gottschewski was used temporarily to bring an end to the open hostility between the NSF and the BdM, so Erich Hilgenfeldt's position as NSF overlord was partly intended to enforce collaboration between the NSF and the NSV. The NSF also became involved in demarcation disputes with other organisations; the Reich Food Estate had a running battle with the NSF over the recruitment of rural women,[102] and the Labour Front earned the RFF's displeasure by claiming the right to organise housewives in its section for domestic workers.[103] The repetitiveness with which 'cooperation' was guaranteed and 'agreements' reached between the NSF and these, and other, organisations[104] testifies to the recurrent nature of the disputes between them.

Deprived of most of its former functions and restricted by the pretensions of other groups, in summer 1934, with the leadership crisis settled, the NSF began to prepare itself for its role as 'spiritual leader' of German women. But it was immediately obvious that most NSF leaders, quite apart from ordinary NSF members, were not themselves equipped for this task. This was partly because the practical demands of the *Kampfzeit* had dominated the NSF's work – as Guida Diehl had complained – so that NSF members were not well enough versed in the Nazi *Weltanschauung* to be able to instruct others. Further, the direction of Nazi propaganda inevitably had to change after January 1933 from destructive criticism of Weimar Governments to unquestioning support for Hitler's regime. NSF members, like other Party workers, would have to be trained in the new orthodoxy predicated by changed circumstances, although some elements of the Nazi *Weltanschauung* – the racist and anti-socialist ones, particularly – did not change materially. In addition, the way in which NSF membership suddenly expanded, in common with the Party's own growth, after the *Machtübernahme*, and also the experience and ability of the expanded membership, demanded careful instruction of the faithful before they could be entrusted with the 'political education' of other women. And once it was felt safe to let NSF enthusiasts loose with their conception of Nazi ideology, there was a constant need to hold refresher courses for even the most reliable, since the changing policies and demands of the regime had to be built into the *Weltanschauung* that was being propagated.

The premium placed on the NSF's new role was reflected in the preoccupation of Gertrud Scholtz-Klink, Hilgenfeldt, Hess and Ley with its membership criteria. These changed at different points in the 1930s to try to ensure that only the most reliable women were included in what was intended to be a tight-knit leadership elite. At first, in 1933, political opportunism generated a kind of enthusiasm for National Socialism among those who had so far held aloof from the Party. In the NSDAP, the influx of new members diluted the strength of the 'old fighters' to such an extent that a moratorium on admission was applied from 1 May 1933.[105] The rush to join the NSF was more modest, but was nevertheless marked, particularly once admission to the Party was closed. From almost 110,000 members at the end of 1932, the NSF's size grew to almost 850,000 a year later, then to over a million and a half at the end of 1934 and to two million a year after that.[106] This growth necessitated the founding of new local branches and districts, particularly in Gaus where the NSF's hold before 1933 had been tenuous: in Hessen-Nassau-North and Lower Franconia, for example, the full energies of the Gau NSF leadership in 1933 were consumed by the need to organise the new recruits into groups.[107] In Saxony, NSF membership increased twentyfold between October 1931 and the end of 1933, to a total of 80,000,[108] giving Lotte Rühlemann plenty to occupy herself with during the period of the NSF's leadership crisis. And in Gau Bayerische Ostmark the modest ten NSF local branches which existed in mid-1932 provided the basis for expansion to as many as 750 early in 1934, with 20,000 members altogether. Further meteoric growth, to 70,000 by August 1934, led GNSFL Thea Friedel to impose a six-month moratorium on admission, 'to give the NSF leaders the chance to prove their suitability'; she found a number of them unable to do so and dismissed them from office.[109]

Strasser had originally intended to make the NSF the collective body of women Party members, although he had relented by allowing a category of 'helpers' in the NSF for non-Party members.[110] By 1935, the balance of membership had altered radically so that out of a million and a half NSF members only 136,197 — half of them 'housewives' — were Party members, as 5.5 per cent of the NSDAP; not one NSF member in ten was a Party member, and only one-third of the 'leaders' in both the NSF and the DFW were Party members. Furthermore, far from all women Party members were NSF enthusiasts. In 1935, as many as 73 per cent of the women in the NSDAP were classed as 'inactive'; they paid their subscription — which gave them free membership of the NSF — and made no other contribution to the work of the Party or its affiliates. By contrast, almost 60 per cent of male Party members were 'active'.[111] There were, then, almost 100,000 women Party members, who were automatically also NSF members, who played no part in the life of the Party or the NSF. There were also non-Party members in the NSF who played no active role in it. One woman teacher who joined the NSF in July 1934 was described as 'anything but a National Socialist', who had taken out NSF membership simply in order to retain her job.[112] No doubt there were many like her.[113] With high graduate unemployment, at a time when the teaching profession, particularly, was being purged and the new regime's attitude to women in the professions seemed hostile, the least that a woman teacher or lawyer or civil servant could do was to join a Party affiliate in addition to her occupational group; while some gave a semblance of loyalty by joining the NSV or the BdM,[114] others chose the NSF. But it was a matter of mutual convenience, since Gertrud Scholtz-Klink desired the services of well-educated women in her organisations, if they were prepared to be active in them. In the later 1930s she worked hard to try to involve professional women in the 'women's work'.[115]

This was not least because of continuing anxiety about the limited educational experience and intellectual ability of the majority of NSF members. While the NSDAP outwardly despised intellectuals, and while the NSF and the BdM were explicitly intended to appeal to the population at large, regardless of social or educational background, it was regarded as a disadvantage that the most enthusiastic NSF workers were engaged in essentially practical occupations and therefore ill-equipped to convey the Nazi *Weltanschauung* in a coherent and convincing way. From the start, the NSF and its precursors had been largely middle-class-based groups, with a number of working-class women attracted during the Depression particularly; these 'old fighters' were diluted by a large number of opportunists from 1933, including a small group of women with professional positions to conserve. But the majority of NSF members were middle-class − often lower middle-class − housewives or clerical workers.[116] Recruiting drives produced some results among the wives of civil servants,[117] but although the NSF's leadership hoped to attract large numbers of wives of higher civil servants, particularly, there was strong resistance in the Reich Ministries to special recruiting drives among them.[118] In many areas, the NSF's enthusiasts remained women 'with avowed good will and a touching readiness for service, for which very often the spiritual basis is, however, lacking',[119] while it seemed impossible to persuade women from the 'educated classes' to work in the NSF.[120] This was hardly surprising; apart from other objections many well-educated women might have had to National Socialism, they were unlikely to volunteer to join an organisation which was already run by women whom they considered their social and intellectual inferiors. And women graduates, particularly, having been used to mixed company at university and, often, at work, would hardly relish segregation in such a claustrophobically single-sex group.

Gertrud Scholtz-Klink faced a problem in that while she wanted to attract better-educated women to the NSF, she wanted them to join willingly and to be active and disciplined members once they had joined. Those who met these requirements were often handsomely rewarded, some with prestigious jobs[121] and others with admission to the Party once the ban on new admissions began to be relaxed.[122] But as a leadership elite, the NSF could not afford to carry passengers, and in February 1935 the RFF and Hilgenfeldt produced a ruling that only women Party members who were active in the NSF were to continue to be members of it,[123] to eliminate the large amount of dead wood which had accumulated. Non-Party NSF members who were inactive could be excluded at the leadership's discretion because they had no automatic right to membership. And the purging process of 1933-4 had removed the hyper-active, those whose indiscipline or feminist militancy did not accord with the new image of a harmonious, highly-disciplined leadership corps dedicated to imbuing German women with the Nazi *Weltanschauung* as defined by the Party's male leaders. But while Gertrud Scholtz-Klink was concerned to slim down the NSF to these dimensions, her policy at the centre seemed to be contradicted by what was happening in some of the regions. In Gaus, like Saxony and Bayerische Ostmark, where the rush to join the NSF had been prodigious, weeding out passengers was desirable; but in other areas, and, it was clear, in some sections of the population, it was hard to persuade enough women to join the NSF to make local branches viable and to build up a respectable NSF membership in Gaus where the women's organisation was struggling. The recruiting drives held in some parts of the Rhineland as late as 1935 were an attempt to build up NSF groups almost from scratch in the face of strong resistance inspired by the Churches.[124]

But regardless of local variations, Gertrud Scholtz-Klink decided that the only way to consolidate the NSF as the women's leadership group was to impose a moratorium on entry, which Hess agreed should have effect from 1 February 1936.[125] From now on, the NSF was to be consolidated as 'a leaders' organisation', bringing together BdM leaders, active women Party members, leading women in the NSV and, from October 1939, all office-holders and 'important women colleagues', in the DFW, the Labour Service, the Nazi Girl Students' Group and all Party affiliates, who had proved their value through 'a year and a half's faultless tenure of office' – if they applied to join the NSF.[126] This was designed to close ranks at a time when the NSF's task was the maintenance of the 'inner front' of ideological conformity, with the need to utilise the services of all experienced, reliable and trained women to instruct the mass of German women, by example and by indoctrination courses. But by this time the other groups with women officials – including the Labour Front, the Labour Service, the NSV and the Nazi Teachers' League – had developed distinctive functions while the NSF, restricted to a large degree to supervision of the DFW's activities and 'political education', had stagnated. If Nazi women activists could satisfy their ambitions and fervour in these organisations, what need was there for them to seek – and pay for – membership of the NSF? Gertrud Scholtz-Klink was trying to maintain the fiction that she and the NSF stood at the pinnacle of the hierarchy of women's organisational life in the Third Reich, whereas by 1939 she was trying to cash in on the status acquired by all these other groups by aiming to entice their office-holders into the NSF. In the end, it looked as if only close association with other, purposeful groups would prevent the impression from gaining currency that the NSF was operating in a backwater.

The main reason for this lay in the DFW's failure to become a genuinely mass organisation of 'followers' of the elite NSF; by the time war broke out, the DFW was still clearly the organisation of only a small minority of German women. There was therefore less difference between the NSF and the DFW than there was between the two of them and the mass of women who were members of neither. This was implicitly recognised early in 1941 when Gertrud Scholtz-Klink proposed to Hess that the NSF and the DFW should be amalgamated, for administrative convenience, she said. Hess's unexpected departure[127] left the matter undecided, but Party Treasurer Schwarz, seeing financial merit in it, raised it with Ley in April 1942.[128] Thereafter, while the 1939 membership criteria remained formally in force, in practice the two organisations worked as one, with NSF leaders in direct charge of the DFW's work at every level. The NSF even abandoned its distinctive badge, dating from Elsbeth Zander's day and bearing her motto 'GHL',[129] and the runic symbol of the DFW became the uniform badge of both organisations.[130] It made belated sense to combine the two into one official women's organisation; the NSF and the DFW had worked closely together from the beginning of the war, and as the war dragged on and the needs of the home front intensified it was desirable that all organised women should work together under unified leadership.

In 1934, however, it was not foreseen that the DFW would remain a very minority concern, thus failing to provide the NSF with high status in the Party and the country and to act as its channel for the indoctrination of Germany's women. Accordingly, an elaborate programme was created to prepare NSF leaders and members for their task of 'political education'. Even the GNSFLs — responsible for the conduct of the DFW's work at the regional level — were deemed not to be fit to instruct those further down the line, and to remedy this the first *Reichsschule* (national college) for training NSF leaders was inaugurated in Coburg at the end of May 1934 with a residential course for the GNSFLs. This was interrupted by the intrusion of the 'Siber affair' into its proceedings,[131] which provided a salutary lesson about the discipline required in the NSF, as elsewhere in the Party. A second national college was opened in Berlin in April 1938,[132] and a third, also in the capital, followed. By the end of 1938, 3,890 women had passed through 111 courses in the *Reichsschulen*.[133] There was also, from January 1935, a twice-yearly, fortnight-long residental Seminar at the *Hochschule für Politik* in Berlin to give NSF members 'the academic and political basis of the National Socialist *Weltanschauung*, and thereby afford them the necessary ammunition for influencing the spiritual and character-building attitudes of our women'.[134]

The content of the Seminar courses provides a useful illustration of the kind of 'political education' to which NSF members were encouraged to submit themselves, to enable them, in turn, to instruct women throughout the country. Much of the time, the participants worked in discussion groups, chiefly led by members of Gertrud Scholtz-Klink's staff in the RFFg, to enable them to gain experience in answering questions and arguing a case before they were confronted by the supposedly interested female population. There were also formal lectures given by some of these same RFFg officials, by Gertrud Scholtz-Klink herself, and by as many Party notables as could be persuaded to participate. Among those who accepted invitations to speak were Alfred Rosenberg, whose talk was entitled *'Weltanschauung* in Foreign Policy', Dr Walter Gross, the population pundit, who lectured on 'Woman in the National Socialist Nation', and Gauleiter Adolf Wagner who led a discussion group on 'World Economy — Raw Materials — Four Year Plan'. Lydia Gottschewski — now Frau Ganzer — was brought out of retirement to lecture on 'Women in the New Regime', and Hedwig Förster, once reprimanded by Strasser, led a discussion of 'The New Educational Goal of Girls' Schooling'. Although a number of topics — women in Nazi society, the population problem, German history from the National Socialist point of view, and exhaustive variations on the theme of 'race and heredity', especially — kept recurring, the subjects covered in the Seminar were wide-ranging, to give the women the official orthodoxy on as many aspects of personal and national life as possible. Trusted 'experts' gave lectures on and led discussions of anything from 'political Catholicism' to German art, literature and drama, from colonial policy to family law, and from 'Bolshevism' to the 'Jewish problem' and the place of the peasant woman in contemporary society. From the exposition of the 'experts', NSF women were expected to grasp the essence of all these subjects and more, as well as the Nazi theory of practical subjects, for example, girls' education, family health, household management and child care. To equip the participants for their task of passing on what they had learned to the wider circle of German women, there was also a course on public speaking conducted by the Seminar's Director, Dr Else Petri.[125]

Of the 3,260 NSF members who had attended the Seminar by summer 1939, more than half were housewives and the rest employed.

The largest representation — 15 per cent of the total — came from clerical workers, while civil servants' wives provided a further 14 per cent of the attendances. By contrast, but not surprisingly, those classed as 'workers' and 'workers' wives' together accounted for only 1.5 per cent of the attendances. The age-group most strongly represented was that of women in their forties, who made up 35 per cent of the total; a further 30 per cent were over 50. The over-40s, then, outnumbered the 20 to 40-year-olds by almost two to one,[136] suggesting again[137] that the most enthusiastic women Nazis were on the whole older than the men. It was, of course, more difficult for young mothers to be away from home for a fortnight than for those with a grown-up family. But the greatest dedication was shown by the employed women, most of whom were spending unpaid time off work to attend an indoctrination course, although many of them would be NSF officials on whom pressure to attend could be exerted. By the end of 1938, the NSF had only 3,500 full-time, salaried staff, of whom 2,000 worked in the Gaus and the remainder in the districts. While in a number of cases in Gaus and districts voluntary workers received an honorarium, in the local branches, where the immediate work of influencing the 'unpolitical' German woman was to be carried out, the NSF's entire staff, including all its local branch leaders, were unpaid volunteers.[138] The Nazis, and Schwarz particularly, did not believe in spending money where they could rather exploit the 'idealism' of their most ardent followers.

The Seminar and *Reichsschule* courses were to serve as models for courses throughout the country, to ensure that DFW sectional leaders and leaders of the affiliated organisations, as well as ordinary NSF members, could be indoctrinated in their own region. For this purpose, 32 *Gauschulen* (Gau colleges) had been opened by 1939, with one in most Gaus, although Mecklenburg, Schleswig-Holstein and Halle-Merseburg had yet to establish one. But in Düsseldorf, Cologne-Aachen, South Hanover-Brunswick and Württemberg-Hohenzollern there was more than one, and one *Gauschule* had already been opened in Austria, with more planned. In the 'old Reich', between 1936 and 1938, *Gauschulen* mounted 6,911 ordinary courses, attended by 350,651 women, with a further 685 'racial-political' courses which attracted 31,442 women.[139] In some cases, it was said, the numbers had had to be limited, since it was felt to be counter-productive to try to 'educate' large numbers of people at once.[140] This sounds like special pleading, since the figures published by the RFFg itself show that the numbers passing through *Reichsschulen, Gauschulen* and Seminar courses were hardly impressive. Fewer than 400,000 attendances at political indoctrination courses by the start of 1939 was highly unsatisfactory in view of the importance attached to 'political education' by the Party; and since the NSF, which was supposed to become an instrument capable of indoctrinating the mass of women, was maintained at a level of just over two million in the later 1930s, it is clear that there was a marked lack of enthusiasm for 'political education' among even the faithful of the Party's elite women's organisation. The attempts which had been made to eliminate dead wood from the NSF had clearly had only limited effect.

On the other hand, there was evidently a hard core of energetic enthusiasts who staffed local branch NSF offices, attended weekly NSF meetings as well as evening courses and occasional residential indoctrination courses, put in voluntary stints with the NSV, visited homes to try to put the National Socialist message across to housewives, and helped to organise the DFW's sectional work in their area.[141] These were the women who devised the NSF's periodic exhibitions of the 'women's work', drummed up support for its fêtes and sales of work, and formed welcoming parties at railway stations for Party notables visiting their area.[142] No doubt they were among the subscribers to the *NS-Frauenwarte*, who numbered 1.2 million in 1938. The 40,000 or so women working in Gau, district and local branch NSF offices − including, in 1938, 32 GNSFLs, their 2,500 assistants, 700 district leaders and their 13,000 assistants and 24,000 local branch NSF leaders[143] − along with the 280,000 cell and block NSF leaders, probably accounted for most of the genuinely committed activists; the official claim that the NSF had 'over a million' enthusiasts seems somewhat extravagant. As unpaid, part-time volunteers, for the most part,[144] these women indeed worked prodigiously, to an extent that justified some of the RFFg's propaganda about their 'tireless' efforts. To them fell the task of bringing the regime's message quite literally home to the mass of women who had resisted recruiting drives and involvement in readymade leisure activities − to say nothing of 'political education' courses. It was up to NSF workers to make personal contact with these women, particularly if they were housebound housewives to whom no other Nazi organisation had access, and to try to generate enthusiasm, or at least interest, among them; this, at any rate, was Ley's view.[145] But penetrating the massive apathy of German women who recalcitrantly remained 'unpolitical' was a formidable task beyond the ability of amateur propagandists from the NSF, and not one which was realistic in time of peace and an improving economic climate. In spite of the energy expended by a small group of dedicated activists, the NSF's attempts at generating active enthusiasm for the regime's policies among the female population at large were predictably unproductive. Winning acquiescence of a more passive kind was possible, and was to a large degree achieved; but a dictatorial government which had taken over or abolished political functions formerly exercised by individuals or their chosen groups was asking too much in expecting these same people to stir themselves to excitement about its own selfish policies. It remained to be seen if the changed circumstances of war, conquest and then retreat would make German women more receptive.

The DFW and the 'Women's Work of the Nation'

If there was something unrealistic about trying to organise women's social life — axiomatically the free conduct of their spare time — then it was positively bizarre to try to channel the leisure time and activities of the women of a relatively sophisticated population into unquestioning service, allegedly for the benefit of the entire community but, in reality, to meet the power-political demands of the regime. It was to this end that the sectional work of the DFW was geared, and it was no misnomer to call the DFW's activities 'the women's work of the nation'. Whether it was learning practical skills or theoretical knowledge through courses, or providing assistance in a variety of areas of social welfare, it all amounted to something very different from conventional leisure pursuits or social life — and, in short, it amounted to work. The NSF's role as 'spiritual leader' of the DFW was to teach German women to accept that this was the natural, responsible and desirable way to spend their free time, rather than frittering it away on trivial entertainment or gossip; the NSF was to persuade women that the satisfaction of duty done and service performed for the good of the nation was far greater than that which could be obtained from following fashion or craving possessions. The moralising tone adopted to explain this justified the term 'spiritual leadership', and probably did much to reconcile the confessional groups to the DFW in the first instance; it contrasted sharply with materialistic Marxism and with the decadence of a society dedicated to consumerism and pleasure.

The aura of spiritual uplift invoked by Gertrud Scholtz-Klink and her close associates was at once sincere and bogus. The cynicism with which the regime's male leadership played on the sentiments as well as the gut instincts of ordinary Germans to encourage voluntary service and payment into 'welfare funds', for example, is as transparent as it is deplorable. Just as the Party had worked hard for victory in the *Kampf-zeit* in order to bring only Hitler and a few other bigwigs to power, so the men and women of Germany were to serve and sacrifice, not for the good of the national community, as was claimed, but for the domestic and foreign ambitions of Hitler and his henchmen. And yet, it seems clear that, with no access to the centres of power in the Third Reich, the women's leaders were not a party to this cynicism; very many of them genuinely believed that women would live better, fuller, happier lives if they allowed themselves to be trained to perform their domestic chores more efficiently and to utilise their spare time to help those in need (provided that they were healthy, 'Aryan' and politically reliable), and to develop an interest in German culture. The words used to express what was expected of women in the 'new Germany' were *Opferfreudigkeit, Einsatzbereitschaft* and *Verantwortungsbewusstsein* (joy in sacrifice, readiness for service and consciousness of responsibility). These were the qualities which the DFW's work was intended to foster, through practical activities and through constant reference to 'the "ideological training" [which] provides the aim and basis . . . of every task in the DFW'.[146] It is little wonder that this confidence trick took in only a minority of German women, however sincere the misguided motivation of the National Women's Leadership.

Partly because of the uneven development of the working sections, with only the RMD, Vw/Hw and GA fully operational by 1937, there was considerable overlap between them. Far from being regarded as undesirable, this duplication was positively encouraged, since most DFW members were active in only the one section. There was, in fact, what amounted to a basic core curriculum for all participants, with further specialisation in an area of particular interest within their chosen section. All women, whatever their speciality, were to be thoroughly versed in the essentials of the regime's requirements as they affected women; however practical some of the activities of the sections might appear, their very direction contained a high degree of 'political education', to bring the National Socialist message home to women by deeds as well as words. For example, the emphasis on child-care and family life in the RMD was used to convey the regime's encouragement for a return to the large families of pre-First World War days, and also to indoctrinate women about Nazi racial policy. In 1936, with the announcement of the Four Year Plan, the Vw/Hw came into its own, propagating a large variety of expedients for using only German produce and finding substitutes for foreign imports. The GA was used to whip up pro-German enthusiasm in the Saar, Austria, the Sudetenland and the Polish Corridor among those who favoured inclusion in a Greater German Reich. However, the women working in the RMD, too, had to be 'nationally conscious', and so there was, for example, strong propaganda to persuade them to collect traditional German toys, especially old ones which had been used by successive generations in a family.[147] In both the RMD and the Vw/Hw sections cookery and sewing courses were provided — at a charge — to try to produce as many proficient housewives committed to using German materials as possible.[148]

With the founding of the other two major service sections, 'Auxiliary Service' (HD) in 1936, and 'Culture/Education/Training' (K/E/S) in 1937, there was further overlap, since part of the work of these sections had already been performed by the existing three. The work of the women in the HD was to some extent in the form of aid to the NSV's 'Mother and Child' section; but women in the RMD had been involved in this since 1934. And the cultivation of German music, literature and customs was already a part of the GA's work, since it aimed to stimulate an interest in German culture among women expatriates; now, the K/E/S section promoted this actively at home.[149] One way and another, the work of each of these five sections managed to include the basic constituents of the regime's policies towards women and the way in which women should respond. Women should attend courses to become capable mothers and proficient housewives, bringing up their children to appreciate their German heritage and to be convinced of Germany's special destiny. They should conduct their households not only in an orderly way, but also, by their patterns of consumption, in a nationally responsible way. They should demonstrate their sense of service to the community by helping in the NSV's social welfare programme, as volunteers, and they should also exhibit national pride by making contact with German women abroad and taking an active interest in Germany history, songs and dances. On the negative side, they should discourage foreign cultural influences — including Paris or London fashions[159] — and avoid buying imported goods. Above all, they should reject 'Bolshevist' culture and morality, and be on their guard against the pollution of the 'race' by non-'Aryans'.

These were the premises from which the more distinctive aspects of the sectional work progressed, each designed to serve one of the regime's political policies. For example, the HD was not merely to provide an auxiliary welfare corps but was also to give women elementary first-aid instruction with the Red Cross and training with the National Air-Raid Protection Society. While there was strong emphasis on the voluntary social service aspects of the HD's work, and especially on the 'neighbourhood aid' scheme of community self-help, the increasingly sinister aspect of work geared to the emergency services necessary in wartime could not be disguised.[151] And the women themselves were clearly aware of the growing relevance of this: by the end of 1938, 66,000 DFW members had been trained as social welfare auxiliaries, 22,000 as auxiliary nurses, and as many as 581,000 had passed through air-raid protection courses; each of these figures was double that recorded as the total by the end of 1937.[152] All of the functions of the HD would become vitally necessary in wartime, but on the scale demonstrated by these figures they would be able to cope adequately only in a victorious war. Once bombing raids began in earnest, the Red Cross and air-raid protection training of a relatively small number of women would be of very limited value, although the provision of 'neighbourhood aid' — much of which had existed long before the DFW insisted on organising it — in terms of services as mundane as baby-sitting had practical value and also helped to maintain community solidarity and morale; in this, at least, the women's organisation enjoyed some success.

The other new section, K/E/S, was said to 'comprehend such a variety of areas that its sphere of competence and internal connections are only barely perceptible at first sight'.[153] This was plausible enough, since the section had evolved from a number of separate 'subject areas' established in the RFFg during 1935 and 1936, including 'genealogical research', 'racial policy' and 'academic questions'.[154] The K/E/S secton became primarily responsible for the fulfilment of 'the cultural task of women' by which great store was laid. This involved the collecting, editing and performing of traditional German songs, dances and music, 'research' to discover authentic German customs, folklore and costumes, and the propagation of German styles in art and interior decoration.[155] The early emphasis on race and heredity in the 'subject areas' constituted the negative side of this activity. Oddly, perhaps, attention to health care and physical training also featured in this section; but since 'in the National Socialist view, ideology and life cannot be separated from each other',[156] presumably the rationale was that a healthy and obedient mind would more probably be found in a healthy and obedient body. K/E/S was also the section in which attempts were made to bridge the gap between women of different educational backgrounds, with Dr Eben-Servaes entrusted with two aspects of this. As leader of the 'Group of Women Lawyers in the DFW', she was to interest her members in the DFW's work, and particularly in its legal ramifications. As leader of the sub-section for 'academic work', she was to appoint a 'woman academic' in each Gau to co-ordinate the work of explaining in lay terms to ordinary DFW members developments currently taking place in universities and in research.[157]

But the major task of K/E/S was 'political education' through local courses and through the Reich and Gau colleges. Indoctrination had always been an integral part of the DFW's purpose, but there was a necessary hiatus between the DFW's inauguration and the provision of 'political education' courses for its members, because of the extent to which those who were to instruct them — NSF members and leaders — were so ill-prepared for the task. From 1937 DFW section leaders and members were strongly encouraged to attend 'political education' courses to ensure that they were versed in the Nazi *Weltanschauung*. There was special emphasis on trying to recruit the 'German housewife and mother', partly because if she was not employed the regime's only access to her was through the women's organisations, but particularly because of her sensitive position as 'the first educator of the nation's youth'. The young had to be brought up to think 'in the National Socialist way' from the start, and the only way of ensuring this, in a society where the family was exalted, was to persuade mothers to allow themselves to be indoctrinated, so that they would bring their children up in 'love for the *Führer*' and enthusiasm for the activities of the Hitler Youth.[158] To some degree, this attitude would be fostered by attendance at RMD courses in practical mothercare, but the RFF and her associates did not want merely to indoctrinate women by rote; they had an almost touching desire to persuade women by allegedly logical explanation of the rightness of the regime's policies, particularly as they affected 'the most critical problem of the National Socialist range of ideas . . . . race and population policy'.[159] Women were, it was said, 'guardians of the race', and so they had to be instructed fully about Germany's racial and population problems so that they would willingly play their part in solving them, not least by having more children.[160]

In conjunction with the Press and Propaganda section, K/E/S workers prepared vast amounts of 'explanatory material' which was circulated to Gau and district libraries. They also took courses to prepare them for public speaking, and invited guests to address them on important aspects of the Nazi *Weltanschauung*, to improve their comprehension.[161] But although the work of K/E/S was still in its early stages in 1938, it seems clear that there was among DFW members —

those who had chosen to be involved at all — only limited enthusiasm for pure indoctrination courses, particularly when attendance figures are compared with those for other sections' activities. While 300,000 women attended air-raid protection courses and half a million passed through RMD courses in 1938, only 100,000 attended ideological training courses, with a further 15,000 attending special racial policy courses mounted in the Gaus.[162] But while 'political education' was regarded as the K/E/S's most important function, the section also provided the nearest thing to conventional social life available in the DFW, with 'community evenings'. While 'politically reliable' leadership ensured that the discussion frequently centred on German history and culture, groups also met to exchange experiences at work, in education, in the home, and particularly once husbands and sons were away from home in wartime these meetings brought some comfort to the women and helped to maintain their morale. Gathering together in groups for sporting activities, music-making or basket-weaving, even under the watchful eye of K/E/S officials,[163] was, again, more akin to normal leisure activity than the interminable round of courses provided to instruct women in how to conduct virtually every aspect of their life, from bathing babies to choosing approved intellectual pursuits, and learning approved recipes and elementary first-aid. This was why genuine leisure interests were to be found in the same section as pure indoctrination, to try to ensure that those who had joined the DFW for the sole purpose of enjoying sociable group activity were also under strong pressure to attend a 'political education' course as well as their sports club or sewing bee.

For those who were convinced of the benefits of National Socialism, the GA section provided the opportunity to try to impress foreigners by them. Reliable women volunteers — no doubt including the 'Miss D.' who escorted Clifford Kirkpatrick's acquaintance round an RMD school and a WLS camp[164] — acted as guides to more than 3,000 visitors from all over the world between summer 1934 and spring 1939. While representatives of the press, social services, education and political parties from more sceptical countries were always welcomed, there was a particularly warm reception for delegations from sympathetic regimes, like Fascist Italy and Franco's Spain.[165] Expatriates visiting the old country and members of ethnic German communities abroad received special attention, to convince them by word and deed that the 'people's community' of the new Germany was a living reality. There was warm hospitality for 640 German women from eastern Europe between 1936 and 1939, and 27 'responsible' women were selected for 'political education' courses to equip them to agitate for their 'reunification' with the Reich when they returned home to their pressure groups in Poland, Memel, Denmark and elsewhere.[166] Raising consciousness in this way was increased in the later 1930s, as Hitler's foreign policy aims became more explicit, but it remained an uphill struggle until the war brought conquests because of the natural hostility of the governments of the countries affected. For the most part, GA workers had to be content with sending literature and musical instruments to ethnic Germans abroad, including those in the former German African colonies. In addition, 57 women who had attended purpose-built 'political education' courses went to Africa to 'train' the colonists, under the auspices of the National Colonial Society, in 1938.[167]

This collaboration between the GA and the National Colonial Society is a typical example of how the sections of one of the NSDAP's affiliated or member-organisations made links with the central office of another organisation deemed particularly relevant to its work. This was to try to ensure that all activities in the same area — colonial policy, consumer policy, cultural policy, among others — were conducted according to a uniform plan. The K/E/S section, for example, had links with the Nazi Teachers' League, to guide its conduct of the sub-section for 'questions of girls' education', while its cultural pursuits were expected to accord with the policies of the Nazi Cultural Community, which had a liaison office in the RFFg. Above all, the K/E/S was to work closely with the ideological training offices of the NSDAP, at every level, to ensure that its 'political education' courses accorded with central Party policy and were updated to meet the demands of political developments at home and abroad. Similarly, agreements with the National Air-Raid Protection Society and the Red Cross —as well as Gertrud Scholtz-Klink's position in the latter — were intended to ensure that the DFW's workers in the HD section operated in unison with these national organisations and served their purposes.[168] The mere reaching of agreements did not always ensure harmony — as strained relations between the NSF and the Labour Front, the NSV, the BdM and the Food Estate demonstrated — but friction tended to lead to new attempts to bring co-operation through the construction of an ever more complicated network of agreements between the RFFg and the central offices of other Party organisations. The extent to which Gertrud Scholtz-Klink's central staff was swollen by representatives of other groups was matched by the number of delegates she sent to sit on others' committees, and was the inevitable wasteful result of absurd attempts to create monopoly organisations to control every conceivable activity chosen by the Party Leadership as suitable for the 'racially desirable' population of Germany.

The bureaucratic implications of creating monopoly organisations were not foreseen when the DFW started life with modest claims to the co-ordination of mothercare and homecraft instruction, in the RMD and Vw/Hw sections in 1934. Few people in authority in any Party affiliate would have disagreed that these two areas should be the concern of the organisation of 'German wives and mothers', present and potential; even the BdM ultimately agreed to its senior members' receiving homecraft instruction through the Vw/Hw.[169] The Party whose leadership had propagated the view that a woman's place was in the home, with her family, had attracted to it women who felt criticised and threatened by the egalitarian demands of radical feminists and communists, and who wanted nothing more than to devote themselves to home and family, with official approval. The raising of the housewife's status, largely through propaganda, and the elevating of everyday housework to the level of a skilled occupation — through the introduction of a course to produce 'Master Housewives'[170] — seemed to vindicate the promises made by Nazi leaders before 1933, and would certainly have pleased the thousands of members of the housewives' organisations whose *raison d'être* this was long before a Nazi women's organisation emerged.[171]

But the strong emphasis on competence in domestic management which was evident in both the RMD and the Vw/Hw's work from the start was not intended merely to produce a nation of well-ordered homes. The homecraft training which was an integral part of the mothercare instruction in the RMD was directed towards using German produce and nourishing healthy children for Germany's future; this was ancillary to the main purpose of the RMD which was the propagation of Nazi population policy and of its intrinsic racialist assumptions, which again lay behind the RMD's practical tasks of providing auxiliary help for the NSV for its work with 'valuable' mothers and children, and running courses in ante- and post-natal care, family health and hygiene.[172] The Vw/Hw derived its most important functions, as well as its emphasis on the value of housewifery as an art rather than a chore, from the old housewives' organisations whose more political purpose had been to act as a virtual employment agency for 'reliable' domestic servants and, during the First World War, to advise women about how to manage in the straitened circumstances of war and blockade.[173] Helping to train girls in elementary housekeeping, and placing them as temporary 'home helps' in large families, in the 'Household Year' scheme, and producing leaflets with advice about buying, preparing and preserving seasonal foods, for example, to promote nutritional self-sufficiency were the main purpose of the Vw/Hw, before the war as well as during it.[174] As the 1930s progressed and the regime's foreign and racial policies began to be pursued more relentlessly, the functions of the RMD and the Vw/Hw diverged significantly, away from the initially strong degree of overlap that there had appeared to be in 1934.

While the Vw/Hw section had increasingly to work according to directives issued by the Ministry of Food, in co-operation with the Food Estate and the Four Year Plan Office, as one of the many agencies promoting the drive for autarky, the RMD had, in part of its role, at least, monopoly status. In its welfare functon, it acted largely as an auxiliary of the NSV, but from 1935 it was designated by Frick as 'the only agency for giving mothercare instruction'.[175] Party endorsement followed, the SS setting an example in 1936 with Himmler's decree that all girls who aspired to marry an SS man must provide proof of attendance at an RMD course before his approval would be given to the match.[176] In spite of complaints that this requirement was likely to have a damaging effect on the professional homecraft schools under the authority of the Education Ministry,[177] other Party agencies, including the Food Estate, the SA and the Order Castles, followed the SS in requiring the fiancées and wives of their members to attend an RMD course.[178] The government helped, too, by providing money through the marriage loan scheme for the fees for an RMD course.[179] And in some cases employers helped to finance RMD courses held on their premises to try to reach women manual workers; there was some success here, with 37 per cent of the employed women attending RMD courses in 1937 being 'workers', although white-collar employees accounted for 45 per cent of attendances.[180] But reaching urban dwellers was relatively easy, as the Gau historian in Bayerische Ostmark pointed out forcefully; rural women had been left to muddle on in ignorance and poverty, and the result, she said, was a consistently 'shocking level of infant mortality' in country areas.[181] The only solution seemed to be to take RMD courses to women in rural areas, using travelling instructors. In Gau Mainfranken, between June 1934 and October 1935, two-thirds of the 150 courses held were of this kind, and there were plans to open a 'model' RMD school in a depressed area of the Gau.[182] In the country as in the towns, RMD courses were provided at any time of day, to suit the available clientèle.[183]

With every effort expended to attract women to RMD courses —

including the waiving of fees for the needy – it is hardly surprising that attendance figures were high; this no doubt also reflected the extent to which women felt that RMD instruction was more relevant and more palatable than 'political education'. By March 1939, over 1.7 million women had attended almost 100,000 RMD courses, with half a million in 1938 alone;[184] after ten years' operation the figure was said to have risen to five million.[185] There were four Reich RMD schools, to act as models for local enterprises, and four residential schools and three 'brides' schools',[186] to give more intensive training – and indoctrination – than was possible at short weekly classes. Mounting the courses was an expensive business, and the fees went only part of the way towards meeting the cost; there was, unusually, some government support, but there was nevertheless the need to resort to street collections and the sale of special postcards to raise money.[187] RMD staff were paid at a modest level, with salaries ranging between 175 and 250 marks a month, but they had longer holidays than most people, as compensation.[188] The staff were recruited, instructed and paid by the RMD's central office in the RFFg, run by Erna Röpke, and edicts on these matters and much besides poured out from her office. GNSFLs had to submit plans for future RMD development to her, and were in turn informed of the RFFg's priorities, given the financial constraints.[189] The RMD section leaders in the Gaus met together regularly to ensure that the RMD was being operated in as uniform a way as possible across the entire country.[190] Attempts at central direction sometimes reached absurd proportions, as in December 1937 when Erna Röpke sent a circular to the GNSFLs and Gau RMD section leaders pointing out that 'an important task of the RMD is to advise parents about their choice of presents for their children at Christmas', and giving detailed instructions about the kind of 'advice' to be offered.[191] But if some aspects of Nazi population policy were horrific and others were absurd, providing instruction in infant and child-care was genuinely constructive. The propaganda was, of course, constant and deplorable, but the large numbers attending RMD courses, the significant fall in infant mortality rates,[192] and the enthusiasm and idealism of RMD organisers, which shines through in their reports,[193] suggests that this was to some degree both a positive and a popular venture, particularly in comparison with other aspects of both population policy and the DFW's activities.

Some aspects of the Vw/Hw's work, too, were fairly popular, with 1.8 million women attending courses, predominantly in cooking, by the end of 1938. In addition to formal instruction, the section offered consumer advice through its 150 bureaux throughout the country,[194] to try to guide housewives' patterns of consumption and to remind them at every turn of the need for thrift and inventiveness in the cause of autarky. This was the stated aim of the Vw/Hw from the start, in 1934, even before the announcement of the Four Year Plan in autumn 1936.[195] Else Vorwerck's central office in the RFFg churned out hundreds of leaflets with information about seasonal foods, home-produced substitutes for imported goods and the use of left-overs, to try to give Germany 'nutritional freedom'. Vw/Hw officials sat on a variety of committees geared to this aim, and the Vw/Hw established its own research office to test thrifty recipes and experiment with substitutes. Although food was the major concern, there was also strong interest in promoting home-produced household goods and clothes.[196] Not only were German women encouraged to buy German products; they were also to be taught how to care for their family's clothes, by being given detailed washing instructions, for example,[197] so that they would get the best — and longest — wear out of them, and not require to make heavy demands on industry for new ones. And this, it was clearly implied,[198] would also help to damp down consumer aspirations, by — it was hoped — removing some of the motive for demands for increased rates of pay.

In the early years of Nazi rule, the depressed standard of living of large numbers of Germans, especially — but not only — the unemployed,[199] meant that there was little scope for the kind of consumption regarded as 'irresponsible' by the regime. But the regime's own success in bringing an upswing in the economy in the later 1930s created the problems that it feared, of a better-off population craving consumer goods. The Vw/Hw's task was to try to suppress these desires in women by labelling them profligate, even unpatriotic, and offering instead at times spurious, but at times ingenious, expedients for avoiding both imports and the kind of demands on home industry deemed excessive in view of the priority given to building up heavy industry. Films and slides were made for local Vw/Hw courses, rehearsing methods of cooking which would avoid waste and conserve nutritional value, and giving instruction about fruit and vegetable preserving.[200] Preserving was an important means of using to the full large quantities of goods when they were in season, particularly if there had been a good crop,[201] thus providing a cupboard substitute for goods which were in short supply and expensive. The section threw itself into support for the Food Authority's campaigns, in autumn 1937, for example, encouraging the gathering of windfall fruit, beechnuts, acorns and chestnuts, and providing advice about the kind of recipes to use for these somewhat unpromising items.[202] And the Vw/Hw's activities as a whole were conducted according to the guidelines set out each month by the Ministry of Food, even in peacetime.[203] These propagated thrifty habits in all areas of the economy, with plans for collecting old clothes, waste paper and virtually any article that could be repaired or re-used, to ease demands on industry.[204]

The tasks which the DFW's sections set themselves – or, in many cases, had set for them by more important Party agencies – were formidable and unrealistic. Elevating the status of the housewife and then expecting her to make do and do without, to scrimp and save food and material not for her own benefit but for that of the 'community', were hardly mutually compatible tactics. Training women to look after one child properly in an RMD course and at the same time exhorting them to have unmanageably large families[205] seem equally incongruous. The contradiction of having creative and cultural pursuits organised by the same people who were recruiting for stultifying indoctrination courses could not have been lost on many DFW members. Gertrud Scholtz-Klink and her staff no doubt believed that the resistance to involvement in these activities shown by the mass of women would be a transient affair, something which would pass with the current generations of adult German women. When girls who were young and those as yet unborn reached adulthood, they would have been brought up 'to think in the National Socialist way', and would automatically welcome the DFW's endeavours and submit themselves to demands made of them. To try to accelerate this process, special attention was paid to the younger members of the DFW by the creation in August 1936 of 'youth groups' to cater for what were deemed to be their particular interests, including singing, dancing and outdoor pursuits. But recreation was a small part of the 18 to 30-year-olds' activities, as of their elders', in the DFW. It is hardly surprising that young women in this age-group who were already DFW members were slow to volunteer for the 'youth groups',[206] given the extent to which they were singled out for special racial-political and mothercare instruction, to remind them constantly of their destiny and their duty as the mothers of Germany's immediate future.[207]

The women eligible for the 'youth groups' were arguably something of a lost cause, like their elders, but the DFW had a more promising long-term prospect in its 'children's groups' for six- to ten-year-old boys and girls who were too young to join the Hitler Youth but old enough to be highly impressionable. In fact, the DFW's role in these groups seems to have been limited to providing the children, since the sensitive task of forming the attitudes of the very young was entrusted to fully ideologically reliable NSF members alone. The primary function of the 'children's groups' was to bring the young up in the National Socialist faith, and to counteract the still strong influence of the Churches over them. The children normally met together for only one afternoon a week for activities including 'ten minutes on contemporary political events',[208] but once the war made heavier demands on working women the groups were increasingly used as nurseries; in January 1940, Ley ordered that accommodation at the disposal of the Labour Front be made available to the 'children's groups' to make the facility more widespread[209] – to encourage more women to volunteer for war work. In January 1938 there were over 9,000 groups catering for almost 350,000 children, and by the end of the year 11,000 groups and over 400,000 children were recorded in the 'old Reich', with a further 1,500 groups and 40,000 children in Austria.[210] By the end of 1940, with 'valuable' children from occupied countries gathered in groups as a particular priority, there were almost 19,000 groups with almost 690,000 children organised for their earliest experience of systematic indoctrination.[211]

The difficulty in dealing with an organisation run by a totalitarian party under conditions of strict censorship is that there is little indication available – apart from membership and attendance figures – as to how far the leadership stimulated its own constituency. The undoubtedly prodigious efforts of the RFFg's staff and the DFW's sectional leaders at Gau and local level elicited a very limited response from the mass of women, but presumably made some impression on DFW members. Nevertheless, a glance at the low level of attendances at exhibitions and fêtes staged by the DFW, and at the circulation figures for the Party's women's press, suggest that even among the organised the level of interest generated remained low, restricted to a small, self-selected group. The RMD's own magazine, *Mutter and Volk* (Mother and People) had 150,000 subscribers in 1938, compared with the half million women who attended RMD courses in that year alone. The Vw/Hw's *Deutsche Hauswirtschaft* attracted 140,000 subscribers in 1938, presumably having inherited something of a captive readership from the days when it had been the magazine of the dissolved housewives' organisation. While DFW members might be interested in the subject-matter of either of these fairly typical women's magazines, they were obviously not greatly interested in the DFW as an organisation, nor, it may be assumed, in the message repetitively hammered home in the RFFg's publications, about the importance of the women's work and the need for all German women to participate in it: the DFW's own magazine, *Frauenkultur im Deutschen Frauenwerk* (Women's Culture in the DFW) had a circulation as low as 23,000 in 1938.[212] Since the DFW's message was not reaching more than a fraction of its membership through its official magazine, there remained one way of trying to reach the rest, and the women of Germany as a whole, on a regular basis. The Press and Propaganda section, with its representative in the National Broadcasting Leadership,[213] produced regular radio programmes for women, compiled from material provided by the working sections. The programmes were transmitted regionally, so that 'For the farmer's wife' featured on Breslau radio, for rural Silesia, but not in the programme for Berlin women. Cookery advice, cultural items, advice about schoolchildren's problems, programmes for 'the very young' with their mothers, occasional political items, and keep-fit instruction, all figured regularly. And as part of the GA activity, the foreign service put out special women's programmes for German nationals abroad.[214] The high level of radio ownership by the later 1930s, as well as Goebbels's acceptance that the aural and visual media had to provide features that were more attractive than repetitive propaganda[215] may well have meant that women at home actually listened to these radio programmes, and that some − albeit diluted − elements of the National Socialist message reached those who neither subscribed to nor read the Party's press.

The picture which emerges of the 'women's work' in the 1930s is one of determined effort within a highly circumscribed area by a few activists who manifested the required readiness for service, consciousness of their responsibility and even joyful sacrifice for a cause to which they devoted themselves with religious zeal. The faithful had to survive repeated disillusionment within their own camp, in the NSF and, more so, in the DFW, quite apart from the uphill struggle against the solid conservatism of the majority of women, who continued to regard the NSDAP simply as a political party − with the strengths and flaws which that implied − rather than as the apocalyptic agent of a new millenium. This should have been predictable given the obvious inclinations of German women before 1933, which had been recognised by Strasser and the NSF leadership as they tried to win a larger share of the female vote in 1932.[216] The adherence of women voters to clerical-conservative parties in the Weimar era could be broken by the dissolution of these parties, just as the destruction of all left-wing parties and organisations could deprive their former supporters of much of their social as well as political activity. But if this left a vacuum in the lives of many women – especially those working-class women who had supported the SPD or the KPD – it was not inevitable that it would be filled by Nazi alternatives. Further, the Labour Front had more direct access to working women than the NSF or the DFW. While some middle-class women were prepared to participate in Nazi-sponsored activities, as individuals or, more, as part of a group membership in the DFW, others either tried to circumvent the DFW's monopoly[217] or else retired into a form of 'inner emigration'. But for those women, of whatever class, who were particularly susceptible to the appeal of a religion, the Churches, with their message of love rather than of hatred and vengeance, were more attractive than National Socialism. The mild accommodation reached between the regime and the Churches in 1933, when there were more apparently dangerous adversaries for the new Government to subdue, extended to collaboration by Evangelical and, to a lesser extent, Catholic groups in the new 'women's work'; the DFW's RMD section could hardly have begun in 1934 without it. But as the regime increasingly turned to attack the Churches – as it had to, given its totalitarian pretensions – Christianity proved, not for the first or the last time, that it is a particularly formidable force when on the defensive. The Churches as institutions behaved less than admirably during the Third Reich,[218] but at the local level, particularly in strongly Catholic areas, ordinary people, especially women, refused to relinquish their habits, let alone their faith, to meet the demands of the new order, and were often either led or backed by a priest or a parson in their resistance.[219]

The continued existence of the Churches, and their holding of normal regular services, even if their organisations were largely forced to disband,[220] created a focus of alternative loyalty which was unique in the Third Reich, as both Nazis and Communists recognised.[221] The commitment of women, particularly, to the Churches, and to the political and social organisations associated with them before 1933, could not be obliterated simply by dissolving those organisations, certainly not when their basis, the Churches themselves, continued to function. This helped to make women, and particularly non-employed housewives, a peculiarly and tenaciously difficult group to enlist for the Nazi cause. Even if they were prepared to engage in DFW-sponsored activities – and only a small minority was – the strong religious affiliation of large numbers of women meant that theirs were not vacant souls potentially receptive to the Nazi *Weltanschauung*; thus the spiritual claims of the NSDAP met an uncomprehending and negative response from people whose allegiance had long been committed, probably since birth. The anxiety voiced about continued clerical influence over the young, after six years of Nazi rule,[222] was also anxiety about the continued religious affiliation of parents, especially mothers. The result was that the radical anti-clericalism which was rampant in some quarters of the NSDAP was soft-pedalled in the women's press, and Gertrud Scholtz-Klink made unconvincing attempts to set National Socialism above the two main confessions, as a God-fearing, non-partisan religious force, in her speeches.[223] The NSF and DFW had to recognise that many of their supporters regarded themselves as Christian[224] and that, not being in a sellers' market, they were in no position to campaign against the Churches among the women they had so far failed to attract.

The NSF and the DFW did attract some women from all sections of society in the 1930s, and most from the middle class; but on the whole the unwillingness – the inability, even – of women with a strong Christian conviction to commit themselves to National Socialism, and to do so, above all, in a way that committed the 'whole person' over whom the Party sought complete mastery, was matched by the apathy of those who had been helpless while *Gleichschaltung* had destroyed their chosen parties and clubs. This meant largely, but not exclusively, working-class women – those working-class women who had been involved in political or social activity; the formerly unorganised continued in this happy state, seeing no reason and no incentive to break the habit of years. There were also better-educated middle-class women whose distaste for the crude tactics and simplistic propaganda of the Party and the women's organisation was as strong as their unwillingness to be organised by women whom they despised intellectually and/or socially. Some of those who had figured in the old liberal feminist movement – and whose participation might not have been welcomed – fell into this category.[225] They found a substitute for their former organised activities within Germany in continuing to work as far as possible with the international organisations with which they had long had ties.[226] For those who had the time and the inclination, who were not as overburdened as the farmer's wife and who did not find their services in increasing demand in industry, offices and professions as the economy picked up, there remained a few outlets for their energies besides the NSF/DFW and other Party affiliates. The totalitarian pretensions of the NSDAP were realised neither in the elimination of every other alternative to Nazi-sponsored activity – although their destruction was comprehensive — nor in the attempt to persuade or cajole the mass of German women into their organisations, nor yet in winning for National Socialism as a creed and as a way of life the hearts and minds of the majority of women who did join them.

Notes

1. Orlow I, pp. 262-3, 274-5.
2. Orlow II, pp. 21ff.
3. Ibid., pp. 14-16.
4. IfZ, MA 130, frames 86492-93, 'Pgn. Scholtz-Klink: Die NS-Frauenschaft', 17 April 1939.
5. BA, op. cit., order of 17 August 1935, op. cit.
6. Winkler, op. cit., pp. 77-81.
7. Mason, op. cit., pp. 43-4; Stephenson, op. cit., pp. 61-2.
8. J.E. Farquharson, *The Plough and the Swastika*, London, 1976, pp. 92, 97, 188-9.
9. Heyen, op. cit., pp. 185, 200, 341, 344. And not only women: see Edward N. Peterson, *The Limits of Hitler's Power*, Princeton, 1969; Jeremy Noakes, 'The Oldenburg Crucifix Struggle . . . ' in Stachura (ed.), *The Shaping of the Nazi State*, op. cit., pp. 210-33.
10. Winkler, op. cit., p. 80; Karl Dietrich Bracher, *The German Dictatorship*, London, 1973, pp. 273-4, 277.
11. Winkler, loc. cit.
12. Evans, op. cit., pp. 235-9.
13. Gertrud Bäumer, 'Das Haus ist zerfallen', *Die Frau*, June 1933, pp. 513-14.
14. Allen, op. cit., pp. 213-26.
15. D. Albrecht (ed.), *Der Notenwechsel zwischen dem Heiligen Stuhl und der Deutschen Regierung*, Mainz, 1965, pp. 10-11; BA, R 22/24, letter from Stuckart to Hess, 14 December 1936.
16. HA/13/254, GH Bayerische Ostmark, p. 3.
17. BDC, AOPG, letter from Paula Siber to Hilgenfeldt, 6 March 1934.
18. Ibid., report by Paula Siber, 15 January 1934.
19. HA/13/254, GH South Hanover-Brunswick, p. 10; GH Saxony, p. 10.
20. Heyen, op. cit., p. 179.
21. Dora Hasselblatt (ed.), *Wir Frauen und die Nationale Bewegung*, Hamburg, 1933, expresses cautious support for National Socialism.
22. See above, pp. 101-2.
23. HA, loc. cit.
24. BDC, op. cit., letter from Buch to Krummacher, 20 September 1933.
25. Reports in *VB*, 11/12 and 24 February, and 3 and 7 March 1934.
26. BDC, op. cit., report of 15 January 1934, op. cit.
27. Kirkpatrick, op. cit., pp. 55-7.
28. BDC, op. cit., depositions by Paula Siber, 28 and 30 April 1934.
29. Ibid., letter from Charlotte Hauser to Paula Siber, 4 March 1934.
30. Ibid., depositions of 28 and 30 April, op. cit.
31. Ibid., letter from Hilgenfeldt to Bormann, 2 June 1934.
32. *Die Frau*, April 1934, loc. cit.
33. *FK*, op. cit., p. 3.
34. Ibid., pp. 4-5.
35. Scholtz-Klink, op. cit., p. 48.

36. BA, *Slg. Sch.*, 230, 'Rundschreiben Nr. 1/34', signed by Ley, 5 January 1934.
37. Allen, op. cit., pp. 225-6.
38. 'Deutsches Frauenwerk', *Das Archiv*, 1934/5 I, 1 July, 1934, p. 468.
39. Report in *Die Frau*, op. cit., pp. 506-7.
40. Stephenson, op. cit., pp. 57, 60-1.
41. Reichsfrauenführung, op. cit., pp. 28-9; Kirkpatrick, op. cit., pp. 74-6.
42. BA, op. cit.,'Liste der dem DFW angeschlossenen Reichsspitzenverbände', April 1935.
43. *FK*, op. cit., p. 3.
44. Evans, op. cit., pp. 212-13, 240-3, 250-2.
45. *FK*, loc. cit.
46. BA, op. cit.
47. This is a very tentative estimate, partly based on figures in Evans, op. cit., p. 251.
48. *FK*, op. cit., p. 4.
49. BA, op. cit., *Reichsfrauenführung Jahresbericht 1938*, p. 28.
50. Reichsfrauenführung, op. cit., p. 24.
51. Report in *Frankfurter Zeitung*, 12 February, 1936.
52. Reichsfrauenführung, op. cit., pp. 29-30.
53. BA, op. cit., April 1935, op. cit.
54. *FK*, loc. cit.
55. Bullock, op. cit., p. 275.
56. *FK*, loc. cit.
57. Broszat, op. cit., pp. 283-4, 291-5.
58. *Partei-Statistik*, vol. III, p. 58.
59. BA, op. cit., *Jahresbericht . . .* , op. cit., p. I.
60. *Partei-Statistik*, op. cit., pp. 29-31; 'Zum Organisationsplan der NS-Frauenschaft/Deutsches Frauenwerk', *Deutsches Frauenschaffen* (hereafter *DF*), 1939, pp. 10-11.
61. Heyen, op. cit., pp. 188-9.
62. BA, op. cit., letter from Sommer to Ley, 28 August 1935.
63. Ibid., letter from Ley to Hess, 8 October 1935.
64. *FK*, loc. cit.
65. BA, op. cit., *Der Führerorden*, 'Satzung des Deutschen Frauenwerks', 11 April 1936, p. 10.
66. BA, R22/24, 'Gesetzentwurf IV', 22 September 1936, sent by Bormann to the Minister of Justice, 15 October 1936.
67. Stockhorst, op. cit., p. 417; see also Broszat, op. cit., pp. 157, 305.
68. Ibid., memorandum by Stuckart, 14 November 1936, and his letter to Hess, 30 November 1936.
69. BA, *Slg. Sch.*, 230, *NS-Frauenschaft*, July 1936, order signed by Gertrud Scholtz-Klink, 'Betrifft: Zugehörigkeit der Hausfrauen zum DFW bzw. zur DAF'; Farquharson, op. cit., pp. 92, 97; see above, pp. 91-2, 114, 132.
70. *FK*, loc. cit.; IfZ, op. cit., frame 86492.
71. I am grateful to Dr Gisela Miller for information about this.
72. 'Mitgliederbewegung des Deutschen Frauenwerks', *DF*, 1939, p. 13.
73. BA, op. cit., *Jahresbericht . . .* , op. cit., p. 15.
74. BA, R22/24, letter to the Minister of Justice from Flöl, Prenzlau Court President, 10 February 1939.
75. Calculated from figures in BA, *Slg. Sch.*, 230, op. cit., pp. 15, 19.
76. Reichsfrauenführung, op. cit., p. 19.
77. BA, op. cit., *NS-Frauenschaft* order, July 1936, op. cit.
78. BA, op. cit., pp. 17-18.

79. 'Zum Organisationsplan . . . ', *DF*, 1939, p. 10, op. cit.
80. Winkler, loc. cit., p. 80.
81. HA/13/254, GH South Hanover-Brunswick, p. 10; GH Saxony, pp. 10-11; Evans, op. cit., p. 256.
82. Hüttenberger, op. cit., pp. 221-3.
83. Diehl-Thiele, op. cit., p. 34.
84. Hüttenberger, op. cit., pp. 118-36.
85. See above, pp. 66-8.
86. BDC, *Slg. Sch.*, 392, 'Goldenes Ehrenzeichen der NSDAP', list of names, 30 January 1938, and letter from Forster to Lammers, 12 March 1939.
87. Diehl-Thiele, op. cit., p. 168.
88. *FK*, op. cit., p. 3.
89. BDC, AOPG, *NSDAP Reichsleitung*, December 1934, p. 340; HA/13/254, 'Anschriftenverzeichnis . . . 1. Juni 1941', op. cit.
90. BA, NS22/vorl. 110, 'Aufgabe des Blockleiters', n.d., p. 2.
91. 'Erziehung zur politischen Verantwortung', *VB*, 27 September 1935.
92. Lore Bauer, 'Die "politische" Frau', *VB*, 6 September 1935.
93. 'Zur politischen Schulung im Reichsmütterdienst', *Die Frau*, November 1936, p. 108.
94. BA, *Slg. Sch.*, 230, order of 5 January 1934, op. cit.
95. BA, NSD 3/5, *V,A,B*, vol. II, order of 3 May 1933, p. 21.
96. HA/13/254, GH South Hanover-Brunswick, p. 11; GH Saxony, p. 11; GH Bayerische Ostmark, p. 3.
97. 'Schwesternschaften der NSDAP aufgelöst', *Das Archiv*, 1933 III, 5 January 1934, p. 1159; 'Schwesternschaft der NSV', op. cit., 1934/5 I, 10 April 1934, pp. 9-10.
98. BA, op. cit., order of 5 October 1936, p. 22.
99. See above, pp. 91-2.
100. See above, pp. 114-15.
101. IfZ, MA 130, frame 86495, 17 April 1939, op. cit.
102. Farquharson, loc. cit.
103. BA, *Slg. Sch.*, 230, *NS-Frauenschaft* order, July 1936, op. cit.
104. *FK*, op. cit., pp. 3-5.
105. Broszat, op. cit., p. 253.
106. 'Mitgliederbewegung der NS-Frauenschaft', *DF*, 1939, p. 12.
107. HA/13/254, GH Kurhessen, p. 4; GH Mainfranken, p. 1.
108. Ibid., GH Saxony, p. 7.
109. Ibid., GH Bayerische Ostmark, p. 2.
110. See above, p. 68.
111. *Partei-Statistik*, vol. I. pp. 31, 212; vol. II, p. 160.
112. Heyen, op. cit., p. 256.
113. Dr Marta Baerlecken-Hechtle, Düsseldorf, has been kind enough to tell me that 'so many teachers' who were her contemporaries joined the NSF as a way of protecting their position, even if they were 'avowed opponents' of the regime.
114. Heyen, op. cit., pp. 256-7.
115. Stephenson, op. cit., pp. 174-6.
116. IfZ, MA 609, frame 56478, 'Bericht über die bisherige Tätigkeit des Seminars für die NS Frauenschaft an der Hochschule für Politik', autumn 1939, gives a useful sample.
117. Heyen, op. cit., p. 291.
118. BA, R22/24, memorandum from Hölscher, President of the Supreme Court, to the Minister of Justice, 20 February 1939.
119. IfZ, MA 138, frame 301117, NSDAP Kreisleitung Lübeck, 'Bericht: NS-Frauenschaft', October 1941.
120. Ibid., frames 301117-18, op. cit.; ibid., frame 300885, report from

Hedwig Schmalmack, GNSFL Schleswig-Holstein to deputy Gauleiter Sieh, 29 November 1941; ibid., frame 300901, 'Wochenbericht', Gau Schleswig-Holstein to the Party Chancellery, 12 December 1941.

121. Stephenson, op. cit., pp. 165, 167.

122. BA, *Slg. Sch.*, 230, *NS-Frauenschaft München*, 'Rundschreiben No. 13/35', 19 August 1935, signed by GNSFL Elsbeth Frick,

123. Ibid., *ROL Information* (6) Nr. 0.18/35, '6. Parteigenossinnen und NS-Frauenschaft', 27 February 1935, p. 2.

124. Heyen, op. cit., pp. 179, 291.

125. BA, op. cit., letter from Friedrichs, in Hess's office, to Ley, 17 January 1936.

126. BDC, *Slg. Sch.*, 230, 'Anordnung Nr. 2/39', signed by Gertrud Scholtz-Klink, 25 October 1939.

127. See James Douglas-Hamilton, *Motive for a Mission*, 2nd edn, Edinburgh, 1979, for 'The Story Behind Rudolf Hess's Flight to Britain'.

128. BA, op. cit., letter of 2 April 1942, op. cit.

129. Reichsorganisationsleiter (ed.), *Organisationsbuch der NSDAP*, Munich, 1937, p. 266.

130. Ibid., 1941 edition, p. 266.

131. See above, pp. 107-8.

132. *FK*, op. cit., p. 5.

133. BA, op. cit., *Jahresbericht . . .* , op. cit., p. II.

134. IfZ, MA 609 frame 56489, op. cit.

135. Ibid., frames 56480-5.

136. Ibid., frame 56478.

137. See above, pp. 36-7.

138. BA, op. cit., pp. I-II.

139. Ibid., p. II.

140. Ibid., p. 32.

141. 'Die Arbeit der NS-Frauenschaft und des Deutschen Frauenwerks im Jahre 1935', *NS-Frauenwarte* (hereafter *NS-FW*), March 1936, pp. 613-14; 'Die Kameradschaftliche Volksmutter', op. cit., May 1936, pp. 774-5, 778; 'Nationalsozialistische Frauenarbeit', op. cit., June 1936. p. 831.

142. So I was told by a former minor NSF official in Munich.

143. BA, op. cit., pp. 28-29, I-II.

144. Scholtz-Klink, op. cit., pp. 74, 76.

145. Diehl-Thiele, op. cit., p. 168; BA, NS22/vorl. 110, op. cit., p. 5.

146. Margarete Weinhandl, 'Kultur-Erziehung-Schulung', *DF*, 1939, p. 93.

147. HA/13/253, 'Rundschreiben FW 70/37', and attached questionnaire, 3 August 1937.

148. Reichsfrauenführung, op. cit., pp. 21-2, 24-6.

149. Margarete Weinhandl, op. cit., p. 95.

150. Stephenson, op. cit., pp. 190-1.

151. Lotte Jahn, 'Hauptabteilung IX Hilfsdienst', *DF*, 1939, pp. 51-5.

152. BA, *Slg. Sch.*, 230, op. cit., pp. 55-6.

153. Margarete Weinhandl, op. cit., p. 92.

154. *FK*, op. cit., pp. 3-4.

155. BA, NS22/vorl. 319, *Reichsfrauenführung Dienststelle Kultur/Erziehung/ Schulung*, 'Nr. KS' and 'Nr. KS1', 4 April 1941.

156. Reichsfrauenführung, op. cit., p. 30.

157. HA/13/253, 'Rundschreiben Nr. FW 76/37', signed by Ilse Eben-Servaes, 12 August 1937; Stephenson, op. cit., p. 175.

158. Annemarie Bechem, 'Die deutsche Mutter als Erzieherin', *NS-FW*, April 1937, pp. 695-6.

159. BDC, op. cit., 'Unser Weg!', report from Gau Franken, n.d. (?1940), p. 5.

160. Eva Kriner-Fischer, *Die Frau als Richterin über Leben und Tod ihres Volkes*, Berlin, 1937.

161. 'Presse-Propaganda 1938', *DF*, 1939, pp. 16-20; BA, op. cit.

162. BA, *Slg. Sch.*, 230, op. cit., pp. 32, 37, 55.

163. 'Hauptabteilung Kultur/Erziehung/Schulung', *DF*, 1940, p. 18; BA, NS22/vorl. 121, 'Nr. GF 13-19', 4 April 1941.

164. Kirkpatrick, op. cit., pp. 69-72, 87-90.

165. *FK*, op. cit., p. 5; 'Hauptabteilung Mütterdienst', *DF*, 1941, p. 57.

166. BA, *Slg. Sch.*, 230, op. cit., pp. V-VI.

167. Ibid., pp. VI-VII.

168. *FK*, pp. 3-5.

169. BA, NSD 3/5, *V,A,B*, 1942, vol. 1, 'A 52/41 vom 6.12.41', pp. 617-22.

170. Reichsfrauenführung, op. cit., p. 27.

171. Evans, op. cit., p. 240.

172. Reichsfrauenführung, op. cit., pp. 21-3.

173. Evans, op. cit., p. 212.

174. Reichsfrauenführung, op. cit., pp. 26-7.

175. *FK*, op. cit., p. 4.

176. Erna Röpke, 'Hauptabteilung Mütterdienst', *DF*, 1939, p. 24.

177. BA, R2/12771, letter from the *Deutscher Gemeindetag* to the Minister of Education, 20 October 1937.

178. Articles in *NS-FW*, May 1937, pp. 733-4; *FK*, loc. cit.; Erna Röpke, op. cit., p. 34.

179. BA, *Slg. Sch.*, 230, circular signed by Himmler, 22 April 1937.

180. Erna Röpke, op. cit., pp. 23, 29.

181. HA/13/254, GH Bayerische Ostmark, pp. 5-7.

182. Ibid., GH Mainfranken, pp. 1-2.

183. HA/13/253, 'Was hat das Deutsche Frauenwerk Reichsmütterdienst unseren Frauen und Müttern zu sagen?', accompanying 'Rundschreiben FW Nr. 72/37', 9 August 1937.

184. BA, op. cit., *Jahresbericht . . .*, op. cit., pp. 37, III.

185. 'Bevölkerungspolitik', *Die Deutsche Sozialpolitik*, July 1944, p. 63.

186. Erna Röpke, op. cit., pp. 21-2, 24-5.

187. HA/13/253, 'Rundschreiben FW Nr. 84/37', 1 October 1937; 'Rundschreiben FW Nr. 100/37', 25 October 1937.

188. Ibid., 'Rundschreiben FW Nr. 48/37', 13 May 1937.

189. See, e.g., HA/13/253, 'Rundschreiben FW Nr. 101/37', 25 October 1937; 'Rundschreiben FW Nr. 118/37', 13 December 1937.

190. Ibid., 'Rundschreiben FW Nr. 103/37', 30 October 1937.

191. Ibid., 'Rundschreiben FW Nr. 116/37', 2 December 1937.

192. *Statistisches Jahrbuch für das Deutsche Reich*: 1935, p. 56; 1937, p. 62; 1939/40, p. 68; 1941/2, p. 90.

193. HA/13/254, GHs Bayerische Ostmark and Mainfranken, loc. cit.

194. BA, op. cit., p. III.

195. Else Vorwerck, 'Hauptabteilung Volkswirtschaft-Hauswirtschaft', *DF*, 1939, pp. 35-6.

196. Reichsfrauenführung, op. cit., p. 26.

197. HA/13/253, 'Rundschreiben FW Nr. 60/37', 28 June 1937.

198. Else Vorwerck, op. cit., p. 39.

199. Mason, op. cit., pp. 165-71.

200. HA/13/253, 'Rundschreiben FW Nr. 54/37', 9 June 1937.

201. Ibid., 'Rundschreiben FW Nr. 98/37', 23 October 1937.

202. Ibid., 'Rundschreiben FW Nr. 71/37', 4 August 1937.

203. Ibid., 'Rundschreiben FW Nr. 79/37', 1 October 1937.

204. Ibid., 'Rundschreiben FW Nr. 80/37', 21 September 1937; 'Rundschreiben FW Nr. 88/37', 6 October 1937; 'Rundschreiben FW Nr. 104/37', 1 November 1937.

205. Jill Stephenson, ' "Reichsbund der Kinderreichen" . . . ', op. cit.

206. Stephenson 1978, pp. 201-2.

207. E.g., HA/13/254, 'Rundschreiben FW Nr. 87/37', 25 September 1937; 'Rundschreiben FW Nr. 115/37', 27 November 1937.

208. BDC, op. cit., 'Unser Weg!' op. cit., p. 9.

209. BA, op. cit., 'Anordnung 1/40', 16 January 1940.

210. Ibid., *Jahresbericht* . . . , pp. 25-6.

211. 'Die Kindergruppen der NSF/DFW', *DF*, 1941, p. 74.

212. BA, op. cit., p. 28; see also Stephenson 1978, pp. 199-203.

213. *FK*, op. cit., p. 3.

214. HA/13/253, 'Der Frauenfunk der Woche, 21.3.-27.3.1937', pp. 1-6.

215. Z.A.B. Zeman, *Nazi Propaganda*, London, 1964, pp. 51-2, 116; Grunberger, op. cit., pp. 506-7.

216. See above, p. 80.

217. See above, pp. 138-9, and the implications of p. 140.

218. Conway, op. cit., pp. 331-8; Ernst Wolf, 'Political and Moral Motives behind the Resistance' in W. Schmitthenner and H. Buchheim (eds.), *The German Resistance to Hitler*, London, 1970, pp. 198-226.

219. Heyen, op. cit., pp. 179, 188-9. Peterson, op. cit., pp. 208-23, 259-63, 417-27.

220. Stephenson, *Women in Nazi Society*, p. 160; *FK*, op. cit., pp. 4-5.

221. Heyen, op. cit., pp. 164-5; Hermann Weber (ed.), *Völker hört die Signale*, Munich, 1967, pp. 214-16.

222. BDC, loc. cit.

223. Scholtz-Klink, op. cit., pp. 512-15, 524-6.

224. See above, pp. 35-6.

225. Beckmann, op. cit., pp. 63-4; BA, *Kleine Erwerbungen*, No. 296-(1), letters from Dorothee von Velsen to Gertrud Bäumer: 8 March 1934; 21 November 1936; 10 March 1939.

226. Ibid., correspondence between Dorothee von Velsen and Gertrud Bäumer: 23 October 1933; 14 July 1934; 15 November 1934.

NAZI WOMEN AT WAR

Limited Effort on the Home Front

The peacetime years of the Third Reich were a time of strange shadow-boxing for the NSDAP and its affiliates. Once actual and potential opponents of the new regime had been neutralised by *Gleichschaltung* in 1933, the Party's restricted sphere of activity became frustratingly delineated. Denied even a share in government and axiomatically required to use persuasion rather than coercion with healthy, politically reliable, 'Aryan' Germans, the NSDAP had been condemned to the virtually impossible task of generating enthusiasm for Party ideas and activities among those who, given a free choice, had elected not to become involved with National Socialism beyond accepting Hitler's Government as a fact of life. This uphill struggle had been mitigated by the acquisition of territory — including the Saar, Austria, the Sudeten-land and Memel — which was relatively unsaturated by Nazi canvassing. The readiness of substantial numbers in these areas not only to welcome German rule but also to involve themselves in Party activities was a consolation prize for Party workers used to the apathetic response of the unconverted in the 'old Reich'. The enthusiasm exuded by a report of the rapid construction of an NSF/DFW organisation in Memel — complete with RMD, Vw/Hw and other sectional activities — made in July 1939[1] is reminiscent of the ardour which characterised the accounts of the Party's early development in the Gau Histories.

The war which began in September 1939 with Hitler's attack on Poland opened up new vistas of fertile territory for the NSDAP, among the millions of '*volksdeutsch*' (ethnic German) inhabitants of eastern Europe. The opportunities provided here — and to some extent in occupied western Europe also — helped to give the Party and its affiliates, including the NSF and the DFW, a new lease of life, in a sense creating a new *Kampfzeit*.[2] But while the acquisition of land for *Lebensraum* and the assertion of the right of all *Volksdeutsche* to 'return to the Reich' formed one motive for war and one determinant of occupation policy, domestic pressures decided the other. The regime's obsession with retaining at least the passive acquiescence of the mass of Germans at home while a victorious war was being waged, demanded that resources in defeated countries be plundered to provide

178

material benefits and that foreigners be either encouraged or compelled to go to Germany to make good the serious shortage of labour there.[3] While the *Blitzkrieg* campaigns failed to bring the final victory in the form desired by Hitler, they provided Germany with a huge European empire to occupy and to exploit. As Germany became bogged down in a many-dimensional war of attrition, this exploitation, of human and material resources, became increasingly severe.[4] Other occupying powers have plundered the vanquished and created an imperial system to be worked for their benefit alone.[5] In Hitler's war, this motive was inextricably bound up with the desire to create a new 'racial community', whose attempted realisation began with a determined and appalling policy of population transfers and deportations, engineered under Himmler's authority.[6] While the Nazi Party's efforts to train sometimes unwilling ethnic Germans both ideologically and practically for 'becoming German again' (*Wiedereindeutschung*) made victims of some of the alleged beneficiaries of this policy,[7] its deliberate and cold-blooded discrimination against those who were not 'racially desirable' relegated them to the status of helots, 'a class of serfs . . . deliberately humiliated and liable to massacre'.[8]

By bringing the women's organisation out of the backwater in which it had been stagnating in the later 1930s and by involving it more centrally in the Party's work, the wartime activities of the NSDAP implicated the NSF and, to a lesser extent, the DFW fully in the effects of Nazi racial policy in practice. NSF members had, of course, been well aware of the NSDAP's racial policies; ideological training courses had been explicitly geared to their propagation. And although DFW members had shown reluctance to attend 'political education' and 'racial policy' courses,[9] each of them had had to declare herself to be of 'German-"Aryan"' stock, while large numbers had been exposed to unsubtle propaganda in RMD courses, especially, about the duty of Germany's wives and mothers to safeguard the 'purity of the race'.[10] But in their activities and their publications, the NSF and the DFW had stopped far short of the crude and crass racialist propaganda which was becoming increasingly prevalent elsewhere in the Party in the later 1930s. During the war, however, the NSF's participation in the Party's activities in newly-annexed lands, in the east particularly, made it an accessory to policies of an indescribably inhuman nature. Dörte Winkler is justified in attributing the Allies' relatively lenient treatment of Gertrud Scholtz-Klink after the war to the impotence of her organisation.[11] But it has been overlooked that the NSF's enthusiastic work among new German settlers in occupied Polish territory, for example, was an integral part of policies involving the maltreatment of the 'racially inferior' inhabitants of the area. Anti-semitism was soft-pedalled in the 'women's work' at home, although it was implicit in it; but Gertrud Scholtz-Klink cannot shake off responsibility simply by claiming that the NSDAP's racialist policies 'were nothing to do with me and equally nothing to do with the *Reichsfrauenführung*'.[12]

As closer collaboration in mainstream Party work implicated the NSF in its most inhuman aspects, so it also reduced the women's organisation increasingly to the role of a clearing-house for directing women into service with other organisations – the NSV, the Red Cross, the Air-raid Protection Society, for example. The DFW's sectional work did continue, with predictable emphasis on population policy, physical exercise and domestic science training, and the Vw/Hw tried to direct consumption patterns to an even greater extent than during the era of the Four Year Plan. Along with other affiliates, the NSF and the DFW played their part in the interminable round of collections – of anything that could be used again or recycled – undertaken by the Party.[13] While the NSF and the DFW worked closely together in these practical activities, thus justifying their virtual merger in 1942,[14] there remained until the end a distinction between NSF and DFW members. The latter engaged exclusively in practical activities and were recipients of theoretical orthodoxy; but NSF members continued to carry special responsibility for 'National Socialist educational work'. NSF members had constantly to refresh and update their comprehension of the Nazi *Weltanschauung* so that they could 'involve themselves most strongly where the effort and attitude of German women is concerned'. Jollying women along, to maintain morale when menfolk were away from home in the armed forces and to encourage them to volunteer for war-work, was elevated to the status of a 'leadership task' on 'the spiritual side' of the NSF's work,[15] no doubt to maintain morale and effort among NSF members themselves. But whatever claims Gertrud Scholtz-Klink has liked to make about how her organisation, after '*barely 6 years of peaceful construction together* . . . was able to fulfil all the requirements made of it',[16] the NSF proved as incapable as the rest of the NSDAP, the Government and Hitler himself of persuading German women to support the war-effort in sufficiently large numbers. Berlin women factory workers showed their contempt for the NSF in 1942 by hissing official spokeswomen to the extent that they were unable to deliver their speeches.[17]

The failure to mobilise women for essential war-work in large numbers – which contrasted with the success enjoyed by Germany's enemies[18] – meant that Germany was consistently short of labour and uncomfortably dependent on prisoners of war and foreign workers from occupied countries.[19] At first, a debate about the desirability of conscripting women into war industry dragged on for years, remaining unresolved until 1943 largely because of Hitler's personal prejudices.[20] And once conscription was introduced, in January 1943, there were sufficient loopholes to permit widespread evasion.[21] This was not least because of the reluctance of the mobilisation officers – the Gauleiters – to use any tactics that would be unpopular with the civilian population, in this context and in others.[22] And yet, the problem of mobilising female labour was of crucial importance to the German war-effort, and was, in a sense, the most important issue affecting women during the war. To the NSF was delegated the task of winning co-operation through persuasion, and a fitful propaganda campaign was launched – to little effect[23] as Himmler's agents graphically reported.[24] It was particularly the same middle-class women who had resisted involvement in the DFW in the 1930s who now refused to volunteer for war-work, and found ingenious expedients for avoiding conscription once it was introduced.[25] The enormous campaign mounted in the *NS-Frauenwarte*[26] was bound to have little effect, since it would reach only the million or so subscribers, who were already involved in Party work and therefore not deemed to be free for other duties, in the early part of the war. The only way to reach the majority of women was to visit them at home, and while 'tireless' campaigning of this kind by block and cell NSF officials probably exerted enough personal pressure to persuade some women to volunteer for occasional stints of work anywhere from factories or fields to DFW sewing groups, it did not convince them that they should go out to work full-time or even part-time on a regular basis. Labour Front propaganda about the willingness of women to serve was downright dishonest, even if some of the claims made about maintaining a high level of labour protection for women in industry[27] were justified.[28]

The Party as a whole, and the NSF as part of it, were hamstrung, as they had so often been since 1933, by Hitler's initial and continuing refusal to allow the NSDAP to assume State functions on a large scale. As Gertrud Scholtz-Klink has said in retrospect:

> Obviously we could guarantee an immediately tangible effort only on the part of our own organised members; the women outside were to be mobilised, if necessary, by measures taken by the State alone, as indeed in all other countries.[29]

The Party's restricted sphere of operations, combined with the failure of the NSF to attract substantial numbers of women to the DFW, meant that the NSF could have little effect on the single most important issue affecting German women during the war. The Women's Labour Service has been quoted as an exception to the Party's failure here,[30] but it is obvious that 100,000 or so young women working short hours and deployed in a wasteful way[31] made little difference to the chronic shortage of labour. And the Labour Service had no connection with the women's organisation by this time, so that the NSF could lay no claim to a share in its 'success'. Paradoxically, then, while the war gave the NSF and the DFW a new sense of purpose, their energies were channelled into piecemeal projects and peripheral issues removed from the major concern of equipping German forces to win a decisive victory.

To Party leaders, however, continuing 'political education' courses in wartime was far from peripheral — Gauleiter Kaufmann was an exception here[32] — and was in fact regarded as even more important, if possible, than previously, to maintain morale and national solidarity in an 'inner front'. As early as March 1939, Hess had decreed the *Schulungsbrief* (ideological training newsletter) to be 'vital in time of war', and contingency plans were made for local NSF officials to take over its distribution in the event of any large-scale call-up of male Party workers.[33] This proved to be necessary in some areas in January 1941 as NSDAP block officials began to be drafted.[34] The NSF continued to hold its own courses, as the Gau reports for 1940 showed;[35] in one *Gauschule* in Hessen, 200 NSF officials attended eleven 'political education' courses,[36] to reinforce their own commitment and update their comprehension of the current elements of the *Weltanschauung*. Once the war seemed to be dragging on indefinitely, in 1941, Ley's office became particularly exercised about the need 'to secure a unified line' through the more direct influence of his Main Training Office on the detailed preparation of 'political education courses'.[37] NSF officials were summoned to a conference on the eve of the invasion of Russia, to report on their work and to receive instructions for the future.[38] But Ley wanted even tighter control over the affiliates' courses — since goodwill was no substitute for expertise, in the NSF — and in August 1941 his deputy, Huber, was instructing the Gau training officers to send representatives to attend the NSF's 'political education' courses to ensure that the prevailing orthodoxy was being purveyed.[39]

The war did bring changes in the nature of the propaganda to be directed by the NSF at women, to prevent defeatism, to encourage participation in some kind of war service, and to try to mitigate discontent about rationing and shortages – if not their effects – by exhaustive public relations exercises explaining the need for these expedients. But the core of the Party's propaganda to women remained essentially what it had been in the 1930s. Women were to become politically aware, so as to appreciate Germany's special destiny and to support the regime's efforts to realise it. They were to accept, as gladly as possible, the demands being made of them, and to bring their children up to do the same. They were to conduct their households responsibly, avoiding making superfluous demands, resisting needless luxuries and, above all, 'buying German'. And, no doubt vitiating alternative propaganda urging them to go out to work to help the war-effort, women were to rest assured that the *Führer* was so determined that their 'physical and spiritual identity' should be safeguarded that he had refused to allow labour conscription to be introduced. Continuing the eternal preoccupation with the 'purity of the race', discreet propaganda warned against fraternisation with foreign workers who had been set to work in Germany.[40] This was a major source of concern throughout the war, since the many prisoners of war and other foreign labourers in the Reich were not of German 'Aryan' stock; but with so many German men away from home it was hardly surprising that sexual relationships developed between 'hereditarily and socially flawless' women and foreigners living and working near them, in spite of the severe penalties imposed on the men if discovered.[41] There was some hostility on the part of Germans towards foreign workers, but, particularly in small communities, there was also sympathy for their plight.[42]

The NSF's 'political education' tasks became increasingly thankless, as the war continued and hardships increased. It was all very well for the Party's training office to offer advice about how to maintain morale among citizens facing the daily irritations of shortages and queues, and how to set a good example by assisting pregnant women in these circumstances. But none of this made the queues disappear, and the NSF official – 'recognisable by her badge'[43] – was placed in the front line against aggrieved women shoppers whom she was supposed to soothe with a public relations exercise learned in a 'political education' course. Once the Government at last grasped the nettle of labour conscription for women, it was the NSF's task to reassure 'anxious mothers' whose daughters were being brought into war work, particularly if they were to be used as auxiliaries with the armed forces outside Germany.[44] With rations being cut, goods unavailable – a partic-

ular grievance at Christmas — and complaints about inadequate protection in areas increasingly subject to bombing raids, particular care
had to be taken to listen to the women's anxieties and complaints, and
to try to raise their morale so that they would not cause defeatism at
the front by writing gloomy letters to their men.[45] The women's
resolve had to be strengthened and their fears allayed by pep-talks from
NSF officials, who in turn had to bear the brunt of worries, discontent
and derision. If they failed to convince aggrieved women that
temporary sacrifices were necessary and that final victory would ultimately justify them[46] it was not necessarily because of their own incompetence; the inconsistency and downright unfairness of some
official policies — especially those concerning war work for women —
eventually led to doubts and despair among some NSF workers themselves.[47]

Since the NSF proved unable to persuade women to sign on for
regular war service in a factory or an office, in public transport or on
the land, it had to be content with trying to attract women to piecemeal participation in projects of its own or another affiliate's devising.
Some pressure could be brought to bear on NSF and DFW members, at
least, and many of them volunteered for a variety of tasks, including
auxiliary work on the land at vital times of the year, especially during
the sowing or harvest season when the shortage of labour in agriculture
was most acutely felt. In 1940, it was reported, 1.2 million members
put in over 57 million hours on the land, while another 420,000 spent
21 million hours helping overburdened farmers' wives. But, once again,
these superficially impressive figures are really rather paltry; each of
these women could spare less than one hour a week throughout the
year. Overall, the total of voluntary work performed by 3.5 million
NSF and DFW members in 1940 was 200 million hours, which meant
that on average each volunteer was prepared to spend only a little over
an hour a week assisting the national war-effort. This was, of course,
at a time when Germany was brilliantly victorious, and propaganda to
this effect must have persuaded many women that their efforts were
not required at all, in spite of insistence in the press to the contrary.
Even so, labour conscription was a live issue in 1940; without the threat
posed by it, perhaps even these 3.5 million women would not have felt
the need to make their not very strenuous effort. And much of their
activity was indeed peripheral, in the realm of aid to mothers of large
families and making and mending in DFW sewing circles. Only 19,000
women felt able to face even a small amount of factory work, putting
in 1.3 million hours altogether to allow full-time working women a

little extra time off.[48]

Unorganised women, too, volunteered for auxiliary work, but on the whole, since they had already chosen not to be involved with the Party's affiliates, they remained unreceptive to the NSF's propaganda and projects. The same middle-class women who managed to evade systematic war-work, before and after conscription was introduced, and who despised the official women's organisation were slow to volunteer even for part-time, non-Party work, although some did so. For these women, work in a traditional 'patriotic' organisation like the Red Cross was particularly attractive.[49] The urgency with which the DFW's K/E/S section tried to forge links with the nurses of the Red Cross, to facilitate their 'ideological training in all womanly areas',[50] derived from the realisation that here at last was a chance to gain access to a group of women who had deliberately remained elusive. This strange priority − in the deteriorating circumstances of August 1942 − was only one of many, as became increasingly clear to dedicated NSF workers. The disillusioned Schleswig-Holstein GNSFL, Hedwig Schmalmack, voiced the frustration of others when she wrote in November 1941 that 'to-day it is unfortunately the case that the idealists are regarded as ridiculous'.[51] The only sanction against those who did not work full-time and would not volunteer for any kind of service was periodic castigation in the press of women who had time to frequent cafes while others worked.[52] Even this was played down in the counter-productive, morale-boosting exercise of boasting about the nation's solidarity and the willingness of everyone to serve,[53] and NSF leaders were left to cope with simmering discontent in their locality about how 'the cafes . . . and the tennis courts are always full of women with nothing to do' − whose husbands apparently encouraged their idleness.[54]

The 'idealists', misguided as they were, continued their activities in the NSF and through the DFW's sections, until they were forced, by increasing shortages, to draw in their horns in spring 1943. Then, some of the small number of full-time staff in the RFFg began to be deployed in the regions, once the insatiable demands of the armed forces led to the call-up of male Gau and district officials, and increasing restrictions on the use of paper hamstrung the RFFg's activities,[55] since a free flow of communication was essential to its highly centralised system. It was perhaps remarkable that the sections continued to operate for so long; although there were warnings in December 1941 that reports would have to be drastically limited because of the paper shortage,[56] reports made in 1942 could still be lengthy,[57] and propaganda material, particularly, continued to pour out from the centre. Only in August 1942 was there a ban on the private use of official stationery[58] − no doubt a recognised perk − although the Vw/Hw section had already had to start giving cookery advice over the radio to reduce the amount of paper it consumed for its advisory leaflets,[59] and each Gau had been allocated a monthly paper allowance.[60] Courses and meetings continued to be held in spite of transport problems and difficulties posed by food rationing, which had been introduced even before the war. It was enough for GNSFLs and Gau section representatives to make periodic compulsory journeys to Berlin for meetings, but HD functionaries were put to great inconvenience by the siting of their major annual meeting near 'Litzmannstadt' (Lodz) in September 1941, to impress on Gau section leaders the importance of the Party's 'work in the East'.[61] On this occasion the participants were at least spared the chore of bringing their own bed-linen, towels, shoe-cleaning equipment, sports gear and rations, which was the lot of most NSF/ DFW officials attending meetings in 1941 and 1942. At first it was enough to provide coupons from the ration card, but increasingly the women were instructed about the exact amounts of sugar, fats, marmalade, meat and cheese they were to bring; they were even expected to carry fresh eggs safely in their baggage.[62]

The NSF/DFW's work in the first half of the war, until the turn of 1942/3, was schizophrenic in character, for two basic reasons. First, the section leaders were obviously planning for the long-term future in a German empire at peace, while at the same time they increasingly had to adapt their activities to the demands of a long and damaging war. This does much to explain an order of priorities which seems at the very least peculiar − although in keeping with Nazi 'logic' − in time of national crisis. And secondly, the RFFg's room for manoeuvre was circumscribed by the overriding preoccupation with minimising discontent among the 'valuable' population in the 'old Reich': the 'stab-in-the-back' myth was taken as an awful warning, by Hitler especially.[63] Every objective had to be achieved by persuasion and propaganda, and that included the involvement of the NSF/DFW's own members in voluntary work. It was one thing to fail to persuade women outside the organisations of the wisdom of the regime's policies and the need for everyone to pull her weight; it was a sure sign of impotence that large numbers of DFW members refused to collaborate to the extent that they were classed as 'inactive'.[64] The frustration felt by the new and energetic district NSF leader in Strasbourg, Rosel Reysz, at the failure of male NSDAP officials to persuade their wives to join the DFW and be active in its work, was doubtless shared by other activists. Even when the wives did join, only a low percentage did more than pay a subscription; in one local branch, of 164 wives of political leaders only 94 joined the DFW, and not one actually worked in it. This was an extreme case, but in most of Strasbourg's local branches only between a quarter and half of such women were active. The men either did not encourage their wives to join the DFW, or else positively forbade them to do so; and those who stayed outside regarded it as something of a joke.[65]

There were activisits and enthusiasts in the DFW, but the problem was that most of them wanted to be chiefs rather than indians. In one local branch in Kochem district, a Frau Ervens, who had proved unsuitable as Vw/Hw section leader, rejected the alternative position offered of block NSF leader as being too menial for her. In the end, the district NSF leader left her without an office of any kind 'since she does not have the right attitude for our work'.[66] But, on the whole, dispensing with people who were prepared to work in the DFW was a luxury that local leaders could not afford. The exigencies of war, with men away and with shortages and rationing making life a succession of queues followed by mending clothes and preserving food at home, meant that even non-employed women had little time or energy to spare for unpaid Party work. Local NSF/DFW organisations suffered difficulties as a result of frequent changes of leadership because the women appointed were overburdened in their daily work – as a farmer's wife or as a teacher, for example – and could not devote the necessary time to the organisations.[67] Hedwig Schmalmack's solution was to suggest that preference be given to NSF/DFW workers in the distribution of domestic servants.[68] There was method in the apparent madness of recruiting and deploying large numbers of domestic servants at a time when industry was starved of labour. Providing help at home for hard-pressed housewives, especially on the land and in large families, was an article of faith at the RFFg, and was also a way of trying to keep these people relatively contented. But as it became clear that the same idle middle-class women – often with only the one child – who refused to assist the war-effort still managed to acquire domestic help, resentment redoubled among those who needed help and who faced other difficulties, for example, in shopping after work.[69] Characteristically, the only palliative which the DFW could offer was for the Vw/Hw to send round a note with ration cards asking housewives to shop early in the day so that working women would not face long queues.[70] This open invitation to the idle to buy up scarce commodities while overburdened women worked only fanned the flames of discontent.[71]

This apparent insensitivity belied the anxiety of the RFFg to keep in touch with women's opinions throughout the country, with requests for consumer feedback about its radio programmes, and for the response to new expedients like distributing fruit and vegetables through underused flower shops.[72] The Vw/Hw required regular information from its local representatives about the availability of different commodities in various areas of the Reich, and devised its advice leaflets to cater for local possibilities. It was greatly regretted that the paper shortage forced the Vw/Hw to give consumer advice over the radio from May 1942, since the desire to try to keep regional variations secret, to avoid discontent in more deprived areas, meant that the regional approach had to be abandoned.[73] When the RMD launched its campaign against the consumption of alcohol and tobacco, in earnest in summer 1942, it was strongly emphasised that it must begin in a low-key manner, since 'opinions which might cause unrest among the population are . . . to be avoided'.[74] The GNSFLs sent reports to Gertrud Scholtz-Klink's personal office each month[75] which sometimes, at least, gave a frank picture of the problems arising from the exigencies of war, from the attitudes of some male NSDAP officials, and from the running sore of discontent about the inequitable treatment of women over war-work, which operated to the advantage of middle-class women. In response to the growing disaffection with official policy on the land, the RFF established a section for 'Rural Women' in October 1941, because 'with the exception of a few Gaus, the involvement of rural women in the work of the NSF/DFW has so far had only very limited practical effect'.[76] But the farmer's wife, by now thoroughly resentful about the lack of assistance she was receiving in wartime with the farm's men called up,[77] was hardly likely to be won over after all these years by the appointment of more bureaucrats in the RFFg and the issuing of propaganda to try to attract urban women to help out on farms at harvest time.[78]

But this device was indicative of the RFFg's preoccupation with bureaucratic niceties, with continuing attempts to draw lines of demarcation satisfactorily between the NSF/DFW and other organisations, especially the Labour Front and the BdM, yet again.[79] There was clearly nothing some of Gertrud Scholtz-Klink's staff liked better than to keep redrawing the 'office plan' which showed who sat on whose staff and who was subordinate to whom.[80] The ultimate in exercises of this kind came in April 1941, with the RFFg's own 'peacetime plan' which ran to scores of pages detailing chains of command, duties and designations.[81] If it was perhaps reasonable to assume that Germany's victory was assured and even imminent in 1941, it was surely negligently trivial to agonise about who was entitled to wear which armband in the HD in July 1942.[82] It was perhaps not over-optimistic in December 1941 to schedule a lengthy, intensive course for intending Vw/Hw staff for April 1942,[83] although members of the 'youth groups' might have been more usefully employed at this time than in making toys for *volksdeutsch* children in occupied Russia.[84] But all of this was a contribution to the construction of 'a good organisation [which] is always the basis of any fruitful and lasting work'.[85] By the same token, it was considered vital that, at a time of increasingly stringent rationing, the Vw/Hw's and RMD's cookery courses should go ahead, and the Minister of Food provided an (albeit diminishing) allowance for the purpose.[86] Instructing women in the thrifty use of wartime materials was only part of the motive; the courses continued to be regarded by Gertrud Scholtz-Klink and her staff as fundamentally important for the long-term education of German women.

But some of the sections' work was more immediately relevant to the present than the idyllic future. The Vw/Hw's advisory bureaux throughout the country sold a multitude of leaflets with information about recipes, washing techniques, repairing clothes and furniture, caring for everything from stockings to electrical equipment, and combating moths.[87] The Vw/Hw also launched campaigns that make sense in the 1980s, to promote wholemeal bread consumption and to conserve energy.[88] The RMD gave special advice about children's diets and rationing, and acted as an information centre for the exchange of second-hand prams, cots and bath-tubs.[89] And its general campaign to help women to protect their own and their children's health sensibly involved concern about smoking and alcohol abuse.[90] HD workers repaired and redistributed army uniforms[91] – probably rather a grim task – and the 'youth groups' provided auxiliaries for Red Cross work.[92] The Vw/Hw organised collections of rags and old clothes for recycling,[93] and the K/E/S collected books for the army, although it managed to run into difficulty in this rather simple exercise.[94] And policies could backfire: complaints were made that the system of clothing coupons worked to the disadvantage of women who made their own clothes, since the methods taught in the DFW's sewing courses led them to need more material than was used in off-the-peg clothes.[95] No doubt, though, the advice given was often welcome as women struggled to make do in increasingly straitened circumstances. And, particularly with men away from home, even 'sewing evenings' and 'cookery demonstrations' provided some diversion, while, hardly surprisingly, DFW film shows, poetry readings and illustrated talks were well attended.[96]

Women both inside and outside the NSF/DFW were prepared to accept advice and to attend social events, but they were not prepared to be working members of the sections in significant numbers, unless they had a position and a title. And yet, much of the sections' work, in the RMD, the HD and the 'youth groups' especially, had always been intended to provide women volunteers for, broadly, social service work, often under NSV supervision. During the war, the DFW did provide members – 200,000 in 1940 – to replace officials in the NSV who had been called up,[97] but increasingly it had to rely on unmarried girls – who might be as young as 16 – who had signed up for two years' service in the RFF's *Frauenhilfsdienst* (Women's Auxiliary Service), which had been introduced in May 1938 to recruit and train auxiliary welfare workers.[98] In 1941 and 1942, most of the HD's work was done by these girls, while its 'neighbourhood aid' scheme was staffed by the BdM and supervised by HD members.[99] The BdM also provided substantial numbers of girls for work on the land,[100] and more were made available by orders making school pupils liable for service in agriculture.[101] Once girls performing the extended period required of Labour Service conscripts from 1941 were drawn out of social service and into work in munitions factories and with the armed forces, in 1942, the HD offered to provide substitutes, again from the auxiliary service girls.[102] Of full DFW members, only the 'youth groups' could be dragooned into service, with the obligation to perform periodic four-week stints in a 'Work-Joy-Comradeship' scheme, and with strong pressure on them to work in the occupied eastern territories.[103] But the 'youth groups' were also expected to attend a variety of Vw/Hw and RMD courses, and to participate in K/E/S activities, with strong emphasis on sport.[104] These, after all, were the young women who would be the mothers of a new generation, and so, war or no war, they had to be trained and influenced accordingly. For the rest of the NSF/DFW's membership, unless they were officials or instructors, it was possible to live their own lives untroubled by more than repeated attempts at persuasion to serve; busy enough with the many cares of war, large numbers of 'organised' women remained 'inactive' even as Germany was thrown onto the defensive.

NSF/DFW Work among the *Volksdeutsche*

If attempts to continue Party activities in the 'old Reich' after 1939 brought enthusiasts uncomfortably face-to-face with the domestic realities of war and an apathetic population, the extension of Nazi rule to newly-occupied territories provided a kind of escapism for fanatics, for Germany's conquests in 1939-41 not only created a new 'Germanic Empire' but also gave the Party and the SS a new sphere of influence. The appointment of 'old Reich' Gauleiters at the head of the civil government in new territories in both east and west gave the Party a decisive advantage over the State there.[105] But Himmler's appointment as 'Commissioner for Strengthening Germandom' made him overlord of population policy and determined its general direction. This dual authority contributed to the development of even more confused bureaucratic structures, not least in the NSF/DFW,[106] and, in the east particularly, at times created intra-Party tensions of explosive proportions.[107] In theory, at least, the Party and the SS were working towards the same goal: the annexed territories in both east and west which created an even Greater Germany were to be purged of all but ethnic Germans, in the east to make room for immigrants from Soviet eastern Poland and the Baltic States — recognised as within the Soviet sphere of interest — who would be 'processed' by the Liaison Office for Ethnic Germans (VoMi), part of Himmler's growing empire.[108] In east and west these ethnic Germans were to be 'made German again' and their life-style and — if possible — their attitudes Nazified; the inhabitants of the new border areas were, in fact, to be subjected to the same pressures that the Germans of the 'old Reich' had experienced since 1933.

Like the other Party affiliates which were pressed into service in this work considered vitally important to Germany's destiny, the NSF/DFW worked largely — particularly in the east — as an agent of Party or SS policy. The erosion of their former rather stultifying autonomy was a price willingly paid for full involvement in top priority Party work. At first, in 1939-40, this meant sending members to help to look after new settlers from eastern Europe who were lodged in reception camps while their credentials as ethnic Germans were verified. In January 1940, 400 NSF/DFW members were working in camps in the eastern border Gaus, cooking and taking 'personal motherly care of those who had been brought home' from Galicia and Volhynia.[109] During 1940, 1,265 NSF/DFW members worked in reception camps or with the transport bringing ethnic Germans from Rumania, the Baltic States and eastern Poland; tribute was paid to the special contribution made by women from Gaus Hamburg, Saxony, Berlin, Brandenburg and Halle-Merseburg.[110] Some members also helped the NSV to secure accommodation and furniture — usually expropriated from non-Germans, including

Jews − to enable new settlers to move from the camps into permanent homes.[111] But this was all in the nature of emergency relief work; the aim was to prepare the new settlers for their role as German citizens, and this would involve mounting courses in the camps for 'ideological and practical training'. The GA was to co-ordinate NSF/DFW sectional work in the border areas especially in the new Warthegau, constructed from former Polish territory. As a start, in 1940, the GA organised visits of three weeks each for two reliable NSF members from each 'old Reich' Gau to the Warthegau, to stimulate interest at home for work in a developing area.[112]

There were similarities in the work done by the NSF/DFW in the new eastern and western border lands, but the differences were greater. In both, the aim was to construct a women's organisation and win over ethnic German women to National Socialism. In both, the basis was provided by attaching annexed areas to an existing 'old Reich' Gau: in the west, Alsace became part of Gau Baden, Lorraine joined Saar-Palatinate and Luxembourg joined Koblenz-Trier; in the east, Silesia, Danzig and East Prussia were each augmented by Polish territory, although the Warthegau was entirely new.[113] Each of the enlarged Gaus and the Warthegau was to be sponsored by two or three 'old Reich' Gaus, whose NSF/DFW members would collect goods and money for the new area and send some of their own number to help to build the organisation and start courses. For example, Hamburg and Mainfranken sponsored Baden in its work in Alsace, while Saxony, Swabia and Tirol were charged with assisting the Warthegau.[114] 'Youth group' members were set to work collecting toys and back numbers of the *NS-Frauen-warte* and making punch-and-judy puppets for their sponsored Gau; but sometimes this misfired, through an excess of zeal on the part of untalented members who made 'unsuitable' toys or through a lack of vigilance which permitted the sending of song books with religious songs. Gratitude for effort was accordingly tempered by exasperation on the the part of the new NSF officials in these 'areas under construction' *(Aufbaugebiete)*.[115] There was no bar to 'old Reich' members' helping other developing Gaus besides the one they were sponsoring, and everyone was strongly encouraged to make a particular effort to assist the Warthegau.[116] Again, the GA supervised this 'comradely' work, which from autumn 1941 came under the authority of Himmler's VoMi.[117]

While the ultimate aims in east and west were similar, the means of achieving them, the pace at which progress was possible and the attitude towards the indigenous population were markedly different. The logistics of the operation in the east were more complicated, while circumstances in the west were more stable. Although there were forced deportations in the west, they were not on the same scale as those in the east, and there was not at the same time a massive influx of hundreds of thousands of homeless, often penniless, settlers.[118] There was nothing in the west to compare with the unbridled loathing of Poland and the Poles in the east, evidenced by the gratuitous derogatory remarks which peppered official communications. NSF workers wrote of the 'danger' of ethnic German children playing with Polish children, and provided nurseries to 'protect' them.[119] Participants in the HD's course near Lodz in September 1941 were warned to bring lockable cases 'since the domestic staff are all Polish'.[120] Quite callously, ethnic German children living in the 'General Government', who were said to be 'undernourished and in poor health' as a result of the 'bad economic circumstances of the Polish period', were to be parted from their parents and looked after by RMD staff for between four and six months while their parents were 'put through the appropriate training' so that the children would find their homes transformed when they returned. 'Old Reich' Gaus were asked to spare RMD instructors, even if they were in short supply, to train the mothers of these families while the children were away.[121]

Such high-handed methods were not employed in the west, where there was, however, a high priority on providing RMD courses for the 'valuable' population in Alsace, Lorraine and Luxembourg; and whereas in the east only ethnic Germans were to enjoy the 'privilege' of RMD instruction, in the west there were other 'desirable' elements who were made eligible. As the first step towards creating a network of RMD schools throughout the Netherlands, one was opened in Amsterdam in February 1941, and 42 RMD courses were provided for 700 women between October 1940 and May 1941. But 69 per cent of these were Germans from the Reich, and only 19 per cent 'pure Netherlanders'; the stay-at-home Dutch housewife[122] was clearly unimpressed by the innovations of the occupying power. And RMD work began 'only hesitatingly' in Lorraine, because, it was alleged, 'of the peculiarities of the Lorrainers'.[123] In these western areas, the NSF/DFW had to try to sell its courses and social events to women who were still living in their own homes; in the east, the audience was literally captive in the camps, or else entirely dependent on the Nazi Party for its accommodation outside them, having left home and possessions behind. While the Nazi aim was to mould all 'desirable' elements to the Party's purpose, in the east ethnic Germans were treated as objects without free will while in the west they were credited with some discretion. This reflected, no doubt unconsciously, the contrast in attitudes towards eastern and western Europe generally, and was partly a product of the special difficulties encountered in dealing with eastern ethnic Germans who did not speak German, and for whom 'reliable' interpreters had to be found.[124] But if the GA workers were at times patronising in their attitude to the new settlers, there was no doubt in their minds that these people had to be rescued from their unfortunate past, the women turned into 'capable German housewives', and, above all, strictly segregated from non-Germans and those in the camps whose origins remained in doubt. Ethnic Germans in transit camps were to receive the dubious benefit of ideological and practical instruction from Party agencies, the GA catering for the women and girls. Those already classed as non-German were ignored, while in camps with an unprocessed population care was to be taken to give only very basic help and instruction, so that Germans would not be totally neglected and non-Germans would not be treated with special care.[125]

The major preoccupation in the east continued to be looking after ethnic Germans in camps and trying to settle them suitably, as late as 1942. Under these circumstances, building up a durable NSF/DFW organisation in districts and local branches could proceed only slowly. By contrast, creating an organisational network and bringing as many women as could be persuaded into sectional activities could proceed soon after hostilities ceased in the west, once the 'undesirable' had been deported to France from Alsace, Lorraine and Luxembourg.[126] In the west, the NSF/DFW had in effect to repeat the process which had been attempted, with varying degrees of success, in the 'old Reich' before and after the *Machtübernahme*. The response was, similarly, in line with previous experience. After some early enthusiasm on the part of those who were susceptible to the ideas of National Socialism and the appeal of the activities offered by the NSF/DFW, there was passive resistance to involvement by those who had not been inclined to participate from the start. It was hardly surprising, in relatively uncanvassed territory, that there seemed to be a gratifying willingness by some women to join the NSF or the DFW and to help to create new local branches and then cells and blocks. This occurred in a more or less orderly fashion in the new Strasbourg district: on 21 February 1941, the Bischheim-West local branch was founded, and Martha Schumacher appointed leader there; but progress was less smooth in Geisweiler, with the NSDAP cell leader reporting in January 1942 that although an NSF cell had been founded in his area in the previous year, no one had yet come to tell the members what kind of work they should be doing.[127]

Viewed from above, the new Strasbourg NSF/DFW developed quickly and effectively in 1940-2. Between October 1941 and April 1942, 17 new local branches were founded, contributing to a total of 98 by the end of September 1942.[128] This was a success; in 'old Reich' Gau Baden at the start of 1938, 27 districts had had only 1,029 local branches between them.[129] So advanced did the NSF's development seem in Strasbourg by November 1941 that the district NSF leader instructed all her local branch leaders to commence the construction of the smallest unit of all, the block. Determined to attract a large membership to her organisations, Rosel Reysz asked her local branch leaders for reports, with names and addresses, on women who refused to join the DFW.[130] In Strasbourg district there was a continuous round of courses and social events, and district leader Bickler was prevailed on to address 'ideological training' courses mounted by the K/E/S on 'the struggle for the German mother-tongue in the west'.[131] There were difficulties in meeting the demand for practical courses in the many rural local branches, and travelling RMD instructors were used widely in Alsace.[132] Bickler clearly valued his NSF, not only sparing time to talk to its meetings but also entrusting to it little tasks, like obtaining a radio for a local hospital.[133] But Rosel Reysz was aware that building an organisation provided only the structure for work, and that the substance, the willing co-operation of the female population, would be harder to achieve. In addition to 'the usual difficulties', she said, there was a 'somewhat tense atmosphere' between Alsatian women and the German NSF/DFW officials drafted in to help to Nazify the area. Some local women were prepared to enter into the new spirit of things, collecting woollen goods for German soldiers on the eastern front, and joining the DFW, the NSF and the Party itself. It was seen as very encouraging that in November 1942 as many as 1,600 Alsatian DFW officials were admitted to the NSF after the required 'year and a half's faultless tenure of office'.[134] But by this time the NSF/DFW's canvassing had reached saturation point, to Rosel Reysz's frustration. Already in summer 1942 she had persuaded Bickler to instruct all his married male subordinates to tell their wives to join the DFW, to try to boost its membership from an accessible source. The results were mortifying, and in March 1943 she prevailed upon him to try again.[135] By this time, the course of the war, with increased casualties, bombing raids and shortages to worry about, and the growing prospect that the new Germanic Empire's days might be numbered, only convinced those who had held aloof from Nazi activities that neutrality was the most prudent course.

However desirable the construction of a Nazi system in the western border areas seemed, it could not compare with the emotive sense of destiny that informed Party activity in the east. 'Making the German east strong' for the *Führer* took on the aura of nineteenth-century missionary work, with a determination to convert people to the Nazi creed and direct their lives according to its precepts, whether they liked it or not, which seemed to justify the claim made by one NSDAP functionary that 'National Socialism is a religion'.[136] The idealism of many, including the young,[137] was genuine if misplaced; more, it was morbid, given its implications for non-Germans. The same GNSFL in the Warthegau who wrote in glowing terms about the benefits derived by new settlers from the hard work of 'old Reich' visiting workers was proud to claim a share for her GA section in the process of separating Germans and Poles according to the definitions of the 'German People's List'. 'The racial-political motive', she wrote, 'must constantly have a decisive influence on all measures in our Gau'.[138] There was particular emphasis on the 'spiritual care of the settlers', who had lived and worked with foreigners all their lives unaware of the inherent undesirability of this; they were to be made aware of their special contribution to Germany's racial mission in eastern Europe. The K/E/S was entrusted with the supervision of all 'spiritual training' for women in the eastern areas, although the GA co-ordinated all the sectional work there and the HD was responsible for the care of settlers still living in camps;[139] there was clearly plenty of room for confusion within the NSF/DFW itself.

The 'spiritual and practical training' to which the women among the new settlers had to submit consisted of little more than the kind of courses offered to 'old Reich' women since 1934. The NSF/DFW leadership had at the same time an impossible goal and limited horizons and imagination, aspiring only to turn all German women within their enlarged constituency into appreciative, pliable citizens whose care of their family, conduct of their household and use of their spare time accorded with the needs of the State as divined by the NSDAP leadership. And so ethnic German women, too, had to be instructed in infant care, sewing and cooking, health and hygiene, taught about the history of the Nazi Party and its women's organisation, and encouraged to take an interest in German history and culture; it was all part of the DFW's standard stock-in-trade. Nazi, or even German, prejudices about eastern Europe showed through in the greater emphasis in courses there on cleanliness and hygiene than was felt necessary in either the 'old Reich' or the west. Similarly, it was stressed that the basic constituents of the 'women's work' in the east were to be presented simply, with care taken to select staff – for RMD courses particularly – who had the knack of conversing with rather simple women.[140] The NSF/DFW leadership was clearly oblivious to the fact that a significant proportion of the early settlers were middle-class white-collar workers and professional people and their families,[141] whose major difficulty lay in adjusting to life on the land,[142] if they were settled there, and not in attaining the intellectual level of NSF/DFW workers. The NSF/DFW may well have helped some of these women to settle into their new role as farmers' wives or as urban housewives in unfamiliar towns, through the instruction and advisory centres provided by the RMD and the Vw/Hw, especially in coping with the shortages of wartime. Pressure from the HD may have encouraged strangers to help each other in a 'neighbourly' way,[143] to their mutual benefit. But these expedients were necessary only because large numbers of ethnic Germans had been uprooted from their previous environment, as a result of 'intimidation and economic promises'.[144] And the motives behind the assistance provided for ethnic Germans were, and were openly admitted to be, first and foremost 'racial-political' (*volkspolitisch*).[145] The interests of the individual, never high on the Nazi scale of priorities, were of no account in this monstrous resettlement project.

The eastern Gauleiters' desire to construct a Party apparatus as quickly as possible in the newly-annexed areas made them dependent on an influx of old hands from the 'old Reich'[146] – uncomfortably so, in the NSF/DFW. Gertrud Scholtz-Klink had liked to boast that only 1.5 per cent of her officials were full-time, salaried staff;[147] in trying to build up the NSF/DFW in the east, the disadvantages of a system which depended on part-time, largely unpaid volunteers became apparent. It was one thing for the ideal 'German housewife and mother' or the single working woman to spare time in evenings or at weekends to maintain NSF/DFW work in her own local branch. It was enough of an effort to try to persuade her to do that, as reports about 'inactive' members showed.[148] But how could such women be expected to take off for the east, for weeks or even months at a time? This was the problem facing the few full-time NSF/DFW officials in the new eastern areas, and particularly the new GNSFL in the Warthegau, Frau Thrö, whose organisation had to begin completely from scratch. She worked hard to try to attract volunteers from the 'old Reich', circulating fulsome reports about the progress of work in her Gau and emphasising its rewarding nature. Above all, she hoped to recruit women for year-long stints as a 'settlers' welfare officer . . . the new occupation for women', among new settlers in urban and rural areas. From 30 welfare officers in December 1940, the numbers rose to 'around two hundred' by April 1942. Some 300 women and girls had been through the scheme, set to work only after attending a ten-day course whose emphasis was 'on the racial-political aspect as a priority'. Their task was to visit new settlers in their homes, to remind the housewives of their German identity and of 'the National Socialist approach to living', about which they had been instructed in the transit camps. On the practical side, the welfare officers were to ensure that homes were kept clean, children were properly looked after, and households conducted in an orderly and thrifty manner. They also acted as a liaison between the woman settler and other agencies, for example the Food Estate or the NSV, which provided material aid where necessary. They submitted reports every month to the GNSFL, to give her an overall picture of progress in the Gau, so that she would know, for example, that in December 1941 37,993 families were visited by 179 welfare officers a total of 126,038 times; and the welfare officers met together every three months to compare notes.

All the advice and instruction provided by the welfare officers was for one purpose: 'to train the woman settler to help herself' in the approved manner. Similarly, they and other NSF/DFW visitors from the 'old Reich', who did shorter tours of duty, had to try to train NSF political leaders and DFW sectional workers from among the most promising women settlers, to try to make the Warthegau independent of the assistance from the 'old Reich' which was so necessary in these early stages of development.[149] The stress on grooming new leaders in the Warthegau and in other eastern developing areas became more urgent as it quickly became apparent that only a small hard core of 'old Reich' volunteers was forthcoming. The central personnel office in the RFFg tried repeatedly to attract recruits to the welfare officers' scheme, but, also repeatedly, had to urge the GNSFLs to try harder to enrol applicants, since the number of volunteers was unaccept- ably low. At first, only NSF members with some leadership experience were deemed suitable for the scheme, but by March 1942 any NSF, DFW or other Party activist who could be prevailed upon to go was welcome.[150] As with work in the 'old Reich', the members of the 'youth groups' were repeatedly urged to help out here, to make good the deficiencies among older members. Trainee leaders in the 'youth groups' were directed into spells of six weeks' service in the east, and there was strong pressure on ordinary members to volunteer for a month's service, especially at harvest time, not just once but every year.[151] In May 1942 the net was extended to make six weeks' service in Upper Silesia compulsory for all trainee leaders and full-time or part-time employees in the 'youth groups' and the 'children's groups', and for all NSF/DFW district and local branch officials under 30.[152] Coercing those with positions to aspire to or, perhaps, to lose was the tactic to which the RFFg was driven in its determination to support the Party's work in the east to the utmost, with the continuing refusal of eligible recruits to volunteer.[153] In April 1943, with the war turning against Germany, there was still an obsessive desire to attract full-time staff for the eastern Gaus. One district NSF leader suggested that this would be a 'lovely task' for war widows; many of them would no doubt feel that they had contributed enough. But in spite of the 'urgency' with which applicants for the east were sought,[154] the increasing call-up of male Party members meant that the few NSF/DFW activists were having to cover for NSDAP workers to such an extent that they could not fulfil 'womanly tasks' at home,[155] let alone spare personnel for work in the developing east.

Nazi Women on the Defensive

Although the Second World War was the product of German aggression, German society was in some respects on the defensive from its start. Rationing foodstuffs and clothing in 1939 revealed the failure of the 1936 Four Year Plan to achieve autarky. Even in time of remarkable success, in 1939 and 1940, there were dead to mourn and wounded to tend. From 1940 there were the effects of 'Black' radio[156] to counter, with enemy attempts to undermine German morale by spreading ugly rumours, about more stringent rationing, for example.[157] As early as May 1940 civilians found themselves periodically in the front line as British bombing raids began, although area bombing did not begin until March 1942, with a heavy raid on Lübeck.[158] The regime, too, was on the defensive at home, as the reports of Himmler's security agents indicate.[159] The war was not popular, and although Germans at home were often said to show 'great interest' in Germany's successes, they were also 'surprised' by each new invasion, and generally anxious for the war to end. As victory turned into defeat, each new reverse was greeted with 'shock' at home.[160] The longer the war went on, the more difficult the mechanics of day-to-day living became: shops closed altogether on certain days of the week as rationing became more severe by late 1943; clothing coupons were no longer issued because what material there was had to be used to help survivors of bomb damage who had lost everything; shortages not only of meat but also of potatoes and other vegetables left mothers wondering desperately how to feed a growing family.[161] The Vw/Hw could busy itself in advising women how best to utilise scarce commodities, but it could not make them more available.

The undercurrent of discontent about practical problems was a constant theme throughout the war, but although difficulties only increased as time went on, anxiety about the course of the war was uppermost in the minds of those at home, particularly once the reverses at Stalingrad and in North Africa in early 1943 were followed by Italy's withdrawal from the war in the summer. There was no 'stab-in-the-back' and very little overt opposition to the regime, but from autumn 1943 onwards there was a discernible withdrawal into the self on the part of the mass of civilians. 'A certain lethargy' settled over them, and they now fully distrusted the official propaganda which had spoken only of victory and done nothing to prepare them for the disasters of 1943.[162] Repeated shocks caused numbness, and women, especially, began to avoid war news items in the press and on the radio: 'it's almost more than I can stand to listen to the army reports. I'll just have to wait until there's better news again', they said.[163] Their distress was, of course, chiefly on personal grounds, with terrible fears about the fate of their menfolk at the front. The geometric progression of casualty figures once Germany's advance into Russia became bogged down in winter 1941/2 caused both mourning and anxiety about those still at the front, and there was particular fear of an intensification of the methods of warfare by the introduction of poison gas.[164] In spite of this, and in spite of talk of 'limits to endurance' as early as 1942, German civilians, including the mass of German women, took the line of least resistance and made no trouble for the regime.[165] Germany was defeated by force of arms, not by subversion or even by a collapse of morale at home.

To this extent, the Party and its affiliates fulfilled their primary purpose in wartime. Maintaining morale and preventing defeatism were vital if the Third Reich were to avoid the breakdown at home that was believed to have destroyed the Second. But the passive resignation and 'negativism' that were so often reported[166] were hardly what the Party had hoped to achieve. There was — as the Party had learned painfully since 1933 — a world of difference between the absence of opposition and the engagement and enthusiasm of the population for things Nazi.

Now, as the Party strengthened its hold on the administration of the 'old Reich' as well as the new territories, and as the authority of its major functionaries, the Gauleiters, was enhanced, the NSDAP began to encounter not merely passivity but even the kind of hostility which it had hoped to leave behind for ever in the *Kampfzeit*. Although faith in Hitler himself remained strong, by 1943 women particularly were beginning to criticise the Party openly, and Party members, uncomfortable with this growing unpopularity, began to abandon the 'Heil Hitler' greeting and even stopped wearing the Party's badge in public.[167] It was noticed, and resented, that Party officials continued to be exempted from military service in large numbers, and that they also had access to facilities – the use of official cars, for example – which contrasted with the straits in which ordinary people found themselves.[168] Complaints about practical problems, the inadequacy of the Party and the long duration of the war in 1943 and 1944 helped to ensure that unpopular measures, like closing down consumer goods factories and enforcing labour conscription for women effectively, were avoided, at the Gauleiters' instigation and to the frustration of Albert Speer.[169]

To the end, then, German industry remained imperfectly geared to the demands of war, and for as long as Germany held on to her wartime conquests their human and material resources were increasingly ruthlessly exploited to cushion the effects of war on the civilian population at home. So much for the qualities which the NSF had chosen[170] to epitomise the ideal German housewife and mother, who figured prominently in the civilian population and among those voicing discontent about the regime's conduct of the domestic side of the war. An 'awareness of responsibility' towards the national community and a 'readiness for service' were conspicuous only by their absence from the attitudes and behaviour of the majority of German women during the war. The political apathy manifested by West Germans after the war[171] clearly had its roots in the negative response of the civilian population to the Nazi regime's repeated pleas for selfless service. As for 'joy in sacrifice', the loud resentment voiced by women on a variety of issues in the early part of the war suggests that the initial minor sacrifices which they were asked to make were borne far from joyfully. The regime had only itself to blame, since it had promised the people only success and the material benefits which would accompany it. As the war dragged on, the insatiable demands of the armed forces for recruits caused added resentment and terrible fear among women whose menfolk were sucked into the military machine; and yet, this could have the effect of binding them more closely to the Nazi cause,[172] since their personal vested interest in a German victory was at stake. The appalling casualty lists returning from the eastern front gripped widows, mothers and daughters of those who had perished in quiet despair, especially if they had more men in the family to lose. And so in one sense German women made the supreme sacrifice for Hitler's ambitious obsessions; three million of their men perished in Hitler's war, prompting the *Führer* not to grieve but to devise, in January 1944, proposals for legalised bigamy for the post-war period, to boost the German birth-rate.[173]

Like the Party as a whole, the NSF/DFW found itself on the defensive in the second half of the war. The character of the 'women's work' as local activity co-ordinated by a central office, the RFFg, was increasingly eroded, with the NSF/DFW working with other affiliates at home, as in the eastern occupied territories, under the authority of the Gauleiter, rather than within the framework of a national women's organisation. Local emergencies, the increasing difficulty of conducting activities on a national scale and the enhanced power of the Gauleiters combined to leave the RFFg as a central office with not much more to administer than itself. Although circulars on a variety of issues connected with the sections' work continued to pour out from the centre throughout 1941 and 1942, and reports fed back the local responses, the increasing restrictions on communications — telephones, paper, transport — vitiated the RFFg's attempts to control the 'women's work' from the centre. The RFFg continued to have an intricate organisation, even with the introduction of the slimmed-down 'wartime plan' in April 1943,[174] and periodic conferences of GNSFLs and Gau section leaders continued to be held. At one such event in March 1944 the participants had to listen to Gertrud Scholtz-Klink's extravagant boasts — which they must have known to be false — about women's enthusiasm for the regime and the NSF/DFW, their admirable solidarity in wartime, and the proved 'necessity' of women's participation in the political life of the nation.[175] This world of make-believe bore no relation to reality. Having lost the battle to attract women to its ranks before the war and then failed to mobilise them for voluntary service on any scale during its early stages, the NSF/DFW was forced to revert to the existence led by the women's auxiliary groups in the 1920s, working with local NSDAP branches and affiliates to mitigate local difficulties and to try to make National Socialism popular through useful deeds and personal contact.

For long-serving NSF functionaries, like Gertrud Scholtz-Klink herself and GNSFLs like Hedwig Schmalmack in Schleswig-Holstein, and a host of minor officials, there must have been an element of *déjà vu* about the *ad hoc* practical work which consumed much of the NSF's energies towards the end of the war. The start of area bombing in March 1942 was an indication of grimmer things to come over the next three years, and the Party busied itself in trying to combat its effects. This was perhaps the one area in which the Party won any popular approval during the war: the NSDAP and its affiliates worked hard and effectively to repair damage and alleviate discomfort resulting from bombing raids, at first especially in the vulnerable western and north-western cities.[176] The NSV was in charge of this relief work, and NSF members acted as their auxiliaries; but as more and more Party officials were called up, in the last months of the war, the women were increasingly left to conduct emergency relief work on their own, in much the way that they had been during the *Kampfzeit*. Those who had passed through the HD's Red Cross and air-raid protection courses were of obvious relevance, but were very thin on the ground; it was chiefly left to the hard core of NSF activists in an area to help to care for the homeless,[177] and to offer sustenance and sympathy to victims of air-raids in general. Some of the older women must have drawn poignant parallels with the soup kitchens and elementary first-aid provided for SA bands fifteen or twenty years earlier. And where in earlier times DFO and then NSF groups had had schemes for sending city-dwelling children to the countryside for a break, now the NSF helped to evacuate women and children from bomb-damaged cities to rural areas. The major difference was that whereas immediate, if often primitive, action had been possible in the hand-to-mouth days before 1933, in the 1940s a virtual 'paper war' raged among government and Party agencies,[178] and complaints about the difficulties of penetrating the Nazi bureaucratic undergrowth abounded from women evacuees who simply wanted to know where they were to go and who was going to help them.[179] In Kochem district a roundabout route led from the NSV's district office, which asked the NSF district leader to help to settle 300 children from bombed areas; she then instructed her local branch leaders to contact the local NSV offices to obtain instructions about how they could most effectively help.[180]

The NSF's functions here included the sensitive problem of persuading families in the reception Gaus to take in a child or a mother with children, often for an indefinite period. And it was the NSF's task to ensure that the newcomers settled in contentedly and that morale was maintained. This emergency work gave the small circle of activists renewed confidence and enthusiasm both for the practical work and for their role as 'spiritual leaders'. Even so, they had to contend with a strong current of discontent about evacuation policies, particularly among women who had been compulsorily evacuated with their children from a large town to more primitive rural surroundings. There was anxiety about husbands who had been left behind to look after themselves, and even greater concern about the DFW's 'neighbourhood aid' scheme, conceived before the war; HD members were supposed to work under NSV supervision, to make sure that men on their own were cared for, but, hardly surprisingly, the wives took a poor view of this. As it happened, the scheme broke down almost before it started, because there were too few women volunteers to make it viable on the scale now required. And the Party which had stressed the importance of the family unit as the basis of society found that its propaganda backfired when women evacuees drifted back to the towns and danger because of discontent at their own circumstances away from home and distress at the break-up of the family.[181] They, and the women who remained in the countryside, can have taken little comfort from the words of the Vw/Hw's leader, Else Vorwerck, in a radio broadcast which stressed the need for co-operation, patience and faith among billeted and host families alike.[182]

Although some Gauleiters and lesser functionaries sank into despair and others worked only to save their own skin in the last months of the war,[183] some Party workers kept going virtually until the end, maintaining an organisation with increasing difficulty and forced to concentrate on emergency relief work. But if the Party did not 'disintegrate' at the beginning of 1945,[184] only its most committed workers were still active by this time, and those in the regions largely operated independently of the centre, with which they had either diminishing contact or, in many areas, no contact at all. Those at the centre, including Gertrud Scholtz-Klink and her staff as well as Bormann and his lieutenants,[185] continued to behave as if National Socialism still had a future; no doubt there was an element of desperation in their self-delusion. The reality consisted of skeleton Gau organisations which assisted an active Gauleiter's final efforts; increasingly in 1945 these ceased to function, and authority devolved automatically to the districts as communications were dislocated. In the border Gau Koblenz-Trier, the Kochem district's headquarters had to move east to Wehr because of 'unfavourable circumstances' in the district's western areas in January 1945. But, undeterred, the district NSF leader insisted on trying to conduct business in an orderly fashion, sending out questionnaires to her local branch leaders at the end of February to ask about the extent of bomb damage in their area. By this time, couriers were being used to deliver messages because of the breakdown of the communications' system, and Frau Müller, the district leader, had lost touch altogether with some of her branches. Still in contact with her Gauleiter, she was determined to maintain morale, and she certainly kept her subordinates busy, demanding reports on bombing, casualties and the measures taken to help survivors, with specific mention of a sewing room and a 'community kitchen'. Above all, she said, 'we must never allow our women to become despondent or to doubt'.

This optimistic tone was tempered by realism: Frau Müller, at least, realised that 'in the future, too, our work must be essentially practical in nature'.[186] By contrast, 'political education' remained the overriding obsession at the RFFg, illustrating once again its failure to carve out a genuinely useful role for itself. In November 1944, with refugees flooding into the Reich from Germany's former eastern territories which were now occupied by the Red Army, the RFFg's interests lay not in organising emergency relief work or in fuelling the remains of the war-effort, but in appointing representatives to provide 'political leadership, psychological influence and care' for the large number of women and children among the refugees, in the camps where they were lodged. To Gertrud Scholtz-Klink, this task was 'unconditionally vital in wartime', and she jibbed at the way in which the Vomi appeared to be assuming complete responsibility for it, without reference to her.[187] Himmler's adjutant at the Vomi not only agreed to the appointment of 800 women 'camp trustees', but also undertook to pay them, since the work involved valuable *Volksdeutsche*[188] who had now, yet again, been uprooted. This was not the first time that the SS had met the RFFg's requests for recognition, and indeed it had been hoped in Derfflinger Street that Gertrud Scholtz-Klink's marriage in 1940 to *Obergruppenführer* Heissmeyer would bring reflected glory and new adherents to the women's organisations. But apart from piecemeal agreements – to bring SS wives into the NSF/DFW's 'youth work' during the war, for example[189] – this did not materialise, to the despair of Gertrud Scholtz-Klink and some of her staff. If this gave rise to recriminations within the RFFg,[190] it was clear that neither the RFF nor anyone else there could give the 'women's work' credibility during this war once Hitler had made his personal decisions about not applying or enforcing labour conscription for women, and not using necessary coercion of other kinds against the 'valuable' – especially the middle-class – population in the interests of the war-effort.

And so Gertrud Scholtz-Klink, supported by Bormann, was left to maintain the fiction which she propagated assiduously up to – and, more recently, after – the end of the war, although at bottom she knew it to be false. To the end she sustained that public image of conformity and success which had most commended her to the Party bosses, in and after 1934. She has boasted that the NSF's activities in the closing stages of the war testify to the 'recognition of the women's work by Party, State and Armed Forces',[191] but here, as elsewhere, the NSF's role was superficial, merely propagandistic. Once Hitler gave his permission for the recruitment of women to operate anti-aircraft batteries, in August 1943, the NSF was supposed to provide volunteers from its own ranks for this task, since the Party felt inhibited about publicly advertising such an obviously 'unwomanly' job.[192] But there were few volunteers, as the appeal two months later to women already employed in other capacities by the air force to volunteer for anti-aircraft work implicitly conceded.[193] The NSF was left to its thankless work of propaganda, to try to convince the female population of the necessity of the regime's current policies, including the need to bring more women into work with the armed forces.[194] But the female population had long since ceased to pay attention to Nazi propaganda, let alone to believe it. Undeterred, the Party embarked in November 1944 on a scheme to provide 'political, ideological and cultural leadership' for women who were brought into work with the forces. On the brink of defeat the NSDAP's preoccupations remained the same as they had been in the days of apparent success: suitable women were to be selected and trained for 'political education' tasks, and the RFFg and the RJFg were to work together and to try to avoid disputes.[195] Apparently oblivious to the crumbling of the Nazi system, in February 1945 Gertrud Scholtz-Klink was concerned with appointing an 'inspector' and her deputy to supervise the entire 'leadership and training' of women working in the armed forces, and with denying Göring's claims to make such appointments at his own discretion.[196]

By this time, the Party's leadership was turning to the most desperate expedients, and the image of German womanhood propagated by the NSDAP from its beginning found its ultimate contradiction in practice when, at the end of February 1945, Hitler approved the formation of experimental 'women's battalions' to fight alongside 15-year-old boys on what was left of Germany's front line. Gertrud Scholtz-Klink was to help with the formation of this women's force, which would be enlarged rapidly if it proved to be satisfactory in practice.[197] Bormann, too, was busy concocting hand-to-mouth expedients, in March 1945 trying to organise sabotage squads – under the nickname '*Werwolf*' – from among remaining Party officials and 'reliable' Labour Front, NSV and NSF workers. But in allegedly sending round a circular to this effect to the Gauleiters[198] he was making little more than a gesture: perhaps a handful of them would receive it, perhaps not even that. The chaos that ruled in Berlin itself[199] was matched by that obtaining in areas under enemy occupation or attack.[200] By the end of April, most women working with the armed forces would hardly need to be told to change out of uniform into civil attire,[201] and those who had played a leading part in the 'women's work' could simply remove their NSF badge and merge with the rest of the distraught population. It was not until July 1945 that Melita Maschmann, in company with the BdM's leader, was apprehended by the Allies, to be interned under their policy of 'automatic arrest' of all NSDAP functionaries, including upper and middle rank NSF leaders.[202] The formal dissolution of the Nazi Party and its affiliates and offices, including the *Reichsfrauenführung*, the *NS-Frauenschaft* and the *Deutsches Frauenwerk* was enacted by the Allied Control Council on 10 October 1945;[203] but this simply ratified a state of affairs which had already existed for some five months.

Notes

1. Ruth Boehme, *NS-FW*, July 1939, pp. 9-10.
2. Professor Dietrich Orlow, Boston, was kind enough to confirm this impression.
3. Mason, op. cit., pp. 302-12 gives a cogent discussion.
4. Gordon Wright, *The Ordeal of Total War 1939-1945*, New York, 1968, pp. 116-23; Peter Calvocoressi and Guy Wint, *Total War*, London, 1974, pp. 244-54.
5. E.g., Alfred Cobban, *History of Modern France*, vol. 2, London, 1965, pp. 51-2.
6. Martin Broszat, *Nationalsozialistische Polenpolitik 1939-1945*, Stuttgart, 1961, pp. 18-25, 62-5, 85-137; Joseph B. Schechtman, *European Population Transfers 1939-1945*, New York, 1946, pp. 27-353; Robert L. Koehl, *RKFDV: German Resettlement and Population Policy 1939-1945*, Cambridge, Mass., 1957, pp. 49-229.
7. Herbert S. Levine, 'Local Authority and the SS State: The Conflict over Population Policy in Danzig-West Prussia, 1939-1945', *Central European History*, December 1969, p. 354.
8. *Chambers Twentieth Century Dictionary*, 1972, p. 606.
9. See above, pp. 160-1.
10. HA/13/253: 'Rundschreiben FW Nr. 87/37', 25 September 1937; 'Rundschreiben FW Nr. 94/37', 14 October 1937.
11. Winkler, op. cit., p. 41.
12. Zentner, op. cit., p. 262.

13. Orlow II, p. 284; HA/13/253: 'Rundschreiben FW Nr. 81/41', 16 July 1941; 'Rundschreiben FW Nr. 24/42', 5 February 1942; 'Rundschreiben Nr. 114/42', 14 May 1942.

14. See above, p. 152.

15. BA, NSD 3/5, *V,A,B*, 'Aufgaben der NS-Frauenschaft, B. 47/40 vom 16.7.1940', p. 659. BA, *Slg. Sch.*, 369, 'Anordnung und Richtlinien für den Einsatz des Ortsgruppenleiters im Kriege . . . NS-Frauenschaft', n.d.

16. Scholtz-Klink, op. cit., p. 54.

17. IfZ, MA 341, frame 2-667392, letter of 2 April 1942, op. cit.

18. Winkler, op. cit., pp. 176-84; Leila Rupp, *Mobilizing Women for War*, Princeton, 1978, pp. 167-75, 183-8.

19. Alan S. Milward, *The German Economy at War*, London, 1965, pp. 41, 46-7, 111-13; Farquharson, op. cit., pp. 235-7.

20. Winkler, op. cit., pp. 102-21.

21. Heinz Boberach (ed.), *Meldungen aus dem Reich*, Munich, 1968, 294-5, 384, 405; IfZ, MA 441/8, frames 2-759517-18, *Meldungen aus dem Reich*, 'Lücken in der Verordnung . . . ', op. cit.

22. Hüttenberger, op. cit., pp. 158-9, 165-8, 183-6; 'Party resistance to full-scale mobilization', Noakes and Pridham, op. cit., pp. 652-3; Tim Mason, 'Women in Germany, 1925-1940: Family, Welfare and Work', *History Workshop*, autumn 1976, pp. 20-1.

23. Rupp, op. cit., pp. 105-12, 127-33, 135-6; Stephenson, op. cit., pp. 106-10.

24. Boberach, op. cit., pp. 146-8; IfZ, MA 441/1, frames 2-750490-1, 2-750862-3, *Meldungen aus dem Reich*: 18 December 1939, 19 February 1940.

25. Boberach, op. cit., pp. 148, 287, 290-5, 405; Rupp, op. cit., p. 172.

26. Articles in *NS-FW*: October 1939, inside cover, pp. 210-11, 214-15; January 1940, pp. 296-7; May 1940, inside cover, pp. 417-19, 436-7.

27. BA, NS22/vorl. 396, *VB*, 26 July 1940, 'Die Partei im Kriege (X): Die Front der Schaffenden'; IfZ, MA 736, Gau South Hanover-Brunswick DAF report for 1942, 'So sorgt die Partei für den Arbeiter', pp. 4-5; ibid., 1940, p. 64.

28. Winkler, op. cit., pp. 154-63.

29. Scholtz-Klink, op. cit., p. 455.

30. Ursula von Gersdorff, *Frauen im Kriegsdienst 1914-1945*, Stuttgart, 1969, p. 68.

31. Jill Stephenson, ' "Einsatzbereitschaft": Women's Labour Service in Nazi Germany', forthcoming in a volume edited by Heilwig Schomerus and Volker Hentschel, 1980; c.f. Farquharson, op. cit., pp. 234-5.

32. Orlow II, p. 278.

33. BA, NS22/2038, circular signed by Gertrud Scholtz-Klink, 14 March 1939.

34. Ibid., 'Mitteilung 20/41' signed by Woweries, 27 January 1941.

35. BA, NS22/2037, 'Jahresbericht der Gauschulungsämter für 1940', pp. 2-35.

36. IfZ, MA 736, 'Jahresbericht des Gauschulungsamtes im Gau Hessen, 1.1.40-30.11.40'.

37. BA, NS22/2038, 'Mitteilung 63/41' signed by Huber, 21 May 1941.

38. Ibid., 'Mitteilung 70/41', 30 May 1941.

39. BA, NS22/2037, 'Rundschreiben Nr. 7/41' signed by Huber, 16 August 1941.

40. BA, *Slg. Sch.*, 230, 'Die Aufgaben der NS-Frauenschaft', speech delivered by an NSF official on 18 June 1942.

41. Boberach, op. cit., pp. 265-7; 'The treatment of Polish labour' in Noakes and Pridham, op. cit., pp. 648-50.

42. Boberach, op. cit., pp. 322, 415. Peterson, op. cit., pp. 415-16, 424-47.

43. BA, NS22/vorl. 110, 'Wo steht die innere Front?', n.d.

44. 'Einsatz, Betreuung und Ruf der Nachrichtenhelferinnen', *V,A,B,* 28 July 1943.

45. Boberach, op. cit., pp. 80, 198, 210-12, 271, 277-8, 283, 361-2, 367.

46. Winkler, op. cit., p. 144.

47. IfZ, MA 341, frames 2-667392-4, letter of 2 April 1942, op. cit.

48. IfZ, MA 253, frames 649-54, 'Der Einsatz der NSF/DFW im Kriegsjahr 1940', 24 April 1941. See also Winkler, op. cit., pp. 107-10.

49. IfZ, MA 138, frame 301118, Kreisleitung Lübeck, 'Bericht 10.1941'.

50. HA/13/253: 'Rundschreiben Nr. F 75/41', 17 June 1941; 'Rundschreiben Nr. F 110/41', 11 September 1941; 'Rundschreiben Nr. 202/42', 29 August 1942.

51. IfZ, op. cit., frame 300886, 'Arbeitsbericht der Gaufrauenschaftsleiterin', Schleswig-Holstein, 29 November 1941, p. 4.

52. 'Der Fraueneinsatz in der Kriegswirtschaft', *NS-FW,* 1 May 1940, p. 417.

53. 'Frauenhände packen zu', *NS-FW,* October 1939, p. 210; Ilse Buresch-Riebe, *Frauenleistung im Kriege,* Berlin, 1942, pp. 29-38, 45-111.

54. IfZ, MA 341, frames 2-667392-3, letter of 2 April 1942, op. cit.; ibid., MA 341, frame 300885, op. cit., p. 3.

55. 'Stillegungs- und Einschränkungsmassnahmen bei der NS-Frauenschaft/ Deutsches Frauenwerk, A.22/43 v. 22.3.43', *V,A,B,* 1943, vol. IV, pp. 252-3.

56. HA/13/253, 'Rundschreiben Nr. F 147/41', 15 December 1941.

57. IfZ, MA 130, frames 86393-406, 'Jahresbericht der Arbeit der Kreis-frauenschaftsleitung Strassburg vom 1.10.41 bis 1.10.42'.

58. HA/13/254, 'Rundschreiben Nr. 198/42', 27 August 1942.

59. Ibid., 'Rundschreiben Nr. 125/42', 26 May 1942.

60. Ibid., 'Rundschreiben Nr. 141/42', 8 June 1942.

61. Ibid., 'Rundschreiben Nr. FW 87/41', 4 August 1941.

62. Ibid.: 'Rundschreiben Nr. F 108/41, 9 September 1941; 'Rundschreiben Nr. FW 121/41', 20 October 1941; 'Rundschreiben Nr. 99/42', 1 May 1942; 'Rund-schreiben Nr. 146/42', 13 June 1942.

63. Mason, op. cit., pp. 17-38.

64. IfZ, op. cit., frames 86368-71, 'Bericht über die Mitarbeit der Frauen v. pol. Leitern auf Grund des Rundschreibens v. 25.6.42', 10 April 1943.

65. Ibid.; ibid., MA 138, frame 300886, op. cit., p. 4.

66. Ibid., MA 130, frames 86329, 86331, letters from Frau Strasser, local NSF branch leader, Treis (Mosel), to the Kochem district NSF leader, and vice-versa, 15 and 17 August 1942.

67. Ibid., frames 86394, 86400, 'Jahresbericht . . . ', op. cit.; ibid., MA 138, frame 300883, op. cit., p. 1.

68. Ibid.

69. Ibid., frames 30086-87, op. cit., pp. 4-5; Boberach, op. cit., p. 294.

70. HA/13/253, 'Rundschreiben Nr. F 76/41', 18 June 1941.

71. Stephenson, *Women in Nazi Society,* p. 110.

72. HA/13/253: 'Rundschreiben Nr. 109/42', 11 May, 1942; 'Rundschreiben Nr. 136/42', 5 June 1942.

73. Ibid., 'Rundschreiben Nr. 125/42', 26 May 1942.

74. Ibid., 'Rundschreiben Nr. 144/42', 15 June 1942.

75. Ibid., 'Rundschreiben Nr. F 111/41', 15 September 1941.

76. Ibid., 'Rundschreiben Nr. F 118/41', 4 October 1941.

77. Stephenson ' "Einsatzbereitschaft" . . . ', op. cit. (Ms Edinburgh, 1979, pp. 15-17).

78. HA/13/253, 'Rundschreiben Nr. 149/42', 20 June 1942.

79. Ibid.: 'Rundschreiben Nr. FW 105/41', 4 September 1941; 'Rundschrei-

ben FW Nr. 124/41', 24 October, 1941; 'Rundschreiben Nr. 85/42', 17 April 1942; 'Rundschreiben Nr. 200/42', 3 September 1942.

80. Ibid.: 'Rundschreiben F 138/41', 21 November 1941; 'Rundschreiben Nr. 183/42', 28 July 1942.

81. BA, NS22/vorl. 318, vorl. 319, 'Friedensmäassiger Organisationsplan: Reichsfrauenführung, 5 April 1941.

82. HA/13/253, 'Rundschreiben Nr. 168/42', 13 July 1942.

83. Ibid., 'Rundschreiben FW 149/41', 19 December 1941.

84. Ibid., 'Rundschreiben Nr. FW 151', 18 December 1941.

85. 'Die Organisation der NS.-Frauenschaft Deutsches Frauenwerk', *DF*, 1941, p. 18.

86. HA/13/253: 'Rundschreiben FW 73/41', 26 June 1941; 'Rundschreiben Nr. 166/42', 17 July 1942.

87. Ibid.: 'Rundschreiben Nr. FW 85/41', 25 July 1941; 'Rundschreiben FW 123/41', 22 October 1941; 'Rundschreiben FW 128/41', 31 October 1941; 'Rundschreiben Nr. FW 140/41', 10 December 1941; 'Rundschreiben Nr. 96/42', 30 April 1942.

88. Ibid.: 'Rundschreiben F 105/41', 10 September 1941; 'Rundschreiben Nr. 160/42', 6 July 1942.

89. Ibid.: 'Rundschreiben FW Nr. 82/41', 23 July 1941; 'Rundschreiben Nr. 111/42', 14 May 1942.

90. Ibid.: 'Rundschreiben FW Nr. 77/41', 3 July 1941; 'Rundschreiben Nr. 144/42', op. cit.

91. Ibid., 'Rundschreiben Nr. 103/42', 4 May 1942.

92. Ibid., 'Rundschreiben Nr. FW 103/41', 28 August 1941.

93. Ibid., 'Rundschreiben FW Nr. 81/41', 16 July 1941.

94. Ibid.: 'Rundschreiben Nr. F 115/41', 26 September 1941; 'Rundschreiben Nr. F 119/41', 15 October 1941.

95. IfZ, MA 441/1, frame 2-750489, *Meldungen aus dem Reich*, 18 December 1939.

96. Ibid., MA 130, frames 86402-3, 'Jahresbericht . . . ', op. cit.

97. Ibid., MA 253, frame 652, 24 April 1941, op. cit.

98. BA, NSD30/1836, *Informationsdienst für die soziale Arbeit der NSV*, January 1939, 'Einsatz des Frauenhilfsdienstes für die Soziale Betriebsarbeit', p. 72; 'Hauptabteilung Hilfsdienst', *DF*, 1941, pp. 30, 32.

99. HA/13/253: 'Rundschreiben Nr. FW 79/41', 4 July 1941; 'Rundschreiben Nr. FW 90/41', 11 August, 1941; 'Rundschreiben Nr. 106/42', 6 May 1942.

100. Ibid., 'Rundschreiben Nr. 1 49/42', op. cit.

101. Farquharson, op. cit., p. 234.

102. HA/13/253, 'Rundschreiben Nr. 95/42', 30 April 1942.

103. Ibid.: 'Rundschreiben Nr. F. 89/41', 30 July 1941; 'Rundschreiben Nr. FW 100/41', 19 August 1941; 'Rundschreiben Nr. 139/42', 6 June 1942.

104. Ibid.: 'Rundschreiben FW Nr. 120/41', 21 October 1941; 'Rundschreiben Nr. FW 137/41', 27 November 1941; 'Rundschreiben Nr. FW 143/41', 8 December 1941; 'Rundschreiben Nr. 82/42', 17 April 1942.

105. Hüttenberger, op. cit., pp. 147-52; Orlow II, pp. 286, 330.

106. HA/13/253, 'Rundschreiben Nr. FW 146/41', 19 December 1941.

107. Hüttenberger, op. cit., pp. 178-82; Levine, op. cit., pp. 331-55.

108. Schechtman, op. cit., pp. 272-80; Koehl, op. cit., pp. 49-88, 104-10.

109. *DF*, op. cit., pp. 33, 35.

110. IfZ, MA 253, frame 650, op. cit.; Koehl, op. cit., p. 98.

111. Schechtman, op. cit., pp. 278, 322.

112. HA/13/253, 'Rundschreiben Nr. FW 68/41', 20 June 1941.

113. Orlow II, pp. 287-94, 318-20.

114. HA/13/253, 'Rundschreiben Nr. 66/42', 23 March 1942.

115. Ibid.: 'Rundschreiben Nr. FW 151', op. cit.; 'Rundschreiben Nr. 58/42', 12 March 1942; 'Rundschreiben Nr. 102/42', 5 May 1942.

116. Ibid.: 'Rundschreiben Nr. F 101/41', 26 August 1941; 'Rundschreiben Nr. 83/42', 8 April 1942.

117. Ibid., 'Rundschreiben Nr. FW 97/41', 16 August 1941.

118. Schechtman, op. cit., 277, 288-92; Koehl, op. cit., pp. 99-101, 117-18, 121-2, 128-33; Eugène Schaeffer, *L'Alsace et La Lorraine (1940-1945)*, Paris, 1953, pp. 100-7.

119. IfZ, MA 225, frame 2-408814, 'Aus der Arbeit der NS-Frauenschaft im Wartheland', 29 April 1942.

120. HA/13/253, 'Rundschreiben Nr. FW 109/41', 10 September 1941.

121. Ibid., 'Rundschreiben FW Nr. 135/41', 22 November 1941.

122. Werner Warmbrunn, *The Dutch under German Occupation*, Stanford, 1963, p. 100.

123. 'Hauptabteilung Mütterdienst', *DF*, 1941, pp. 66-7.

124. HA/13/253, 'Rundschreiben Nr. FW 145/41', 19 December 1941.

125. Ibid., 'Rundschreiben Nr. 40/42', 24 February 1942.

126. Koehl, op. cit., p. 128; Schaeffer, op. cit., p. 91.

127. IfZ, MA 130: frame 86478, letter from the Bischheim-West local branch leader to the Strasbourg district leader, 26 February 1941; frame 86445, memorandum from the Strasbourg district leader to Rosel Reysz, 16 January 1942.

128. Ibid., frames 86393-4, 'Jahresbericht . . . ', op. cit.

129. Reichsorganisationsleiter (ed.), *Gau- und Kreisverzeichnis der NSDAP*, Munich, 1938, pp. 70-1.

130. IfZ, op. cit., frame 86456, circular from the Strasbourg NSF district leadership to the NSF local branch leaders, November 1941.

131. Ibid., frames 86407-18, reports of the NSF/DFW's sectional work in Strasbourg district, 1941-2; ibid., frames 86475, 86482, 86484-5, 86487-8: correspondence between Strasbourg district leader Bickler and NSF officials, 4 April 1941; 6 November 1941; 30 October 1942; 23 September 1942; 19 September 1942; 23 September 1942, respectively.

132. Ibid., frame 86353, letter from the local branch NSF leader, Treis-Mosel, to the Strasbourg district NSF leader, 15 August 1942; *DF*, op. cit., p. 66.

133. Ibid., frames 86438-9, letter from Rosel Reysz to Bickler, 3 March, 1942, and vice-versa, 28 February, 1942.

134. Ibid., frames 86393-5, 'Jahresbericht . . . ', op. cit.

135. Ibid., frames 86368-71, 'Bericht . . . ', 10 April 1943, op. cit.

136. Heyen, op. cit., pp. 170-1.

137. Melita Maschmann, *Fazit. Keine Rechtferigungsversuch*, Stuttgart, 1963, pp. 56-7.

138. IfZ, MA 225, frames, 2-408809-15, op. cit.

139. HA/13/253: 'Rundschreiben Nr. F 86/41', 28 July 1941; 'Rundschreiben Nr. 46/42', 24 February 1942; 'Rundschreiben Nr. 162/42', 3 July 1942.

140. Ibid., 'Rundschreiben Nr. F 86/41', op. cit.

141. Schechtman, op. cit., pp. 317-18, 326-8; Koehl, op. cit., p. 99.

142. Maschmann, op. cit., p. 38.

143. IfZ, op. cit., frames 2-408811-13, op. cit.

144. Koehl, loc. cit.

145. HA/13/253, 'Rundschreiben Nr. 178/42', 21 July 1942.

146. Orlow II, pp. 291-3.

147. IfZ, MA 130, frame 86493, 17 April 1939, op. cit.

148. See above, pp. 149-50, 186-7, 190, 195.

149. IfZ, MA 225, frames 2-408809-15, op. cit.; HA/13/253, op. cit.

150. Ibid.: 'Rundschreiben Nr. F 101/41', 26 August 1941; 'Rundschreiben F 129/41', 4 November 1941; 'Rundschreiben Nr. 6/42', 9 January 1942; 'Rundschreiben Nr. 57/42', 10 March 1942.

151. Ibid.: 'Rundschreiben Nr. FW 100/41', 19 August 1941; 'Rundschreiben Nr. 83/42', op. cit.

152. Ibid., 'Rundschreiben Nr. 123/42', 22 May 1942.

153. Ibid.: 'Rundschreiben Nr. 122/42', 20 May, 1942; 'Rundschreiben Nr. 157/42', 1 July 1942.

154. IfZ, MA 130, frame 86345, 'Rundschreiben Nr. 21/43', from the Kochem district NSF leader to her local branch leaders, 27 April, 1943.

155. IfZ, op. cit., frame 86375, report by the Strasbourg NSF leadership to the NSDAP district leader, 7 April 1943.

156. Michael Balfour, *Propaganda in War 1939-1945*, London, 1979, pp. 90-9.

157. IfZ, op. cit., frame 86393, 'Jahresbericht . . . ', op. cit.; HA/13/253, 'Rundschreiben Nr. 96/42', 30 April 1942.

158. Balfour, op. cit., pp. 200, 262-4.

159. Boberach, op. cit.

160. Ibid., pp. 75-8, 80-2, 151-5, 289, 340.

161. Ibid., p. 362.

162. Orlow II, pp. 411-12, 416-17; Hüttenberger, op. cit., p. 160.

163. Boberach, op. cit., p. 438.

164. Ibid., pp. 271, 319, 419.

165. Balfour, op. cit., pp. 268, 403.

166. Orlow II, p. 407.

167. Ibid., pp. 413-16; Hüttenberger, op. cit., pp. 158-61; Boberach, op. cit. pp. 346, 350, 361.

168. Orlow II, pp. 415, 425-6, 456; Boberach, op. cit., pp. 346, 405, 411.

169. Albert Speer, *Inside the Third Reich*, London, 1970, pp. 220-2, 274, 312-13; Noakes and Pridham, loc. cit.

170. See above, p. 157.

171. Ralf Dahrendorf, *Society and Democracy in Germany*, London, 1967, pp. 330-44.

172. IfZ, op. cit., frame 86394, op. cit.

173. Oron J. Hale, 'Adolf Hitler and the Post-war German Birth-rate: An Unpublished Memorandum', *Journal of Central European Affairs*, July 1957, pp. 166-73.

174. BA, NS22/2008, 'Anordnung 3/43', 22 April 1943.

175. 'Tagung der Gaufrauenschaftsleiterinnen', *Das Archiv*, 1943/44, 4 March 1944, pp. 939-40.

176. Orlow II, pp. 438, 441; Arthur Marwick, *War and Social Change in the Twentieth Century*, London, 1974, pp. 114-17.

177. Hüttenberger, op. cit., pp. 169-70.

178. Ibid., p. 171.

179. Boberach, op. cit., pp. 365-6.

180. IfZ, op. cit., frame 86325, circular from the Kochem NSF district leader to her local branch leaders, 20 July 1943.

181. Boberach, op. cit., pp. 363-70.

182. Else Vorwerck, 'Zusammenbruch der Familie', *Reichsprogramm*, 19.00 − 13 May 1944.

183. Orlow II, pp. 470, 482; Hüttenberger, op. cit., pp. 172, 209-11.

184. Orlow II, p. 478. C.f. Domarus, vol. 2, op. cit., p. 2179.

185. Orlow II, pp. 478-80.

186. IfZ, op. cit., frame 86490, circular from the Kochem NSF district leader to her local branch leaders, 26 February 1945.

187. BA, *Slg. Sch.*, 230, memo from the section leader, 'Volkstum und Ausland' to the section 'Organisation/Personal' in the RFFg, 17 November 1944.

188. Ibid., letter to the NSDAP's Reichsschatzmeister from Ravsinski at the Vomi, 11 December 1944.

189. IfZ, MA 341, frame 2-667381, memo from Himmler, 3 June 1942.

190. Ibid., frames 2-667390-94, letter of 2 April 1942, op. cit.

191. Scholtz-Klink, op. cit., pp. 455-6.

192. Gersdorff, op. cit., p. 411.

193. Ibid., pp. 417-18.

194. Ibid., p. 466.

195. Ibid., p. 470.

196. Ibid., p. 503.

197. BA, *Slg. Sch.*, 368, memo for Friedrichs and Klopfer at the Party Chancellery, 28 February 1945.

198. Gersdorff, op. cit., pp. 517-18.

199. Maschmann, op. cit., p. 160.

200. Speer, op. cit., Chapters 29-32, pp. 433-89.

201. Gersdorff, op. cit., pp. 532-3.

202. Maschmann, op. cit., pp. 180, 185.

203. *Anti-faschistische Russell-Reihe* (Dokumentation), Hamburg, 1978, pp. 31-3.

POSTSCRIPT

If the rise to power of the NSDAP had been meteoric, its demise was instantaneous, at the moment of German defeat in May 1945. Some of its major officers were apprehended and brought to trial at Nuremberg, but large numbers, of whom Martin Bormann was the most significant, simply disappeared. Even Himmler managed to disguise himself and evade arrest for a short time.[1] The ensuing trials of the major war criminals involved only men; many women passed through denazification courts — including some who had not been members of the NSDAP or its affiliates, like Leni Riefenstahl[2] — but they were treated as the very small fry they had been in the Nazi system. A distinction was rightly made between NSF and DFW members,[3] but neither were treated with severity; this appropriately signalled the minimal impact which the women's organisations had had on Party policy and on the female population of Germany. Accordingly, Gertrud Scholtz-Klink was treated more as the figurehead of an impotent organisation than as a malefactor. She and her SS-officer husband almost escaped detection, living in her home state of Baden under an assumed name for almost three years. The two of them were actually denazified under their false name, and when their deceit was discovered, early in 1948 by the French occupation authorities, it was on this account that she was imprisoned for eighteen months. Now that she was discovered, she was tried as a major war criminal by a court in Tübingen, but this status was a formality accorded because of her former title. The court's decision confirmed the political unimportance of her former role by sentencing her to eighteen months' imprisonment — a sentence she was deemed to have already served, in autumn 1949, because of her term in prison for the earlier offence.[4] No doubt this leniency owed something to the changed mood in the West, with the Cold War, and not vengeance against former Nazis, now the chief preoccupation.

But if the court did not find Gertrud Scholtz-Klink particularly culpable for the wickedness of the Third Reich, the new Federal Republic's Political Cleansing Commission showed in June 1950 that there were Germans who did not regard her as completely innocuous. It banned her from public office for life, and prohibited her from entering teaching, journalism or allied occupations and from starting a business of her own, for ten years. Hardly surprisingly, she was also denied

214

pension rights from her former occupation, and she was disenfranchised and banned from membership of any political party, trade union or commercial or professional organisation. A fine was imposed on her, and she was restricted to the district in which she lived for two and a half years. This, she has complained bitterly, is how 'idealists' are treated when they end up on the losing side. The memoir of the former BdM and Labour Service official, Melita Maschmann, bears the sub-title 'Not an Attempt at Justification';[5] Gertrud Scholtz-Klink has shown no such contrition.[6] She regards her past activities as those of a champion of women's rights against the uninformed male chauvinism of the Party's men, and as a brave attempt to provide, through her organisations, a unifying force for women in a deeply divided society. But in claiming that NSF local branch leaders were on an equal footing with male NSDAP local branch leaders, and in implying that the sectional leaders in the RFFg influenced the policies of government ministries and Party offices,[7] she manifests either total naivety, a bad memory, or downright dishonesty. She herself showed frustration with the lack of influence which women, the women's organisations and the National Women's Leader continued to wield in the Nazis' male-dominated, male chauvinist system, on those rare, private occasions when she let the mask of compliance and satisfaction slip.[8]

It is true, though, that German society was deeply divided after the First World War, in the 1920s and during the Depression. But these divisions were not going to be healed by the negative creed of National Socialism, with its crude racism and brutality, its desire for revenge and its xenophobia. Dissolving parties, unions and organisations by force and intimidation could remove the outward manifestations of political, social or religious differences but would not eliminate the differences themselves. Creating massive, monolithic, monopoly organisations could give an impression of unity which police terror effectively reinforced, by discouraging dissidence. But the entire Nazi system was based on diversion and disguise, temporary expedients to control the people until they – or, more likely, a new generation – were sufficiently re-educated for the myth to assume the proportions of reality. Once everyone *believed* that class and denominational differences were irrelevant, and that being German was the only attribute that mattered, then there would be no more class conflict, no need for a narrow denominational approach to religion – no need, ultimately, for the Christian religion with its flabby virtues of submissiveness and humility. Until that time, national solidarity was to be maintained by the diversion of antagonism towards others, chiefly Jews, Slavs, Russian 'Bolsheviks'. Aggression against the Poles in 1939 conveniently served three purposes: it won Germany the territory she had lost to Poland at Versailles, and more; it gave the 'master race' the chance to bully and humiliate the despised Poles; and it began to provide material benefits which were to persuade the working class that they were too well off to be able to afford a class war.

But class divisions remained, and class consciousness was, if anything, heightened by wartime policies which discriminated between the classes. The way in which middle-class women were consistently able to evade war-work created widespread and continuing discontent which working women were not afraid to voice in the strongest terms.[9] And in trying to wean women and children away from the Christian Churches the Party met not only resistance but also open hostility.[10] On the whole, as long as the Government governed and refrained from making demands of them, Germans went along with it. Once the regime asked for sacrifices, in wartime, the people, and especially women, responded with resounding resentment. The Nazi Party and the regime whose policies it tried to popularise found themselves caught in their own trap. Winning people over by promising what they want is a common and often enough successful political tactic. Succeeding here and then trying to change people's attitudes so that they will accept disadvantages – shortages, service, sacrifice – at least sullenly and preferably gladly is a Sysiphean task. But it was the one above all others which the NSDAP set itself. Robert Ley was not justified in claiming that 'there are no more private citizens. The time when anybody could do or not do what he pleased is past',[11] but he clearly indicated by this boast what his ideal Nazi system would be. If the racism and the brutality were the most horrifying aspects of National Socialism, the totalitarian aim of engaging and organising everyone in a 'people's community' is highly disturbing.

To the NSDAP's leadership, the kind of peaceful anarchy where private citizens pursue individual interests when and how they choose was anathema. Goebbels might maintain that 'organisation is a means to an end . . . It has the task of forming human groups into units so that they may be brought purposefully and successfully to a starting-point',[12] but the 'end' would be one where people obediently conformed to the official view of all aspects of life voluntarily, once 'organisation' had done its work of indoctrination. 'A good organisation', so prized by the NSF's leadership,[13] would make people accessible to propaganda for as long as it took for resistance to be worn down. But it would hardly be able to 'wither away' once indoctrination had proved successful, since the changing demands of the regime would require constant updating of the message to be purveyed. Organisation, as a concept and a structural form, would be a permanent feature of the Nazi system. Everyone would ultimately be brought into at least one organisation, so that he or she would, as an atomised individual, be directly exposed to the inexorable pressure of the regime. The enormity of this ambition is hard to grasp, and was particularly full of destructive implications for the German family. The majority of Germans showed a healthy contempt for it by continuing to live private family lives in peacetime and by complaining bitterly when the war separated members of a family for long periods.[14] Here, again, the Party was caught in its own trap. Having consistently stressed the importance to society of the family unit, and having equally consistently attacked Soviet Russian family legislation for allegedly undermining the family, the NSDAP found that its demands on those who were prepared to be organised were threatening family life. As early as November 1934 Hess reported 'several complaints' about the heavy demands Party organisations were making on individuals, to the extent that families found it difficult to spend time together; he ordered district leaders to ensure that certain days each week were left free of all Party commitments to enable 'healthy family life' to be maintained.[15] Himmler reached a similar conclusion in 1938, as he became exercised about the marriage and birth-rates. Young people, he found, were spending so much time on their single-sex Party activities that they were not meeting potential marriage partners. Arranging joint meetings of the SS and the BdM, the NSF and the SA, for example, would not provide a solution, he said, since 'valuable girls . . . would not want it to be thought that they were trying to ensnare a husband', and would therefore stay away.[16]

These problems afflicted only a minority of Germans as the rest abstained from Nazi-sponsored organised activities, as far as the need to pay lip-service to the regime through an occupational group allowed. Under the eye of the Gestapo, social intercourse of the simplest kind — conversation 'over a glass of beer . . . family visits'[17] — was possible, if uncomfortable. Human beings, as is their wont, adapted to the constraints of a system which might not have been destined to last for a thousand years, but which could hardly have been expected to effect its own destruction in a mere twelve. Gertrud Scholtz-Klink was so convinced that the social development of the 1930s was on the right lines that she has said that she would have been willing to continue her activities further, after 1945, if she had been given the chance.[18] Allowing for the complete lack of realism in this offer, it has to be asked what future such organisations as hers could have had outside the Nazi system. In anything other than a dictatorship her organisations would not have existed; it has been suggested that there is a direct line of inheritance from the NSF to the *Demokratischer Frauenbund* (Democratic Women's Association) of the German Democratic Republic which was founded in 1947 at the behest of the Soviet occupation authorities.[19] Be that as it may, in a pluralist society where there is a choice of organisations to join, or to abstain from joining, Gertrud Scholtz-Klink's organisations could not have begun to exist. There would be no 'official' women's organisation, like the NSF, with a monopoly of propaganda and sole access to a variety of facilities. Nor would a *Deutsches Frauenwerk* be a live proposition, because it came into existence only as a result of the forcible banding together of organisations which, given the choice, would not have associated with each other. The old *Bund deutscher Frauenvereine* brought together, voluntarily, a host of women's groups, but large numbers of others – most significantly the Socialist ones – remained outside, and were able to remain outside and in existence in a way that was abruptly terminated in spring 1933.

Had there been a Nazi victory in the early 1940s, no doubt the status of the NSDAP in the 'Germanic Empire' would have been enhanced and the Party and the SS would have continued their jurisdictional squabbles in the newly-annexed territories. But Germans at home would have been so relieved that peace and a kind of normality had been restored that they would have reverted to their private lives, with the survivors of families reunited, and would have felt no more disposed to participate joyfully in the work of organisations than they had been before the war. The surplus of women in the population would have provided more opportunities for women – in skilled and professional work, for example – at least until a new generation of men grew up to displace them, and would also have made women more responsible in family life, with large numbers of fatherless families, especially if Hitler's scheme for legalised bigamy had been introduced. These were, in any case, the effects of the war with Germany the loser.[20] But any improvement in the status of women would not have been, and was not, due to the efforts of the women's organisation; it was directly attributable to the effects of the war. This is where Gertrud Scholtz-Klink's aspiration to 'continue further' is at its most illusory. The overwhelming emphasis of the 'women's work' had been on practical housewifery and child-care; if these were, and remain,

major preoccupations of large masses of women everywhere, they are
not activities which open up new opportunities for women and promise
to raise their status in the community at large. By making the traditional activities of the 'housewife and mother' the central concern of
her organisations, with the support of her male superiors in the Party,
Gertrud Scholtz-Klink herself rendered nugatory her stated aim of
'coming forward more quickly'.[21] But National Socialism was a mass of
inherent contradictions, a movement constantly facing self-imposed
dilemmas presented by its own conflicting priorities. Improving
women's status by backward-looking policies which vitiated the
German war-effort was the double contradiction which most obviously
informed the nature of the Nazi women's organisations. But there were
other dilemmas — achieving compliance without coercion, isolating
obedient individuals but valuing 'healthy family life', craving enthusiasm without allowing the choices which stimulate it — which, while
often at their most obvious in the women's organisations, pervaded the
entire Nazi system.

Notes

1. H.R. Trevor-Roper, *The Last Days of Hitler*, London, 1962, pp. 236-45, 250-7.
2. BDC, Leni Riefenstahl's file, including her denazification papers. She was classed in 1949 as a 'Mitläufer' by the Tribunal, but acquitted of the charge of 'promoting the NS dictatorship'.
3. *Antifaschistische Russell-Reihe*, op. cit., pp. 48-9.
4. Wiener Library Personality File G15, reports on Gertrud Scholtz-Klink in: *New York Times*, 3 February 1948; *Neue Zeitung*, 18 November 1948; *Die Welt*, 18 November 1949; *New York Herald Tribune*, 18 November 1949.
5. Maschmann, op. cit.
6. Scholtz-Klink, op. cit., pp. 479-84.
7. Zentner, op. cit., pp. 262-4.
8. BA, R43II/427, letter of 24 January, 1938, op. cit.; IfZ, MA 341, frames 2-667392-3, op. cit.
9. Boberach, op. cit., pp. 148, 287, 290-5, 405; see above, pp. 183-4, 187-8.
10. Boberach, op. cit., pp. 364-5.
11. Quoted in Schoenbaum, op. cit., p. 113.
12. Quoted in George L. Mosse (ed.), *Nazi Culture*, London, 1966, p. 151.
13. *DF*, 1941, p. 18, op. cit.
14. Boberach, op. cit., pp. 361-70.
15. BA, *Slg. Sch.*, 191, 'Anordnung' signed by Hess, 25 November 1934.
16. Ibid., 368, *PKK*, 'Notiz für den Stabsleiter', 16 December 1938.
17. 'Passive resistance from Social Democrats' in Noakes and Pridham, op. cit., p. 301.
18. Zentner, op. cit., p. 264.
19. Vorstand der SPD, Bonn, *Von der NS-Frauenschaft zum kommunistischen DFD*, Hanover, n.d.

20. B. Rich, 'Civil Liberties in Germany', *Political Science Quarterly*, 1950, p. 81.

21. Zentner, loc. cit.

APPENDIX 1: The Gaus of the NSDAP, 1938 (Germany and Austria)

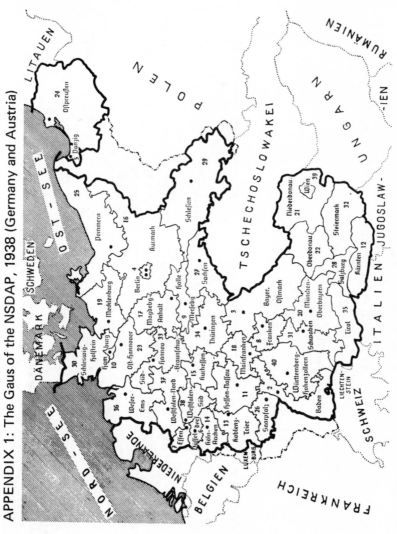

Source: Reichsorganisationsleiter (ed.), *Organisationsbuch der NSDAP* (Munich, 1938), pp. 84-5.

APPENDIX 2: The 1937 Organisation Plan of the National Women's Leadership (*Reichsfrauenführung*)

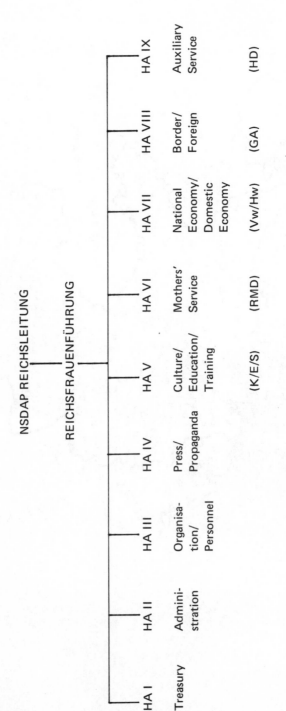

NSDAP REICHSLEITUNG

REICHSFRAUENFÜHRUNG

HA I	HA II	HA III	HA IV	HA V	HA VI	HA VII	HA VIII	HA IX
Treasury	Admini-stration	Organisa-tion/Personnel	Press/Propaganda	Culture/Education/Training	Mothers' Service	National Economy/Domestic Economy	Border/Foreign	Auxiliary Service
				(K/E/S)	(RMD)	(Vw/Hw)	(GA)	(HD)

Notes: 1. HA = Hauptabteilung (Main Department).

2. Abbreviations (e.g., K/E/S) are those used in the text and derive from the German names.

Source: *Deutsches Frauenschaffen*, 1939.

APPENDIX 3: The 1941 Organisation Plan of the National Women's Leadership (*Reichsfrauenführung*)

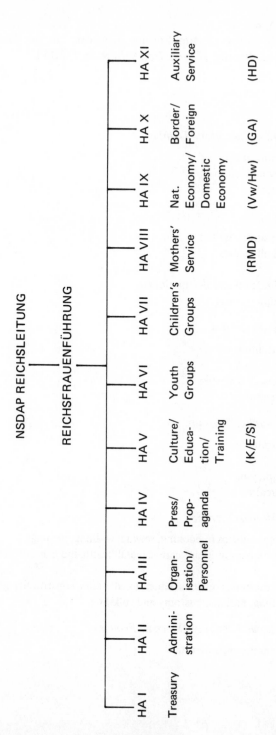

NSDAP REICHSLEITUNG

REICHSFRAUENFÜHRUNG

HA I	HA II	HA III	HA IV	HA V	HA VI	HA VII	HA VIII	HA IX	HA X	HA XI
Treasury	Administration	Organisation/Personnel	Press/Propaganda	Culture/Education/Training	Youth Groups	Children's Groups	Mothers' Service	Nat. Economy/Domestic Economy	Border/Foreign Economy	Auxiliary Service
				(K/E/S)			(RMD)	(Vw/Hw)	(GA)	(HD)

Notes: 1. HA = Hauptabteilung (Main Department).
        2. Abbreviations (e.g., K/E/S) are those used in the text and derive from the German names.
Source: *Deutsches Frauenschaffen*, 1941.

The Sub-divisions of the Service Sections of the National
Women's Leadership (*Reichsfrauenführung*), 1941

HA V – Culture/Education/Training

Ideological education
Racial policy education
Physical education
Projects
National folk-lore
Music and leisure activities
Graphic and allied arts
Literature
Women's education and occupations
National training colleges

HA VI – Youth Groups

Leadership training
Handwork
Music and leisure activities
Physical education

HA VIII – Children's Groups

Leadership training
Handwork
Singing and playing
Physical education

HA VIII – Mothers' Service

Housekeeping: courses in cooking, sewing, washing, ironing
Health care: courses in infant care, general health and care of the sick at
   home
Educational matters: courses in educational affairs, constructive hobbies,
   homemaking, national customs and folk-lore

HA IX – National Economy/Domestic Economy

National economy information
Nutrition

Clothing
Housing
Domestic science training
Domestic science advice
Advice for settlers' wives
Domestic science research and experiment

HA X – Border/Foreign

Foreign work
Border work
Ethnic German work
Colonial work
Liaison offices with the Association for Germans Abroad and the
National Colonial Association

HA XI– Auxiliary Service

Neighbourhood Aid
Collaboration with the NSV
Women's Auxiliary Service for welfare and care of the sick
Liaison Office with the German Red Cross
Liaison Office with the National Air-raid Protection Society

Source: *Deutsches Frauenschaffen*, 1941

GLOSSARY AND LIST OF ABBREVIATIONS

AOPG	*Akten des Obersten Parteigerichts* (proceedings of the NSDAP's High Court), found in BDC
BA	Bundesarchiv, Koblenz
BDC	Berlin Document Center
BDF	*Bund deutscher Frauenvereine* (Federation of German Women's Associations), a middle-class feminist grouping founded in 1894, dissolved in May 1933
BdM	*Bund deutscher Mädel* (League of German Girls), female branch of the Hitler Youth, for girls over 14 years of age
BKL	*Bund Königin Luise* (Queen Luise League), a patriotic conservative women's association, founded in 1923, dissolved in April 1934
Deutsche Frauenfront	Nazi-led federation of women's organisations, in existence during summer 1933
DF	*Deutsches Frauenschaffen*, the annual of the RFFg
DFO	*Deutscher Frauenorden* (German Women's Order), *völkisch* women's organisation founded in 1923 by Elsbeth Zander, merged with other groups into the NSF in 1931
DFW	*Deutsches Frauenwerk* (German Women's Enterprise) the Nazi-led federation of women's groups from 1934 to 1945
DVP	*Deutsche Volkspartei* (German People's Party), a conservative-liberal party of the Weimar Republic
FAG	*Frauenarbeitsgemeinschaft* (Women's Working Group), a form of local Nazi women's group, merged with other groups into the NSF in 1931
FK	*Frauenkultur im Deutschen Frauenwerk*, the magazine of the DFW
Frauengruppe	(Women's Group), a form of local Nazi women's group, merged with other groups into the NSF in 1931

GA
: *Grenz- und Ausland* (Border and Foreign), one of the sections into which the DFW's work was divided

Gau
: (region), the major territorial division of the national NSDAP organisation; there were 32 Gaus in 1933, 40 in the Greater German Reich of 1938. Nomenclature of Gaus in the text is on a contemporary basis where possible, following information in Hüttenberger, *Die Gauleiter*, pp. 221-4. E.g., at the end of 1931 Gau Ruhr was divided into North Westphalia and South Westphalia; events in 1930 refer to Gau Ruhr, but in 1932 to the Westphalias. And referring to the Gau Histories (see below, GH), the 1935-6 name is used even when the History is discussing an event in, e.g., 1931

Gauleiter
: regional NSDAP leader

GH
: Gau History, one of a number of records of Nazi women's work in the *Kampfzeit* compiled in 1935-6

Gleichschaltung
: (co-ordination), the process by which a Nazi monopoly was created in political, social and organisational life from 1933

GNSFL
: *Gaufrauenschaftsleiterin* (regional NSF leader)

HA
: NSDAP Hauptarchiv, the Party's own archival collection, started in January 1934

HA III
: *Hauptabteilung III* (Main Department III) of the NSDAP's organisation in 1932

HA VIII
: *Hauptabteilung VIII* (Main Department VIII) of the NSDAP's organisation in 1932

HD
: *Hilfsdienst* (Auxiliary Service), one of the sections into which the DFW's work was divided

HJ
: Hitler Jugend (Hitler Youth), the Nazi Party's youth organisation

IfZ
: Institut für Zeitgeschichte Archive

Kampfzeit
: (time of struggle), the years from the founding of the NSDAP until the *Machtübernahme*

K/E/S
: *Kultur/Erziehung/Schulung* (culture, education, training), one of the sections into which the DFW's work was divided

KPD
: *Kommunistische Partei Deutschlands* (German

	Communist Party)
Kreis	(district), territorial unit of the NSDAP into which the Gaus were divided
Machtübernahme	(takeover of power), generally referring to Hitler's appointment as Chancellor on 30 January 1933
männerbündisch	(male chauvinist)
n.d.	date of publication not given
Neulandbund	(Newland Movement), *völkisch* women's association founded by Guida Diehl in 1914
n.p.	place of publication not given
NSBO	*Nationalsozialistische Betriebszellenorganisation* (the Nazi Factory Cell Organisation)
NSDAP	*Nationalsozialistische Deutsche Arbeiterpartei* (the Nazi Party)
NSF	*Nationalsozialistische Frauenschaft* (Nazi Women's Group), the monopoly Party organisation for women founded in 1931
NS-FW	*NS-Frauenwarte*, the magazine of the NSF
NSLB	*NS-Lehrerbund* (Nazi Teachers' League)
NSS	*NS-Schülerbund* (Nazi School Pupils' League)
NSSi	*NS-Schülerinnenbund* (Nazi Schoolgirls' League)
NSV	*NS-Volkswohlfahrt*, the Nazi welfare organisation
Ortsgruppe	(local branch), territorial unit of the NSDAP into which the districts were divided
PKK	*Partei-Kanzlei Korrespondenz*, correspondence within the NSDAP's Chancellery, Hess's office from 1933, Bormann's from 1941
RDH	*Reichsbund Deutscher Hausfrauen* (National Association of German Housewives)
Reichsleitung	(National Leadership), the highest decision-making level of the NSDAP
RFF	*Reichsfrauenführerin* (National Women's Leader), the title conferred on Gertrud Scholtz-Klink in November 1934
RFFg	*Reichsfrauenführung* (National Women's Leadership), the title conferred on Gertrud Scholtz-Klink's Berlin office in June 1936
RJF	*Reichsjugendführer* (National Youth Leader), the title conferred on Baldur von Schirach in October 1931

RJFg   *Reichsjugendführung* (National Youth Leadership), Schirach's office

RMD   *Reichsmütterdienst* (National Mothers' Service), one of the sections into which the DFW's work was divided

ROL   *Reichsorganisationsleitung* (NSDAP's National Organisation Office), whose leader was Gregor Strasser until his resignation in December 1932

SA   *Sturm Abteilungen* (Storm Troopers), paramilitary formation of the NSDAP

Schutz- und Trutzbund   (Protective and Offensive Association), *völkisch* organisation in the 1920s

Slg. Sch.   *Schumacher Sammlung* (collection of documents about Nazi organisations and projects, found in BA and BDC)

SPD   *Sozialdemokratische Partei Deutschlands* (German Social Democratic Party)

SS   *Schutzstaffeln*, Nazi elite paramilitary formation, under the leadership of Heinrich Himmler

Uschla   *Untersuchungs- und Schlichtungsausschuss*, the system of intra-party courts within the NSDAP

V,A,B   *Verfügungen, Anordnungen, Bekanntgaben*, gazetteer of NSDAP orders and decrees

VB   *Völkischer Beobachter*, official Nazi Party newspaper

völkisch   (racist-nationalist), the generic term used to describe aims and groups similar to those of the NSDAP, especially in the 1920s

Völkischer Frauenbund   (Racist-nationalist Women's Association), particularly used to describe the group in Nuremberg in the 1920s

volksdeutsch   (ethnic German), used by the NSDAP to describe people of German stock living outside the Reich

Volksgemeinschaft   (national people's community), term used by the NSDAP to describe German society purged of 'alien' elements, to create a feeling of national solidarity

Vw/Hw   *Volkswirtschaft/Hauswirtschaft* (National Economy/Domestic Economy), one of the sections into which the DFW's work was divided

Weltanschauung   (view of life), term used to describe the Nazis'
all-embracing philosophy of Germany's destiny,
and to lend superficial coherence to what was
really a hotch-potch of variable prejudices

WLS   Women's Labour Service, known from January
1934 to April 1936 as *Deutscher Frauenarbeits-
dienst*, and thereafter as *Reichsarbeitsdienst für
die weibliche Jugend*

BIBLIOGRAPHY

Bibliographical Note

Primary sources, which form the largest part of the material used for this work, are, characteristically, often thin on the ground for important aspects and relatively rich for trivial ones. For the early development of women's group activity and the conflicts between different factions, there is substantial material in the Bundesarchiv NS22 files, vorl. 348, 349, 355, 356 and 357. The Gau Histories, in the NSDAP Hauptarchiv (reel 13, fol. 254), are often usefully complementary to this, by no means always giving a purely propagandistic account. The Schumacher collection, to be found in both the Bundesarchiv and the Berlin Document Center, has a sprinkling of useful official documents from the mid-1920s until 1939 in file no. 230 for the women's organisation, as well as material on the *Bund deutscher Mädel* in nos. 251 and 257; but more revealing material on the relations between the NSF and the BdM appears in BA NS22/342. With the Nazi assumption of power in 1933, unselfconscious revelations in documents are very much rarer than they are in the pre-1933 years; no doubt a deliberate purge of indiscreet documents was effected. The almost total absence of official papers for the women's organisation for the period from Strasser's resignation to Gertrud Scholtz-Klink's appointment, from December 1932 to February 1934, suggests that this was the case as far as the women's organisation was concerned. Fortunately, however, revealing material on this period has survived in a relatively obscure source, the proceedings of the Party's High Court in the Berlin Document Center, in the case between Paula Siber and Erich Hilgenfeldt in 1934, AOPG 2684/34. This rehearses several of the events of 1933 plausibly enough, and is the basis for the reconstruction of these in Chapter 3, part 1. Thereafter, with a few exceptions, there are overwhelmingly bland, self-censored documents, in Schumacher no. 230 and in the Hauptarchiv, reel 13, fol. 253, with a large number of circulars sent out by the *Reichsfrauenführung* in 1937, 1941 and 1942. For the early war years, there is a rich seam in the Institut für Zeitgeschichte MA 130 and MA 138 records, with interesting material from Schleswig-Holstein, Baden and Koblenz-Trier at the local level. But the last two years of the war are very poorly served, apart from the documents in the Freiburg

Military Archive published by Ursula von Gersdorff (*Frauen im Kriegs-dienst 1914-1945*), which are of limited value except to the extent that there is little else.

Complete List of Archival Sources Used

NSDAP Hauptarchiv	reel 13, fol. 253-7
	reel 89
Berlin Document Center	Schumacher Sammlung, 211, 230
	Akten des Obersten Parteigerichts 2684/34, 736/1936
	Party membership and NSF cards
	Partei-Kanzlei Korrespondenz
	Party Census forms, 1939
Bundesarchiv	NS22/342, 1044, 2008, 2037, 2038
	NS22/vorl. 110, 121, 318, 319, 348, 349, 355, 356, 357, 396
	NS25/75
	NSD 3/5, 30/1836
	R2/12771, R22/24, R43II/427, R45II/64
	Kleine Erwerbungen, no. 296-(1)
	Schumacher Sammlung, 191, 230, 251, 257, 262, 368, 369, 392
Institut für Zeitgeschichte	MA 130, 135, 138, 225, 253, 341, 441/1, 441/8, 609, 736
Wiener Library	Personality File G15

Contemporary Journals

Das Archiv
Deutsches Frauenschaffen
Die Deutsche Frauenfront
Die Frau
Frankfurter Zeitung
Frauenkultur im Deutschen Frauenwerk
Nachrichtendienst der Reichsfrauenführerin
NS-Frauenwarte
Statistisches Jahrbuch für das Deutsche Reich
Völkischer Beobachter

Contemporary Articles

Grosse, F., Review of Ernst Kahn, *Der Internationale Geburtenstreik*, Frankfurt, 1930, *Die Arbeit*, 1931

Hilgenfeldt, Mercedes, 'So wurden wir', *Mädel Eure Welt*, 1940

Röbke, Hanna, 'Arbeitsdienst für die weibliche Jugend', *Jahrbuch des Reichsarbeitsdienstes*, 1936

Vorwerck, Else, 'Zusammenbruch der Familie', *Reichsprogramm*, 13 May 1944

'Bevölkerungspolitik', *Die Deutsche Sozialpolitik*, July 1944

Contemporary Books

Baumgart, Gertrud, *Frauenbewegung Gestern und Heute*, Heidelberg, 1933

Buresch-Riebe, Ilse, *Frauenleistung im Kriege*, Berlin, 1942

Diehl, Guida, *Erlösung vom Wirrwahn*, Eisenach, 1931

Gottschewski, Lydia, *Die Frauenbewegung und Wir*, n.p., n.d.

——, *Männerbund und Frauenfrage*, Munich, 1934

Hadeln, Charlotte von (ed.), *Deutsche Frauen-Deutsche Treue*, Berlin, 1935

Hasselblatt, Dora (ed.), *Wir Frauen und die Nationale Bewegung*, Hamburg, 1933

Kirkpatrick, Clifford, *Woman in Nazi Germany*, London, 1939

Kriner-Fischer, Eva, *Die Frau als Richterin über Leben und Tod ihres Volkes*, Berlin, 1937

Reichenau, Irmgard (ed.), *Deutsche Frauen an Adolf Hitler*, Leipzig, 1934

Reichsfrauenführung (ed.), *NS-Frauenschaft*, Berlin, 1937

Reichsorganisationsleiter (ed.), *Gau- und Kreisverzeichnis der NSDAP*, Munich, 1938

——, *NSDAP Partei-Statistik*, Munich, 1935

——, *Organisationsbuch der NSDAP*, Munich, 1937, 1938 and 1941

Siber, Paula, *Die Frauenfrage und ihre Lösung durch den Nationalsozialismus*, Berlin, 1933

Post-1945 Articles

Childers, Thomas, 'The Social Bases of the National Socialist Vote',

Journal of Contemporary History, October 1976

Evans, Richard J., 'German Women and the Triumph of Hitler', *Journal of Modern History*, accepted for demand publication. Abstract printed in vol. 48, no. 1, March 1976

Fischer, Conan, and Hicks, C., 'Statistics and the Historian. The SA's Rank and File', *Social History*, January 1980

Glass, D.V., 'Family Planning Programmes in Western Europe', *Population Studies*, 1966

Hale, Oron J., 'Adolf Hitler and the Post-war German Birth-rate: An Unpublished Memorandum', *Journal of Central European Affairs* July 1957

Jones, M.S., Review of Peter Stachura (ed.), *The Shaping of the Nazi State*, London, 1978, *New German Studies*, vol. 6, no. 2

Koonz, Claudia, 'Nazi Women before 1933: Rebels against Emancipation', *Social Science Quarterly*, March 1976

——, 'Mothers in the Fatherland: Women in Nazi Germany', in Renate Bridenthal and Claudia Koonz (eds.), *Becoming Visible. Women in European History*, Boston, 1977

Levine, Herbert S. 'Local Authority and the SS State: The Conflict over Population Policy in Danzig-West Prussia, 1939-1945', *Central European History*, December 1969

Mason, Tim, 'Women in Germany, 1925-1940: Family, Welfare and Work', *History Workshop*, spring and autumn, 1976

McIntyre, Jill, 'Women and the Professions in Germany, 1930-40' in Anthony Nicholls and Erich Matthias (eds.), *German Democracy and the Triumph of Hitler*, London, 1971

Peel, J., 'The Manufacturing and Retailing of Contraceptives in England', *Population Studies*, 1963-4

Pryce-Jones, David, 'Mothers for the Reich', *Times Literary Supplement*, 2 July 1976

Reiche, E.G., 'From "Spontaneous" to Legal Terror: SA, Police, and the Judiciary in Nürnberg, 1933-34', *European Studies Review*, April 1979

Rich, B., 'Civil Liberties in Germany', *Political Science Quarterly*, 1950

Stephenson, Jill, ' "Reichsbund der Kinderreichen": the League of Large Families in the Population Policy of Nazi Germany', *European Studies Review*, July 1979

——, ' "Einsatzbereitschaft": Women's Labour Service in Nazi Germany', in a volume edited by Heilwig Schomerus and Volker Hentschel (forthcoming, 1980)

Stokes, Lawrence D., 'The Social Composition of the Nazi Party in

Eutin, 1925-32', *International Review of Social History*, 1978, no. 1

Winkler, Heinrich August, 'German Society, Hitler and the Illusion of Restoration 1930-33', *Journal of Contemporary History*, October 1976

Post-1945 Books

Albrecht, D. (ed.), *Der Notenwechsel zwischen dem Heiligen Stuhl und der Deutschen Regierung*, Mainz, 1965

Allen, William, S., *The Nazi Seizure of Power: The Experience of a Single German Town 1930-1935*, London, 1966

Antifaschistische Russell-Reihe, vol. 1, Hamburg, 1978

Balfour, Michael, *Propaganda in War 1939-1945*, London, 1979

Beckmann, Emmy (ed.), *Des Lebens wie der Liebe Band* (letters of Gertrud Bäumer), Tübingen, 1956

Boberach, Heinz (ed.), *Meldungen aus dem Reich*, Munich, 1968

Böhnke, Wilfried, *Die NSDAP im Ruhrgebiet 1920-1933*, Bonn-Bad Godesberg, 1974

Bracher, K.D., *The German Dictatorship*, London, 1973

——, Sauer, Wolfgang, and Schulz, Gerhard, *Die Nationalsozialistische Machtergreifung*, Cologne and Opladen, 1960

Brandenburg, H.C., *Die Geschichte der HJ*, Cologne, 1968

Broszat, Martin, *Nationalsozialistische Polenpolitik 1939-1945*, Stuttgart, 1961

——, *Der Staat Hitlers*, Munich, 1969

Bullock, Alan, *Hitler, a Study in Tyranny*, London, 1962

Calvocoressi, Peter, and Wint, Guy, *Total War*, London, 1974

Carr, E.H., *Socialism in One Country*, vol. 1, London, 1970

Cobban, Alfred, *History of Modern France*, vol. 2, London, 1965

Conway, J.S., *The Nazi Persecution of the Churches*, London, 1968

Dahrendorf, Ralf, *Society and Democracy in Germany*, London, 1967

Diehl-Thiele, Peter, *Partei und Staat im Dritten Reich*, Munich, 1971

Domarus, Max, *Hitler. Reden und Proklamationen 1932-1945* (2 vols.), Würzburg, 1963

Douglas-Hamilton, James, *Motive for a Mission* (2nd edn), Edinburgh, 1979

Evans, Richard J., *The Feminist Movement in Germany 1894-1933*, London, 1976

Farquharson, J.E., *The Plough and the Swastika*, London, 1976

Fest, Joachim C., *The Face of the Third Reich*, London, 1970

——, *Hitler*, London, 1977

Franz-Willing, Georg, *Die Hitlerbewegung. Der Ursprung 1919-1922*, Hamburg, 1962

Gersdorff, Ursula von, *Frauen im Kriegsdienst 1914-1945*, Stuttgart, 1969

Grunberger, Richard, *A Social History of the Third Reich*, London, 1971

Heyen, Franz Josef, *Nationalsozialismus im Alltag*, Boppard, 1967

Hierl, Konstantin, *Im Dienst für Deutschland 1918-1945*, Heidelberg, 1954

Horn, Wolfgang, *Führerideologie und Parteiorganisation in der NSDAP (1919-1933)*, Düsseldorf, 1972

Hunt, Richard N., *German Social Democracy 1918-1933*, Chicago, 1970

Hüttenberger, Peter, *Die Gauleiter. Studie zum Wandel des Machtgefüges in der NSDAP*, Stuttgart, 1969

Koehl, Robert L. *RKFDV: German Resettlement and Population Policy 1939-1945*, Cambridge, Mass., 1957

Krebs, Albert, *Tendenzen und Gestalten der NSDAP*, Stuttgart, 1959

Marwick, Arthur, *War and Social Change in the Twentieth Century*, London, 1974

Maschmann, Melita, *Fazit. Keine Rechtfertigungsversuch*, Stuttgart, 1963

Maser, Werner, *Die Frühgeschichte der NSDAP. Hitlers Weg bis 1924*, Frankfurt am Main, 1965

Mason, Timothy W., *Sozialpolitik im Dritten Reich*, Opladen, 1977

Merkl, Peter, *Political Violence under the Swastika*, Princeton, 1975

Middleton, Lucy (ed.), *Women in the Labour Movement*, London, 1977

Milward, Alan S., *The German Economy at War*, London, 1965

Mosse, George L. (ed.), *Nazi Culture*, London, 1966

Noakes, Jeremy, *The Nazi Party in Lower Saxony 1921-1933*, Oxford, 1971

Noakes, Jeremy, and Pridham, Geoffrey (eds.), *Documents on Nazism 1919-1945*, London, 1974

Orlow, Dietrich, *The History of the Nazi Party 1919-1933*, Newton Abbott, 1971

——, *The History of the Nazi Party 1933-1945*, Newton Abbott, 1973

Peterson, Edward N., *The Limits of Hitler's Power*, Princeton, 1969

Pridham, Geoffrey, *Hitler's Rise to Power. The Nazi Movement in Bavaria, 1923-33*, London, 1973

Rupp, Leila, *Mobilizing Women for War*, Princeton, 1978

Schaeffer, Eugène, *L'Alsace et La Lorraine (1940-1945)*, Paris, 1953

Schechtman, Joseph B., *European Population Transfers 1939-1945*, New York, 1946

Schmitthenner, W., and Buchheim, H. (eds.), *The German Resistance to Hitler*, London, 1970

Schoenbaum, David, *Hitler's Social Revolution*, London, 1967

Scholtz-Klink, Gertrud, *Die Frau im Dritten Reich*, Tübingen, 1978

Schön, Eberhard, *Die Entstehung des Nationalsozialismus in Hessen*, Meisenheim am Glan, 1972

Speer, Albert, *Inside the Third Reich*, London, 1970

Stachura, Peter D., *Nazi Youth in the Weimar Republic*, Santa Barbara and Oxford, 1975

——, (ed.), *The Shaping of the Nazi State*, London, 1978

Stephenson, A. Jill R., 'Women in German Society, 1930-40', PhD Thesis, Edinburgh University, 1974

Stephenson, Jill, *Women in Nazi Society*, London, 1975

Stockhorst, Erich, *Fünftausend Köpfe. Wer war was im Dritten Reich*, Bruchsal, 1967

Thönnessen, Werner, *Frauenemanzipation*, Frankfurt, 1969

Trevor-Roper, H.R., *The Last Days of Hitler*, London, 1962

Tyrell, Albrecht (ed.), *Führer Befiehl . . .* , Düsseldorf, 1969

Vorstand der SPD, Bonn, *Von der NS-Frauenschaft zum kommunistischen DFD*, Hanover, n.d.

Warmbrunn, Werner, *The Dutch under German Occupation*, Stanford, 1963

Weber, Hermann (ed.), *Völker hört die Signale*, Munich, 1967

Winkler, Dörte, *Frauenarbeit im 'Dritten Reich'*, Hamburg, 1977

Wright, Gordon, *The Ordeal of Total War 1939-1945*, New York, 1968

Wright, J.R.C., *'Above Parties': The Political Attitudes of the German Protestant Church Leadership 1918-1933*, Oxford, 1974

Zeman, Z.A.B., *Nazi Propaganda*, London, 1964

Zentner, Christian (ed.), *Das Dritte Reich*, Hamburg, 1975

INDEX